TURNPIKE TROOPER

RACIAL PROFILING & THE NEW JERSEY STATE POLICE

AN INSIDE LOOK AT THE INFAMOUS "NJ TURNPIKE SHOOTING"
AND THE POLITICIANS WHO INFLUENCED THE OUTCOME

BY: BADGE #5068 - TROOPER JOHN I. HOGAN

TURNPIKE TROOPER

RACIAL PROFILING & THE NEW JERSEY STATE POLICE

AN INSIDE LOOK AT THE INFAMOUS "NEW JERSEY TURNPIKE SHOOTING"
AND THE POLITICIANS WHO INFLUENCED THE OUTCOME

WRITTEN BY:
JOHN I. HOGAN
EXCLUSIVELY FOR:
BACK AT YOU PRODUCTIONS, LLC

Copyright © 2005 by John I. Hogan.

Library of Congress Number: 2004195708
ISBN :   Hardcover   1-4134-8208-2
               Softcover   1-4134-8207-4

All rights reserved. No part of this book may be reproduced or transmitted in any form or by any means, electronic or mechanical, including photocopying, recording, or by any information storage and retrieval system, without permission in writing from the copyright owner.

Contents is the rights of
Back At You Production, LLC.
backatyou2005@comcast.net

This book was printed in the United States of America.

To order additional copies of this book, contact:
Xlibris Corporation
1-888-795-4274
www.Xlibris.com
Orders@Xlibris.com

Contents

Introduction 9

CHAPTERS:

   1:   The Selection Process 13
   2:   Politics 101 22
   3:   The New Jersey State Police Academy 45
   4:   Playing a Trooper 62
   5:   The Black Dragon 69
   6:   Just Another Day 82
   7:   King of the Big Road 95
   8:   Final Patrol: The "Turnpike Shooting" 103
   9:   The Investigation 121
  10:   Racial Profiling: Real Or Imagined? 188

DEDICATION

In loving memory of William P. Hogan Sr.
Dad, thanks for enduring so much pain and holding on as long as you did. The strength and courage you demonstrated was amazing, and we all miss and love you dearly.

With special thanks to:
Robert L. Galantucci and Mary Jane Wainwright. No one will ever truly know the countless sacrifices the two of you made over the years to ensure my personal well-being. The care, compassion, and dedication you both showed toward my cause will forever be remembered. Words cannot express the gratitude I owe you both.

To my mother and Ashley, I could not have completed this venture without your love and support. To my family, friends, and loyal supporters, your generosity, kindness, and backing allowed me to endure this travesty. The volumes of letters, e-mails, cards, and donations that poured in was astonishing and will forever be a part of my life and memories. When I reflect back over the course of this historical incident, it was all of your goodwill that proved to me that us "little people" do matter in society.

Police Officer's Life
(a moment for reflection)

I have been where you fear to be
I have seen what you fear to see
I have done what you fear to do
All these things I have done for you.

I am the one you lean upon
The one you cast your scorn upon
The one you bring your troubles to
All these people I've been for you.

The one you ask to stand apart
The one you feel should have no heart
The one you call the officer in blue
But I am human just like you.

And through the years I've come to see
That I am not what you ask of me
So take this badge and take this gun
Will you take it? Will anyone?
And when you watch a person die
And hear a battered baby cry
Then do you think that you can be
All these things that you ask of me?

—Author unknown

INTRODUCTION

His piercing steel blue eyes ripped through my soul like shards of jagged glass. My heart pounded erratically as a cold sweat beaded upon my forehead. To put it mildly, I was awestruck. His small but impeccable frame was outfitted with crisp, creased pants and highly polished black leather shoes. The white dress shirt was immaculately starched, and his multi-colored tie perfectly matched the dark blue suit he donned. Though small in stature, this man towered with power, confidence, charisma, and pride. As he spoke to me, I felt as if I were being analyzed by the world's most renowned psychologist. At fourteen years of age, I had just met the man I most admired and respected in life: Colonel Clinton L. Pagano, superintendent of the New Jersey State Police. Ironically, this life-altering experience transpired in the small town of Florence, Burlington County, in the kitchen of my best friend's house.

Unlike most adolescents, I never aspired to become a professional athlete, surgeon, or multimillionaire businessman. Even though I thrived in sports, I knew my academic and physical limitations. From the day I first laid eyes on a uniformed New Jersey state trooper, I knew that was what I wanted to do with my adult life. Still to this day, after all my experiences, both positive and negative, I cannot identify the reasons for my passion about being a New Jersey state trooper.

Back in 1969, my parents, William Phillip Sr. and Dorothy Elizabeth Hogan, relocated to the tiny town of Florence, New Jersey, from South Philadelphia where they had both grown up and met through mutual neighborhood friends. The A&P warehouse in Yeadon, Pennsylvania, where my father had worked for years closed, and in order to remain with the company, he had to transfer to another warehouse, which was located in Florence. At the time, my mother was pregnant with her fifth child; and yours truly, John Ignatius Hogan, was born in Trenton City, New Jersey, at St. Francis Hospital on November 3, 1969.

Growing up on the banks of the Delaware River, we were a lower middle-class family. Our small house on Chestnut Street was dissected into four small bedrooms, two bathrooms, and an unfinished basement. Nestled between Burlington and Bordentown townships, Florence was quite a contrast from the city life my parents were used to, but in retrospect, getting out of their Whitby Avenue house in South Philadelphia was a blessing in disguise if you are familiar with the neighborhood in its current state.

Aside from being a snotty-nosed wise guy but always respectful to adults, my earliest recollections of growing up already had my oldest sibling, Dorothy Anne, attending nursing school where she lived in Coatesville, Pennsylvania. Before I knew it, she had married her high-school sweetheart, Mark Bodrog, and they began to have a family of their own. At the same time, my next oldest sibling, Catherine Marie (Cathy), was about to graduate from Stockton State College with her degree in psychology. I can still remember the displeasure my parents had when she decided to put her degree aside and began working as a blackjack dealer in the new booming Atlantic City casino market. To date, Cathy has several casino dealer licenses, three children and resides in a small community just outside of Atlantic City, New Jersey with her husband Stephen.

With Dottie Anne and Cathy moving forward with their careers and families, I finally had my own bedroom back on Chestnut Street. Billy (William Jr.) was my only brother, and since he was almost seven years older than me, we were not that close growing up. Unlike all of my sisters, Billy chose not to attend Florence High School and instead graduated from Burlington County Vo-Tech High School and immediately began working as a stationary engineer. Tragically, at the ripe age of nineteen, my brother was diagnosed with lymphoma, a rare form of facial cancer, and was undergoing intense chemotherapy and radiation treatments.

I still remember taking the train to Pennsylvania University Hospital with my entire family to watch him receive his cancer treatments. To observe someone that loved his long black flowing hair lose it by the clump load still has a numbing effect on me today. I now believe the pain, suffering, vomiting, and overall physical and psychological effect his diagnosis had on our family taught us to be a stronger, closer, and more harmonious family. Fortunately, Billy's cancer to date is still in total remission, and now he only has a yearly checkup to ensure his good health.

As my brother was going through the battle of his life, I had graduated from Marcella L. Duffy Grammar School and entered Florence High School as a freshman in the fall of 1984. Mary Jane, the sibling closest in age to me, had just graduated from Florence that spring and began pursuing her career goal as a court stenographer at Popkins Stenography School in Cherry Hill. Upon attaining her certification as a court stenographer, Mary Jane married Douglas Wainwright and began a family of her own as well. Mary, like my other two sisters has two sons and one daughter.

Entering the cement walls of Florence High, which rests directly on the banks of the Delaware River, was not a big adjustment for me. In fact, it was a very easy transition. Of the four hundred students that populated our tiny school, because of sports and my older siblings, I already knew just about everyone in town as did most of the popular kids in our township. My best friend, Jimmy Rockhill, was already a junior at Florence, and most of my closer friends were older anyway. The key to being known in Florence was to be active in sports. It was a very close community that thrived on high-school sports, almost *Hoosier*-like if you are familiar with the movie. The town practically shut down on Saturday afternoons for football games, and during basketball season, lines formed outside of our tiny gym just so our loyal and crazed fans could get a seat.

Athletically speaking, during my sophomore year, Florence High was equivalent to a group 1 (small schools) dynasty. We won back-to-back state championships in baseball and sandwiched football and basketball state championships in-between those two. We were given rings, jackets, rides through the town on fire trucks, and even free haircuts. With winning came all of the normal fun things as well. We partied at Green Acre's Park, drank cheap beer, loitered at Rocco's pizzeria, and got into our fair share of mischief. In the back of my mind, however, I always knew to never cross the line; getting in any kind of trouble could have ruined my chance of attaining my ultimate goal, becoming a New Jersey state trooper. Having strict parents and positive role models in my teachers and coaches such as Art Bobik, Joe Frappolli, Ron Luyber and Steve Ordog also helped instill pride, fear, discipline and respect into my character.

It was this upbringing and mentality that formed the strongest of bonds between Jimmy Rockhill and me. I envied him for two reasons: he had connections to the state police, and because he was older, this meant he would be a trooper first! We were inseparable, and our goal in life was identical, which allowed us to continually remind each other of what to do and not to do. The fact that his mother was Colonel Pagano's personal secretary also served as a constant reminder and allowed me to feel close to the "state-police family" that his mom and aunts, who also worked for the state police, always referred to at family parties and social gatherings.

Academically speaking, while at Florence High, any reports or research papers I had to do always focused on the New Jersey State Police. I was infatuated with this organization that I knew so little about. While others were playing basketball at Duffy Middle School, pretending to be Julius Erving, I was practicing mock traffic stops on the New Jersey Turnpike in my basement where I would get involved in shoot-outs while seizing trunkloads of cocaine from drug couriers.

After Jimmy and my older friends graduated, aside from playing sports, high school almost became a nuisance for me. Since I turned eighteen during my senior year, getting my diploma was the only prerequisite I needed to take the written examination to become a New Jersey trooper. Though I had accomplished numerous things in high school, mainly in athletics while maintaining a B+ average academically, when it came time to identify my proudest moment for my 1988 high-school graduation-yearbook photo, I wrote, "When I become a New Jersey trooper."

Having led a relatively sheltered life for the past eighteen years while tucked away in the tiny confines of Florence Township and without any traumatic experiences aside from my brother's battle with cancer, I busted through the doors of Florence High ready to take on the world as a New Jersey state trooper. Barely old enough to vote and still unable to legally drink or gamble, at five feet ten inches and 165 pounds, my intense light blue eyes and black flattop haircut gave the image and appearance of a wannabe cop as I walked with a cocky arrogance, knowing that upon graduating from Florence High in late June 1988, my sole objective in life was to become a New Jersey state trooper.

CHAPTER 1

The Selection Process

Though I didn't look down on college or the values of higher education, I already made up my mind where I was headed in life. Even before I had my high-school diploma in hand, I knew the next state-police written test was scheduled for July 9, 1988, and I planned on being the first in line. I was eighteen years old and a high-school graduate, which was all that was required to participate in this initial phase of the yearlong selection process to become a New Jersey state trooper. Most of my friends headed off to college; and in all honesty, had my parents been able to afford to send me to a four-year university, I may have considered leaving New Jersey to get a degree in criminal justice while attempting to play football in college, but given the totality of circumstances, I truthfully didn't see the point in waiting to attain my lifelong dream.

In the days leading up to the written multiple-choice test for the 113th Recruit Class, I paid a man known only as "Captain" Sam del Rio $300 to take a "test prep" class he ran from the basement of his home near Princeton, New Jersey. This course was nothing more than a memorization class because he *somehow* had numerous copies of the original test in his physical possession. The barrel-chested captain was approximately five feet ten inches tall, roughly 230 pounds and in his late forties or early fifties when I met him at the side entrance of his home, which led to the basement that doubled as a classroom setup. To put it mildly, he had a great business going for himself. On this day alone, roughly twenty applicants crammed into his basement for the preparation course. The premise of the class was to repeatedly "study" only the correct answers that were highlighted on the identical test we would be taking in just a few days. Though nervous about utilizing this concept for something that meant the world to me, prior to departing Captain del Rio's "classroom," we were assured by him that the correct answer would "jump out at us" when we took the actual test in a few days. His only request was that we purposely get one wrong to make it look good!

On Saturday, July 9, 1988, my alarm clock jarred me awake at roughly 5:30 AM. During the previous night, I tossed and turned with nervous anticipation, fearing I would forget the principles I learned from Captain del Rio's class. After a quick shower and a bowl of cereal, I drove to Trenton High School on Chambers Street where the test was being conducted. As I neared the test site, my stomach churned, and my body twitched out of fear and excitement. Even though I arrived an hour and a half early for the 8:00 AM test, hundreds of people were already in line. Being a trooper in New Jersey was the dream of thousands, if not tens of thousands, of men and women. The charisma, aura, reputation, and desire to join this "outfit" were phenomenal. In theory, troopers were like Greek gods to those of us infatuated with the state police and the respect a uniformed trooper commanded. At eighteen, the thought of having so much power enthralled me.

As I exited my black 1985 Mitsubishi Starion and walked to the rear of the line, I humbly assessed each person I passed. Having conducted so many mock traffic stops, shoot-outs, and drug seizures in my basement, I was overconfident that I was already better suited to be a trooper than anyone already in line. Once I finally reached the rear, a sense of pride and anxiousness took over my spirit; I was on my way to becoming a New Jersey state trooper, and nothing was going to stand in my way.

As the minutes passed, thousands of people arrived at Trenton High; and the line appeared to wrap completely around the school on this bright, sunny, and warm summer morning. In addition to Trenton High, the test was also being offered at three other sites across the state. Each facility had a limited number of seats, and a second seating was held at noon on this same day across the state. Completely naive and lethargic to the concept of military bearing, my eyes wandered aimlessly as I stood in line, constantly evaluating my competition.

The test to become a trooper attracted all kinds of unique personalities and physical appearances: fat bald men; skinny guys dressed like dorks; cool guys wearing shades with long hair; and, of course, the typical model "trooper wannabe"—short stocky muscleheads who appeared to be on steroids with shaved heads. You name it—tall, short, plump, old, white, Asian, black, Hispanic—they were all there at Trenton High School on July 9, 1988, to take the written exam to become New Jersey troopers.

As we stood outside, waiting to be seated inside the cafeteria, uniformed troopers walked up and down the masses. Due to the volume of people, fortunately,

I didn't stand out. At times, in the distance, I could hear individuals getting yelled at or made fun of for one reason or another. The theme of this unwanted attention was always the same as troopers screamed, "None of you have what it takes to be Jersey troopers. Stop wasting our time and your time and just go home now!" My heart pounded, and a huge lump formed in my throat. A myriad of things were running through my mind. *What if they yell at me! What if I fail to remember the answers? Did I get here early enough to make the 8:00 AM seating, or am I going to have to wait until the noon test?*

As the yelling and screaming subsided, I could see in the distance that the doors to the cafeteria had opened, and we began to file in. Once inside, we were given strict instructions not to touch anything. A sharpened yellow no. 2 pencil and sealed test lay before each of us fortunate enough to be seated in the testing room. The trooper running the test barked very illicit and stern directions to us, and once he finished, we were permitted to open the test and begin. My heart was racing with nervous anxiety as I read and answered the first multiple-choice question, then the second, third, and fourth questions.

A calming sense of confidence overcame my body, and I even chuckled to myself because, as promised, the answers jumped right off the page, and I quickly completed the first section of the test. *I would have paid five thousand dollars for a guarantee like this!* The test itself was laughable. Basic verbal analogies comprised part one, and the second part were made up of general math and word problems. *What in the hell does this have to do with being a cop?* I quickly finished both sections as the answers literally jumped from the test sheet as promised by Captain del Rio. Being the good little soldier, I purposely got one wrong; and a few weeks later, I learned via a formal letter from the state police that I received an 88 out of 90 correct, thus, allowing me to move onto phase two of the selection process: the physical-agility test.

Unofficially, eight thousand individuals took the written test across the state that day. Due to a federal consent-decree order, whatever that is or meant, the passing score for a white male was 82 out of 90, but for all others, a 69 out of 90 enabled them to move forward to the next phase of the selection process. As basic of a test as it was, without Captain del Rio's class, I am certain that attaining the passing score as a white male would have been extremely challenging for me and most other nonminorities fortunate enough to have this much-needed edge. Though I had never heard of or wasn't aware of the reasons for the federal consent decree, I was just thankful that I was able to attend Captain del Rio's class.

On August 1, 1988, I received my official letter from the Department of Law and Public Safety, Division of State Police, stating I was invited to continue in the selection process for the 113th Recruit Class. Also contained in this package was the official twenty-six-page application to become a New Jersey trooper that each applicant had to complete. I was instructed to report to Division Headquarters in West Trenton at 10:15 AM on August 16 for a physical-agility test and was ordered to wear only a white T-shirt, athletic shoes, and shorts. This test consisted of pull-ups, push-ups, sit-ups, shuttle run, broad and vertical jumps, and ended with vision-and-color awareness test to ensure no one was color-blind.

Though physically prepared for this test, the events of this day were a total wake-up call to my mental well-being. From the second we were ordered out of our cars at exactly 10:15 AM, troopers dressed in full uniform screamed, yelled, and once again told all of us to go home because we were not worthy of being New Jersey troopers. Alphabetically, we stood at attention in complete silence for approximately one hour during which time, instructors walked up and down, belittling each and every one of us. As the light rain fell, we were given clear ziplock bags to keep our completed twenty-six-page application dry. Applicants who failed to wear white T-shirts, bring the proper identification or those stupid enough to arrive with either long hair or facial hair of any kind received the most attention from the twenty-plus troopers who appeared to love every minute of the mocking and razzing that they dealt out.

I recall standing there and physically shaking from pure fear and nervousness. At the same time, however, this is why I wanted to be a New Jersey trooper. I loved the discipline and knew it took a special type of person who was willing to endure the harsh realities that made the New Jersey State Police (NJSP) nationally known for having the most rigorous and intense selection process and training regiment in the country. And for those individuals who stood there with me that day, if they didn't already realize this, they did by the time they left West Trenton later in the day.

Upon finally filing into the gymnasium at Division Headquarters, instructors were screaming like maniacs as they broke us up into groups of fifteen. Identically dressed in captivating yellow T-shirts emblazoned with the infamous triangle of the NJSP, their shirts had bold black lettering that read, "Instructor." My group was shuffled like cattle directly to the left side of the gym where the pull-up station was located. A miserable-looking tall thin trooper with a scowl that could scare a pit bull was in charge of this exercise. After calling us all "dopes" and "idiots," he explained that we must fully extend our arms and completely lift our chins over the bar for the exercise to count. In terms of scoring, nineteen pull-ups was the maximum, and eight was the minimum score for passing.

With my whopping five-foot-ten, 165-pound frame, I had done twenty pull-ups a day at least five times a week recently in preparation for this test. *I couldn't wait to get up on that bar and impress this miserable trooper.* As the sixth individual in line, I quickly realized that no one had to worry about getting credit for nineteen pull-ups though. Even if you did twenty-five flawlessly, this trooper was not going to allow anyone to obtain a perfect score. When it was my turn, I immediately jumped up on the bar and started doing my pull-ups. In the midst of my second one, the trooper bellowed, "Get off there, you asshole! I never told you to jump up there!" He then further chastised me, stating, "You look like a little kid. How old are you?" Without being given time to answer, he finished by adding, "You look like you're gonna cry, you baby-faced prick!"

After finally allowing me to jump up on *his* pull-up bar, I started out strong. I was more than prepared due to my intense training for this day and knew I could easily do nineteen repetitions. When I got to my thirteenth pull-up, the trooper screamed, "STOP!" As I dangled aimlessly from the bar, I was afraid to let go, and my arms began to tire. The instructor belittled me for doing them incorrectly, and he ordered me, "Start all over and do them properly this time, you jackass!" When all was said and done, I had completed roughly twenty-six pull-ups, but on my score sheet, this bastard of a man gave me credit for eight pull-ups, the minimum passing score. *That bastard! What an auspicious beginning! What if I fail? Shit, I've prepared all summer for this damn test. I was in great physical shape, and he just gave me the absolute minimum score for passing.*

Fortunately, my preparedness paid off in all the other exercises. I cruised through the push-ups, sit-ups, shuttle run, and required jumping exercises. Though each instructor was just as callous and verbally abusive (yet comical) as the first trooper, they were much fairer in their scoring. I finished that horrific day with an 88 average and left the confines of Division Headquarters with an even more incredible passion to be a trooper. As I drove home, mentally I told myself that one day, I would be an instructor at the nation's toughest academy and be able to rib new recruits just as I had been for the past few hours.

On August 20, 1988, I received a letter congratulating me on passing the physical examination and was informed that the next phase was a written psychological examination called the Minnesota Multiphasic Personality Inventory MMPI. I was instructed to report to Trenton Central High School at 6:30 pm on August 24—just four days from now! The letter concluded with "failure to appear could result in termination from the selection process." Thanks for all the notice!

On the twenty-fourth of August, I confidently reported to Trenton High School, and the mood was much lighter and far less intense than at the physical exam. We stood outside at attention in the same area where the written exam was given for approximately forty-five minutes in complete silence. Unlike the first two phases, here, there were only a few troopers present, and any verbal furies that were unleashed appeared to be far more personal and direct yet low-key.

As we stood there, the troopers who were present walked up and down the line, looking for any imperfection in our physical appearance or clothing. As one trooper approached my area, I made the grave mistake of making eye contact for a mere split second. For an instant, I stood eye to eye with one of the most squared-away and intimidating human beings I have ever encountered. His brass nameplate glistened "R. Billings," but I already knew who he was: a menacing tall black man whose arm muscles bulged through his long-sleeve wool uniform shirt. He was the picture-perfect image of a trooper: the physique of a bodybuilder, the confidence of a professional boxer, and the attitude of a trained killer. Without hesitation, he briskly walked up to me and asked if I had a problem to which I immediately answered, "No, sir!" He then whispered ever so gently to me that I would never make it to become a New Jersey trooper because I was weak and lacked discipline. Prior to walking away from me, Sergeant Billings whispered in my ear something I would never forget, "If I catch you looking at me or any other trooper again, I am going to squeeze your neck until your eyeballs pop out!"

Now I had to go inside this building and take a psychological exam! Mentally, I was in shock! Even though I knew and understood it was all a mind game, this madman who was as muscular and ferocious as Godzilla had just threatened to pop my eyeballs from my skull! *How did he pass this phase?* Needless to say, at the ripe age of eighteen, I was shell-shocked but, as each moment and experienced passed, I became even more obsessed with becoming a trooper.

The MMPI was a 550-question multiple-choice test. It supposedly graded each individual by building a mental "profile" according to your answers. Many of the questions were repetitive, and I often found myself second-guessing an answer to the same previously asked question. After all, "Do you like the color yellow?" is not something I asked myself on a daily basis!

When the test was completed, we viewed a slide show depicting daily life at the State Police Academy and were told what would be expected of us if we secured an appointment. We also learned that as of this night, there would be approximately five hundred recruits left for the estimated 150 appointments to the 113th New Jersey State Police Academy Class, which was scheduled to begin in March of 1989. Passing the MMPI meant that I was now halfway through the selection process, and I didn't anticipate things would be getting any easier, but now my lifelong dream was within my grasp. Mentally, I kept telling myself that all I wanted was a chance to prove that I had what it takes to become a trooper. If I didn't make it, then it wasn't meant to be, but at the very least, I needed to get through the selection process and into the academy. Once at the academy, the rest would be up to me, and despite my age and any lack of maturity, I felt I was ready for the fierce challenges of being a law-enforcement officer.

On October 19, 1988, just fourteen days before my nineteenth birthday, I received a letter stating I had passed the MMPI and was invited to the oral-interview phase of the selection process. This, as I was told by friends who were already troopers and even Mrs. Rockhill, would most likely be my pitfall due to my age and lack of "life experience." This was the phase where the NJSP could, for any reason, dismiss a potential applicant because it was simply a pass-or-fail interview. Other critical factors were an individual's gender and ethnicity because state-police recruit classes had to be multicultural in appearance due to that same federal consent decree that forced white males to score higher on the written exam.

While waiting for the day of my oral board to arrive, an intense background check was being conducted. In addition to all of my financial and academic records being collected, former teachers, girlfriends, and friends were contacted as character references. A state-police detective then came to my parents' home and personally interviewed me, as well as my mother and father. Even questions about any imperfections in my siblings' backgrounds were identified, and even though I was the youngest of the five, I was forced to answer for their actions. When the interview had concluded, the detective inspected the interior of my personal vehicle and then knocked on doors throughout my neighborhood. It appeared as if no stone was unturned, and it's safe to say if I had a character flaw, it would have been revealed.

In preparation for the upcoming oral interview, I had gone out and spent nearly my entire life's savings. At Jack & Jules Men's Shop in Hamilton, Mercer County, I purchased a two-piece $550 navy blue Italian suit. Along with the suit, I was fitted with a pair of $150 black leather shoes, a $45 maroon tie with matching maroon socks, and a crisp new white dress shirt. I planned to look as sharp as possible, but how to make myself look older and more mature was what weighed heavily on my mind.

Going in, I knew the average interview lasted roughly thirty minutes; anything longer usually meant that you had issues that would get you tossed from the selection process, and anything shorter meant you were probably an idiot and didn't have a snowball's chance in hell of making it past the panel. My goal was to be in the interview for exactly thirty minutes!

For nearly *ninety minutes* on December 2, 1988, state police's superior officers grilled me on various topics and subjects. Also present during the interview were two psychologists who just sat, listened, observed, and interpreted my body language. *How unnerving is that!* These officers repeatedly put me in life-and-death situations and asked me how I would react. *I don't know. What in the hell would any cop do if an older married couple begins throwing pots and pans at them when arriving to break up a domestic argument!* Scenario after scenario, I confidently answered their questions without wavering or stumbling over my words. Most importantly, no matter how hard they tried to persuade me to do so, I never reneged on any answers even if I felt I had answered improperly. Showing a lack in self-confidence by changing your answers was a surefire way to get immediately bounced by the board.

Once the barrage of questions that were obviously directed toward my age and maturity ceased, I exited the interview room confident but curious. I had no idea ninety minutes had passed until I peered at my shiny gold Jules Jergensen watch that was neatly tucked under the sleeve of my white dress shirt. I thought I did well and felt the experiences of the selection process thus far only added to my confidence and maturity. I was composed, calm, and articulate; and I knew one thing's for sure. I looked damn good! Before leaving the grounds of Division Headquarters, I did what I am sure no other applicant from the 113th Recruit Class did: I went directly to the office of none other than Colonel Clinton L. Pagano.

Mrs. Rockhill had arranged for me to come see her and the colonel immediately following my oral interview. With Mrs. Rockhill on my side, I thought passing the oral boards was a humongous bonus. After signing in at the reception area, I went to the top floor of building no. 13 where the office of the superintendent was located. Upon reaching the top floor, I was greeted by Mrs. Rockhill. Just a few feet from her desk lay a brown door with a frosted glass panel inscribed, "Colonel Clinton L. Pagano, Superintendent, New Jersey State Police."

After a quick knock on the door, I was led into his office. Mrs. Rockhill left me to fend for myself, and I was once again awestruck. Though by now I had met him several times outside of Division Headquarters, I was still captivated by his presence. The office was decorated with numerous plaques and pictures of the colonel posing with high-ranking political figures and other officers of the state police. Being in the colonel's office was the pinnacle of my young life, and after a brief review of my oral examination, the colonel deflated me by stating he feels I may be a little young for the academy, but he would leave that decision up to the board who conducted my interview. Upon departing the colonel's office, he assured me that sooner or later, he knew I had the intestinal fortitude to one day be a trooper in his "outfit."

I left the grounds of Division and drove southbound on Route 29 along the banks of the Delaware River, pondering if I was years away from my dream or just a few months. In my heart, I knew I had done everything in my power to prepare, but it was now out of my hands. I would just have to wait and see what happens and if the board feels I am mature enough to proceed, but mentally, the weeks or months of waiting that lie ahead would be very difficult.

I returned home after the twenty-five-minute drive and hung my expensive suit up in the closet of my bedroom. Though mentally drained, I did what had become second nature by now in my preparations for the academy and went for a five-mile run. The cold December air pounded on my chest cavity, but my mind and body were warmed by my burning desire to prove that I could make it to the academy. As my feet pounded on the icy, cold pavement, I repeatedly ran through each scenario and question of the oral board, rethinking my answers.

By the time I had showered and settled in from my run, the phone rang, and I nonchalantly walked to the kitchen where my mom was preparing for our daily 4:30 PM dinner routine. Much to my surprise, the voice on the other end of the phone was Mrs. Rockhill who informed me she just had a discussion with the captain of my oral board. She relayed to me that they were very impressed with me, and despite my age, I appeared very mature and handled myself extremely well during the examination. When all was said and done, the board had agreed—reluctantly, due to my age—to give me the thumbs up and allowed me to enter the final phase of the selection process.

Three days after Christmas 1988, I received my official confirmation that I had passed the oral interview and was now invited to the final phase of the selection process: the medical examination. This was held on January 7, 1989, and was an extremely comprehensive exam of the bones, muscles, limbs, and joints. Doctors also reviewed medical records we were ordered to bring from family physicians. The state-police doctors who controlled this phase had the authority to dismiss any recruit who had previous surgery or injuries, which they felt might impede a recruit from being able to deal with the intense physical rigors of the academy. This final phase proved to be the easiest for me, and it was now only weeks before my dream would begin. Our class was slated to begin training on March 15, 1989; and before I had ever voted, drank, or gambled legally, I was on my way to becoming a New Jersey state trooper; and nothing could stand in my way.

CHAPTER 2

Politics 101

On February 21, 1989, I thought I received the letter I waited a lifetime for from the Division of State Police. Instead of it being my official "entry package" for the academy, it proved that the swirling rumors about our class being delayed were correct. The letter stated that Governor Thomas Kean had mandated a hiring freeze throughout the entire state of New Jersey due to projected revenue shortfalls. Budget cuts were imposed, and we were informed via this letter that the 113th Recruit Class had been postponed. This event was not uncommon; in fact, I learned most classes were always delayed a month or so, but the delay never lingered more than a few months. Initially, we learned that the hiring freeze would be lifted shortly, and our class would begin by the end of summer. Not fully understanding what politics had to do with the state police, I paid attention to politics the first time in my life and, for obvious reasons, had an instant disliking to all elected officials because of this action. *I could understand tightening the belt when it came to state spending, but how can a politician, especially one who is surrounded 24/7 by troopers like the governor is, have the audacity to cut funding to the state police?* The idea of this, to me, seemed ludicrous.

Weeks quickly turned into months, and now I wasn't sure what in the hell was going on. No one from Mrs. Rockhill down to the most junior trooper—which now included my best friend, Jimmy, and a mutual friend named Joe Repici who had both graduated from the 111th Recruit Class—had any idea as to what was going on. Finally, on August 25, 1989, I received another letter from the division that stated,

In response to budgetary restrictions, a moratorium on hiring remains in effect throughout the Division of State Police; consequently, the 113th recruit class has been deferred indefinitely. You should be proud of your progress thus far in the selection process. We hope you maintain a high degree of interest in a career with our organization.

Deferred? What in the hell does that mean? Proud of my progress? Are you freaking kidding me? I was sad, upset, and depressed; but I was only nineteen years old. I still had my whole life ahead of me, and when projecting into the future, after serving twenty-five years as a trooper, I would still be able to retire at age forty-four. My family and close friends actually thought the delay would be good for me, allowing more time for me to grow up and mature. *Screw them; I just wanted to be a trooper!*

For the remainder of 1989, in anticipation for the academy, I was relentless in my workouts. My desire, will, and obsession of becoming a trooper only grew stronger. Rumors continually swirled as to when the hiring freeze would be lifted, but we, the members of the 113th Recruit Class, would never receive another letter from the "Pagano regime."

Before I knew it, months had passed, as did my twentieth birthday. Despite my numerous contacts within the state police, absolutely no one knew when our class would be entering the academy. The year 1990 as now upon us, and it was an election year in the state of New Jersey for the position of governor. In the months leading up to the election, I saw and listened to numerous campaign spots and realized just how full of shit politicians were. I couldn't change the radio or television stations quick enough each time the candidates came on to trash their counterpart. I quickly realized they never discussed the issues and, instead, only spoke negatively about one another. Having never even voted, I swore off politics for a lifetime. *Whatever lying scumbag who was going to put my class in first was who I wanted to win. Once I became a trooper, I would never again have to worry about the despicable actions of these individuals who somehow chose politics as a career.*

In November 1990, Republican governor Thomas Kean's tenure was ending, and political control throughout the state was assumed by the Democrats when James Florio won the election versus James Courier. Unbelievably, after being officially sworn in as governor in January 1991, as one of his first acts as the new leader, Florio ousted the state police's historic and famed leader of fourteen years: Colonel Clinton L. Pagano. James Florio, as was his right as governor, appointed a new colonel and selected longtime crony and retired trooper Justin J. Dintino to return to the ranks and lead the New Jersey State Police.

Colonel Pagano was a legend. How could he do this? As someone who already despised politicians to begin with, my anger and resentment grew by leaps and bounds, but I just hoped for a silver lining in all of this madness. A new governor and a new colonel—maybe this is what it was going to take for our class to finally move forward!

As the months of 1991 now passed, roughly 150 individuals, myself included, who had already been selected for appointment to the NJSP Academy still had absolutely no idea what was going on. For more than a year since being appointed as the new colonel, Justin Dintino had not sent one single letter to us, and we were left hanging in the balance. Supposedly, due to the alleged budget crisis, the hiring freeze throughout the state police remained in effect, but what was really transpiring was anyone's guess. For nearly two-plus years now, those of us who had dedicated our lives to becoming troopers waited patiently, but the new administration never once acknowledged our existence. Then, in January 1992, exactly one year after the new Democratic administration was sworn in, the unthinkable happened right before my eyes as I glared at a local television station.

"Tough luck!" was the response Colonel Justin Dintino, superintendent of the New Jersey State Police, gave to the reporter from New York's channel 9 news station. These words were worse than a dagger to my heart because he was referring to the fate of the 113th New Jersey State Police Recruit Class of which I was a member.

The interview addressed a bitter dispute that was brewing in the media and on the airwaves throughout New Jersey. Reportedly, state-police officers and troopers who were Colonel Pagano's loyalists were not receptive to the changes that were being made among the ranks by Colonel Dintino. Included in these proposed changes was a new criterion for selection and appointment to the NJSP Academy. The interview addressed these changes as well as the legitimacy of a vicious rumor: did the new colonel despise Pagano to the point that he insisted a new recruit class be tested and selected for appointment because he didn't want "Pagano selected" recruits?

Obviously caught in the midst of this political firestorm were the defenseless 150 individuals who already made up the 113th Recruit Class. While I do not speak for the entire class, I can admit that each day of those four years had been dedicated to my becoming a trooper. Without hesitation, I can say that the years of stress; uncertainty; endless miles of running; and countless push-ups, pull-ups, and sit-ups had definitely taken their toll on my young mind and body. And to think, after all this time, this insensitive, callous bastard had the audacity to say, "Tough Luck!" when directly asked by the reporter about those of us who had already passed through the grueling selection process and were waiting appointment to the academy.

What became evident to everyone associated with the state police was that Colonel Dintino was brought on-board by Florio to be a hatchet man. Elder troopers retired by the droves and specialized units like Drug Interdiction (DITU), Criminal Enterprise and Racketeering Bureau (CERB), and other aggressive proactive units were consolidated and phased out. The hard-core, aggressive, and stop at no cost programs to get illegal drugs and activity out of New Jersey that defined the Pagano regime were decimated and came to a screeching halt under Dintino's leadership.

Through friends, I learned that road troopers were bitter; and all activity had stopped, even on the infamous New Jersey Turnpike, also known as the Black Dragon, where daily massive drug seizures were the norm. As I later learned, as a political maneuver to secure the Democratic vote during his campaign, Florio had promised the American Civil Liberties Union (ACLU) and Democrats alike that his administration—in exchange for their votes, of course—would look into years of an alleged practice called racial profiling by New Jersey state troopers. Ultimately, the aforementioned specialized units were terminated in hopes of reducing the amount of complaints that were rampant among the minority community that New Jersey troopers unjustifiably targeted them for motor-vehicle stops and searched their vehicles without probable cause. Obviously, without removing Pagano, who was notorious for backing the aggressive nature of his troopers, this wouldn't have been possible. As I followed and learned more about all of this, my resentment toward politicians was at an all-time high and rightfully so. Exchanging favors for votes—does that really happen in politics? My naïveté was quickly being exposed as I was being introduced to a whole new societal demon known as ruthless politics.

Speculation quickly grew as to what would happen with our class now that the new colonel had been appointed and publicly stated he wanted to revamp the qualifications for the selection process. Considering all the time and money the state had already spent on our testing and selection process, it only seemed logical for our class to enter the academy once the hiring freeze was lifted, *right*? Under normal circumstances, it shouldn't have mattered; but it was obvious that Dintino, for whatever reason, had an ax to grind, and no one was safe, especially a bunch of trooper wannabes.

Nearly three entire years had now passed since the 113th Recruit Class last assembled together in West Trenton for the final phase of the selection process. Even more disheartening was the fact that we hadn't received an official letter from the state police since August of 1989. Fellow recruits, whom I became friendly with during the selection process, all remained optimistic, for this was our dream! No matter how long we had to wait, each of us just wanted a shot to prove ourselves worthy of becoming a New Jersey trooper.

On December 15, 1991, I woke up and went to my job as a uniformed security-guard supervisor in Langhorne, Pennsylvania. Rather than go to college during the entire delay, I had decided to continue working full-time. Once my 7:00 AM to 3:00 PM shift had ended, I rushed home, shucked off the dorky polyester uniform I was forced to wear, and did just as I had done at least five times a week for the past three-plus years: went out for my five-mile run. As I walked down Chestnut Street toward my parents' house, I saw that the mailman had just delivered to our house, and I retrieved the mail before entering the house. Much to my delight, there was *finally* a letter from the state police! All the prayers and years of patience had finally paid off. *At last, my official notice to report to the academy had come!*

Still sweating and out of breath from my run, I carefully tore the envelope open. For this was an envelope and letter that I would keep forever. My heart pounded, and I couldn't wait to read my congratulatory letter, formally inviting me to be a recruit for the 113th NJSP Training Class! My eyes couldn't have been more deceived as I read the following letter *(official copy):*

State of New Jersey
DEPARTMENT OF LAW AND PUBLIC SAFETY
DIVISION OF STATE POLICE
POST OFFICE BOX 7068
WEST TRENTON, NEW JERSEY 08628-0068
(609) 882-2000

ROBERT J. DEL TUFO
Attorney General

COLONEL JUSTIN J. DINTINO
Superintendent

December 13, 1991

Mr. John I. Hogan

Dear Mr. Hogan:

The hiring freeze which has affected the Division of State Police since February of 1989 was recently rescinded. In the near future, we hope to institute a new recruit class. Before a new class is undertaken, however, it is necessary to resolve a number of outstanding issues regarding the selection process. Among these issues is the formulation of a new, job-related written examination which satisfies the Consent Decree between the Division and the United States Department of Justice.

Due to the above factors, as well as the significant amount of time which has elapsed since the previous selection process and the attrition which has taken place in the group previously selected, a new selection process will be required for the 113th State Police recruit class. As soon as the plans for this new class are finalized, you will be notified and invited to apply.

You should take pride in what you have accomplished in the past selection process. We encourage you to maintain a high degree of interest in our organization.

Thank you for your understanding and continued interest in the New Jersey State Police.

Sincerely,

FOR COL. JUSTIN J. DINTINO
SUPERINTENDENT

Roy D. Bloom, Major
Administration Section Supv.

New Jersey Is An Equal Opportunity Employer

Tears ran down my face as my mother came outside and hugged me. Attempting to make me feel better, she stated, "God does these things for a reason. If it's meant to be, you'll get in the next time." I wasn't so forgiving, however. I was bitter, angry, and disgusted. Had Governor Kean just let our class proceed, none of this bullshit would have happened. Goddamn politics!

Forty-one months had passed since I had taken the written exam on July 9, 1988. I was now twenty-two years old and, to no one's fault but my own, allowed all this time to pass without pursuing other career goals or interests. The problem was that aside from being a trooper, I had no other aspirations—*none*! My only goal and dream was to get an opportunity to prove myself worthy of being a New Jersey state trooper.

With news of the criterion that was being suggested to now be a trooper, I soon realized that as a result of my lack of desire to attend college or strive to be anything other than a trooper, I may never even qualify under the new educational standards that Colonel Dintino was attempting to implement. Among other things, a four-year college degree was made mandatory to even take the written test. *I'm fucked! All those miles in the heat, rain, snow, and sleet! Thousands, if not tens of thousands, of push-ups, sit-ups, pull-ups all for naught! They can't do this! How can they just throw us aside like this? Is this just? What about all the time and money spent on our testing process?* Many of my "classmates" had been passed over for promotions and even terminated because their employers knew they would soon be leaving to enter the academy. *How can Dintino not care about everything we went through to get selected? Is he really that callous? What am I going to do now? My high-school friends were beginning to graduate college and land good jobs! Goddamn it! I was supposed to be a trooper years ago!*

I was at a total loss. I had no drive, ambition, or faintest idea as to what I would now do with my life. I had a total of eighteen college credits from a county college where I was just going through the motions to make it look good. Also, I was trapped at a job that paid decent for my age but offered me no gratification or was something I would ever want to make a career of. Even the thought of joining a police department other than the New Jersey State Police made me nauseous. The proverbial "Don't put all your eggs in one basket" had just surfaced to kick me right—square in the nuts! Deeply depressed and feeling an overwhelming sense of failure, I opted to give up hope. My dreams were crushed, and I would never get a chance to prove myself worthy of being a New Jersey trooper all because of the sickening and incredulous acts of New Jersey politicians.

Part II

Brice to the Rescue

A few days had now passed since receiving the letter that obliterated my hopes, dreams, and goals. My five-mile runs immediately ceased, and I stopped working out altogether. Each morning, I listlessly awakened and went to work with no ambition, spirit, or guidance. Upon coming home from work one day in late December, the phone rang at my parents' house. The voice at the other end was deep and unfamiliar as he asked to speak with John Hogan. I quickly learned it belonged to a guy from my hometown named Brice Cote. I always saw Brice out running but never talked to him. I learned through mutual friends who he was and saw him at the various testing sites during the selection process, so I knew he was a hopeful member of the now-defunct 113th class. *What does he want, and why is he calling me? Didn't this dope get the letter? Hey, pal, we're not a class, and we sure as hell ain't going to the academy together! In fact, I don't even feel like talking about the freaking state police!*

After acknowledging the letter we both received, Brice said something to me that I will never forget, "John, they can't do this!" His voice was calm, stern, and very matter-of-fact. Brice added, "I am not sure what I have to do, but I am not going to allow them to get away with this!" As these words spewed from Brice's mouth, I am sure I was on the other end, rolling my eyes. *This guy is off his rocker! What in the hell can one person do? Go vent somewhere else. I have my own issues!* At the time, I figured he was just angry; after all, he was talking about fighting the entire state of New Jersey as well as the fucking colonel of the New Jersey State Police. *Good luck, pal, but I need to decide what I am going to do with my life!*

Unlike me, Brice was already married and had three children. He made great money as a horse trainer/jockey, and his wife was a registered nurse. With his being thirty-three years of age, why was he so upset? What we did have in common, though, was the burning passion to become New Jersey troopers—period! Plain and simple! It is this type of motivation, commitment, and persistence that separates individuals. Brice and I realized our dreams, aspirations, and goals; but unlike me, Brice was not going to give up just yet. Though I thought he was insane, I sat and listened intently to him vehemently denounce the actions of Colonel Dintino and the state police. Brice concluded our conversation by saying that he was looking into some things and would call me in a few days. Before hanging up, Brice's exact words to me were "John, we are not going to take this decision lying down!"

To say the least, Brice made quite a first impression on me. While I knew his intentions were good, the truth is, I thought he was crazy. After all, we were powerless. *What could he possibly be looking into?* I was certain he would just go back to his life, and I probably wouldn't ever hear from him again. I was positive he was just blowing off steam and was pissed about being jerked off by the state for the past four years like the rest of us. At this point, the only thing I knew about Brice Cote was that he was thirty-three, in great physical shape, and as serious as a heart attack. *Did he mean what he said?* I figured I was doing myself an injustice if I lend credibility to this person. After all, I suffered enough over the past four years. My dreams were already shattered. I didn't need to buy into false hope, especially from someone I hardly knew. As expected, a few days passed by, and Brice never called as promised.

From out of nowhere, in the waning days of 1991, front-page newspaper articles from the state's largest publications printed stories titled STATE WASTES $550,000 ON TROOPER TRAINING and CHIEF OF STATE POLICE COPS A COSTLY ATTITUDE, which had the subtitle "Colonel Dintino may dump two hundred qualified recruits whom he considers part of his predecessor's regime."

Where in the hell are they getting this information? Who is behind this? The articles kept referring to "anonymous sources." Who in the hell would have the balls to go to the media and report these facts and, in essence, challenge the morality of the colonel and the entire state of New Jersey?

Another day had passed. The phone rang at my parents' house. Brice Cote was on the other end and said, "I told you I wasn't going down without a fight!" *Was I to believe that he had single-handedly brought this issue to the forefront using the media? No freaking way! This man is out of his gourd! How did he do it? Where did he get the information and resources?*

To put it mildly, Brice knew a lot of people. I quickly learned that Brice Cote was a man of his word and had "friends" in important places. I could hear the excitement in his voice, and he insisted that I immediately come to his house and see what he was in possession of. As could be expected, I jumped in my car and arrived at his house on Riverbank Drive minutes later.

From individuals with ties to the state police, whose names will continue to remain anonymous after all these years, Brice was given numerous pages of confidential documents pertaining to the 113th Recruit Class. Included in these documents were the names and addresses of fellow recruits who made it through the selection process with Brice and me. Now we had the ammunition to fight Dintino's claim that "due to the attrition that has taken place in the group previously selected," a new class must be chosen. If we could prove his reasons for wanting a new selection process were bogus, the real truth as to why he wanted his "own recruits" chosen would surface. The simple underlying truth was Dintino despised the Pagano regime and vindictively held a long-standing grudge against Pagano. This grudge stemmed from a class-action, age-discrimination lawsuit that Dintino was a part of back in the 1980s before he and other troopers were forced to retire upon turning fifty-five years old.

Apparently, Justin Dintino, who was a senior member of the state police at the time, spearheaded a class-action lawsuit that was filed by elder troopers against the state of New Jersey. This group claimed that the mandatory retirement age of fifty-five for all troopers, excluding the colonel who was a political appointee, was unfair and discriminatory. Colonel Pagano, however—whose legend was built on his relentless defense of young, brash, and aggressively trained road troopers—pushed for the mandatory retirement policy so he could continue to reload the ranks with youth. Feeling betrayed and unsupported by the Pagano regime, Dintino's group lost their battle; and speculation was that upon turning fifty-five years old, Justin Dintino retired bitter, angry, and with a strong resentment toward Pagano. In defense of his stance, Colonel Pagano publicly stated that "the NJSP needed young and energetic troopers who were aggressive and could maintain the high level of tradition that the New Jersey State Police was nationally renowned for." While touching on this feud between Pagano and Dintino, news reports and printed articles confirmed that "the 113th Recruit Class had lost a battle with bureaucracy before ever getting a chance to fight crime." Basically, I learned that bureaucracy was just a fancy word for the callous, backstabbing, and manipulative actions of our elected officials.

In response to the mounting media attention this issue was now getting, Colonel Dintino began offering excuses such as "the testing cycle for the 113th class was unfair to minorities!" He stated that a new test must be designed to meet the requirements of the long-standing consent decree the state police had signed with the United States Department of Justice. *Lies! Backtracking! Utter bullshit! The same testing process had been used for decades. Now, suddenly, it's unfair? If anything, the current test was discriminatory toward non-minorities. Remember, white males needed to get an 82 out of 90 correct just to move onto the next phase!*

Publicly, as a result of these front-page headlines, this issue became a hot topic. Almost daily, the debate raged on radio talk shows such as NJ 101.5 and throughout the local news stations. As a result of this firestorm, our class garnered an identity and became known as the Fighting 113th.

As public support for our class grew immensely, Colonel Dintino did not back off, however. If anything, he became even more aggressive, resentful, and bitter. In an attempt to end the onslaught of negative press, he wrote an editorial that was printed in the *Trentonian* in which he stated, "I too share the concerns of the 1989 recruit candidates. More importantly, I am committed to a testing and selection process for State Police Troopers that is fair, honest, open and objective. I intend to diligently pursue that goal—the public safety deserves nothing less." *Was Brice Cote out of magic? Was that the final nail in the 113th's coffin? Where do we go from here?*

Part III

The Fighting 113th Rejuvenated

The phone rang; it was Brice! "Put a shirt and tie on. We are meeting with Senator John Dimon at five thirty tonight at his office!" *How in the hell did he pull this one off? To put it mildly, Brice was as relentless and determined as an angry pit bull!* Every call I received from Brice, whether at work or at home, had a hidden new adventure attached to it.

"You need public support! *Politicians will only listen to you if they think it can in turn help themselves!"* These words came directly from the mouth of elderly senator John Dimon, whose office was located right in Florence, about three-tenths of a mile from Brice's house. Persistence, once again, had paid off for Brice. After several phone calls to his office (unbeknownst to me), Brice finally got the senator to listen to our plight! While I appreciated his candor, my opinion of politicians took yet another nosedive! *Self-serving bastards! Greedy, egomaniacal, and immoral! If your issue can't produce a way for them to get votes, then they had no time for you!*

A day following our meeting with Senator Dimon, I found myself sitting next to Brice in the office of one of New Jersey's most notorious, sought-after, and high-profile attorney named Francis J. Hartman. Located in Moorestown, New Jersey, Brice somehow convinced Mr. Hartman to listen to our dilemma, and he agreed to meet with us. After reviewing all the letters and documentation we presented to him, Mr. Hartman was sympathetic to our situation. He told us that if we could get the rest of our classmates together, he would willingly represent the Fighting 113th in a class-action lawsuit against the state of New Jersey and the New Jersey State Police. *Sue the state and the state police? It was all just happening way too quickly. Do I really want to do that? Are there repercussions for this, and if so, how bad could they be?*

Within days of this meeting, using the confidential documents that "mysteriously" arrived on Brice's door-steps, we sent a letter to every one of our potential classmate's homes. The letter was plain, simple, and almost generic looking; and stapled to it was the business card of our attorney, Francis J. Hartman (official copy, including the misspelling!).

If you have recently received a letter from the STATE POLICE that has terminated the 113th class of recruits, or you received a phone call from recruiting Nov, Dec, of 1990.

And you are still interested in becoming a state Trooper please contact;

Francis J. Hartman
ATTORNEY AT LAW
300 CHESTER AVENUE
MOORESTOWN, NEW JERSEY 08057

THE LAW OFFICES OF   (609) 235-0220
HARTMAN, MARKS & NUGENT   FAX (609) 273-8617

If this concerns you, please act fast. If you haven't had any of these contacts from recruiting disregaurd this letter.

The Fighting 113th

Francis J. Hartman
ATTORNEY AT LAW
300 CHESTER AVENUE
MOORESTOWN, NEW JERSEY 08057

THE LAW OFFICES OF   (609) 235-0220
HARTMAN, MARKS & NUGENT   FAX (609) 273-8617

Within a week's time, Brice received confirmation from Mr. Hartman that enough recruits had called his office, and he was officially retained to pursue this issue on our behalf. Miraculously, with Brice's lead, the two of us had circled the wagons, and the members of the "terminated" 113th Recruit Class were quickly coming together. *Look out, Dintino. We're coming for you! Your credibility and reputation are at stake! Don't screw with the 113th!* My mind, spirit, and soul had been recharged; and as usual, my mom told me, "See? God works in mysterious ways!"

By the first of the year, 1992, my personal computer had a database setup with the names, addresses, and home and work numbers for the remaining members of our class. We even went as far as to rent out a conference room at the New Brunswick Hilton, located just off the New Jersey Turnpike, exit no. 9, where a meeting with the revitalized Fighting 113th met. We were very organized; totally sure of what we were doing; and, most importantly, refused to be denied our right to enter the academy. Basically, we were fighting city hall and all the bureaucratic bullshit that came with it and ready for the challenges that lay ahead.

On January 6, 1992, Brice Cote, the self-appointed president of the Fighting 113th, received this letter from the law office of our attorney, Francis J. Hartman (official copy):

The Law Offices Of
Hartman, Marks & Nugent

FRANCIS J. HARTMAN*
ROBIN G. MARKS*
CHARLES H. NUGENT, JR.*

JOY E. MCGINNIS*
STEPHEN H. DUNBAR*

*ALSO A MEMBER OF PENNSYLVANIA BAR

300 CHESTER AVENUE
MOORESTOWN, NJ 08057-0415

609-235-0220

FAX 609-273-8617

OF COUNSEL
W. THOMAS MCGANN

January 6, 1992

The Fighting 113th
c/o Brice L. Cote
115 Riverbank Drive
Roebling, N.J. 08554

Re: The Fighting 113th v. Col. Justin Dintino

Dear 113th Class Members:

It is my understanding that many of the members who completed all of the prerequisites to reporting on March 8, 1989 to Sea Girt to attend the State Police Academy, have determined not to take lying down the decision by Colonel Justin Dintino that they will have to reapply for admission to that recruit class.

It is my further understanding that following the medical examination, a representative of the State Police assured each member of the class that they were "in" and that they were to report on March 8, 1989. Thereafter, sometime in early January of 1989, a letter was received saying that the class would be delayed. Subsequent communications have been received reassuring each of you that you should stay in shape because as soon as the freeze on hiring is lifted, you would begin attending class.

It is my proposal that we proceed on three fronts: (a) by seeking public support; (b) by seeking political support; and (c) by litigation.

Our lawsuit would seek to require that the Colonel include everyone in the 113th Class who was "accepted", and is still interested, in the next class of recruits without further requirement of any kind.

The lawsuit will be a class action. Each person who wishes to be specifically named as a plaintiff can be, but the action will be brought even for those who do not individually wish to be plaintiffs. I think one or more taxpayers should be included as plaintiffs as well. The suit would seek not only to have each of you admitted to the class but, in the alternative, would seek

THE LAW OFFICES OF

Hartman, Marks & Nugent   Page 2.

damages both for the action of the State in having you qualify when there was a freeze, as well as damages for what happened to you after you qualified until the present time. I know that most of you are not interested in damages, but I feel this is one more pressure we can use to resolve the matter by accepting you into the class.

It is my hope that you will select a small committee which will communicate with me and then in turn communicate with your members. I understand that you will undertake to raise funds not only from members of the class but from family, friends and other supporters. The commitment of money, usually commits a person otherwise to the cause. On the subject of money, it is my understanding that at your initial meeting you will try to raise a war chest of at least $10,000 for legal fees and costs and some money for the organizational effort of telephoning, postage, copying, etc. The money raised will be held by your officers to be paid upon presentation of bills for time and out-of-pocket costs.

This is obviously a less-than-complete letter, but it is intended to indicate our willingness to represent your group and to indicate briefly how we intend to proceed.

We await confirmation that you wish us to proceed as proposed.

Very truly yours,

HARTMAN, MARKS & NUGENT

Francis J. Hartman, Esquire

FJH/jtt

Public support! We had to get public support! How do we do this? Where do we start? Are politicians really that transparent that they'll swing with whatever is better for their future? Over the next few weeks, members of the Fighting 113th were everywhere, gaining momentum with public support. Each time Governor Florio made a public appearance, no matter where in the state he was, a fellow recruit was there to ask him to take a position on our class. "Governor, sir, doesn't it bother you that almost a million dollars of taxpayers' money would be wasted if this class is terminated?" What could he possibly say in front of an auditorium full of average hardworking taxpayers? Letters seeking support for our cause were written to every member of the Senate, assembly, Congress— you name it! I even wrote a personal letter to Governor Florio and Colonel Dintino. *What in the hell was I thinking?*

Other recruits wrote to legislatures and lobbyists in an attempt to draw attention to our plight. A petition drive was also initiated; and one recruit, Michael Coloner, even wrote to the Gulf War hero general H. Norman Schwarzkopf, whose father founded the New Jersey State Police in 1921 on the principles of "honor, duty, and fidelity."

Enclosed are exact copies of sent letters:

GENERAL H. NORMAN SCHWARZKOPF   MICHAEL L. COLANER

FEBRUARY 7, 1992

Dear General:

I am writing to you on behalf of the 113th New Jersey State Police recruit class to inform you of, what we believe to be, an injustice imposed upon us. Knowing the Generals close association with the New Jersey State Police, we hope that you may feel as we do the need to contest the present decision of the current administration.

My fellow recruits and I were selected for academy assignment in January of 1989 after meeting all of the requirements to be accepted into the 113th class.

On February 21, 1989, due to projected revenue shortfalls, former Governor Thomas Kean, at Governor James Florio's request, mandated a hiring freeze and budget cuts for the State of New Jersey. The State Police, then under Superintendent Clinton Pagano, kept us informed through letters as to the on-going status. (See enclosure)

In the three years since then, Governor Florio has taken office and replaced Colonel Pagano with Colonel Justin Dintino. Governor Florio recently lifted the hiring freeze and provided the State Police with the funds necessary to train the 113th recruit class.

Since the hiring freeze has been lifted, we have been informed that we are no longer the 113th State Police recruit class. The State Police cite three factors in our termination; they are as follows:

1. The formulation of a new job related written examination which satisfies the Consent Decree between the Division of State Police and the United States Department of Justice.

2. The significant amount of time which has elapsed since the previous selection process.

3. Attrition in the group selected.

In addition to these factors, a college degree is now being required.

We provide the following for your consideration in our support:

1. According to New Jersey Congresswoman Marge Roukema there is currently no dispute over the current written exam and the Consent Decree between the Division of State Police and the United States Department of Justice.

2. As for the significant amount of time elapsed, we cite the case of the 92nd State Police recruit class that was selected in 1973 and graduated the State Police Academy in 1977. This was also due to budget restrictions. We believe that this shows that a significant amount of time can elapse and not negatively impact, but enhance the quality of the prospective State Trooper. We know of few people, if any, that would put their lives on hold for three years for the opportunity of becoming a State Trooper.

February 7, 1992
Page Two
To: General H. Norman Schwarzkopf
From: Michael L. Colaner

3. The State Police also know of no attrition, for they haven't contacted us since November of 1990, at which time they encouraged us to maintain a high degree of interest in a career with the State Police and advised us that we would enter the academy as soon as funds were available. We have contacted 131 of the 154 recruits without the help of the State Police in locating them, disproving attrition.

We believe, as your father did when he set forth 70 years ago, that State Troopers need to be tested in the areas of general intelligence, reasoning, and elementary mathematics.

I myself have a Military Police background with the United States Marine Corps. I left the Marine Corps after achieving the rank of corporal and four years of dedicated service in law enforcement.

If the State Police are looking for a college degree as a prerequisite to becoming a trooper, they should go even further and limit the degree to criminal sciences. For if an individual who spent four years going to school and achieving a bachelor of arts degree in fine arts is more qualified then any individual with any military background, they are mistaken. I am in no way discounting the importance of a college degree. In fact, I have been pursuing one myself, but it was not a requirement when we were selected to enter the 113th class in 1989. I know of no individual college that teaches the three points the New Jersey State Police was founded on, Honor, Duty, and Fidelity.

In conclusion General, we are looking for any help you can give us. It would be greatly appreciated. I have enclosed the requirements presented to us at the time of our initial testing as well as articles on our class. I have also enclosed letters from our senators and lawyers to the State Police and our Governor, asking them to please review our case and overturn the present decision of the current administration. If you need to contact me for further information, my address and telephone number is listed below.

I have enclosed names and telephone numbers of people associated with our cause.

Thank you for your time and consideration.

Sincerely,

Michael L. Colaner
The Fighting 113th

FRANK R. LAUTENBERG
NEW JERSEY

COMMITTEE:
APPROPRIATIONS
SUBCOMMITTEES:
TRANSPORTATION, CHAIRMAN
COMMERCE, JUSTICE, STATE AND JUDICIARY
DEFENSE
FOREIGN OPERATIONS
VA, HUD AND INDEPENDENT AGENCIES

United States Senate
WASHINGTON, DC 20510-3002

COMMITTEE:
BUDGET

COMMITTEE:
ENVIRONMENT AND PUBLIC WORKS
SUBCOMMITTEES:
SUPERFUND, OCEAN AND WATER PROTECTION, CHAIRMAN
ENVIRONMENTAL PROTECTION
WATER RESOURCES, TRANSPORTATION AND INFRASTRUCTURE

HELSINKI COMMISSION

January 14, 1992

Dear Mr. Russano:

Thank you for contacting me regarding the termination of the 113th State Police Academy training class.

I am looking into this matter with the appropriate authorities and will be back in touch with you as soon as possible.

In the meantime, should you have any additional information that might be helpful during my review, please forward the information directly to my Newark office.

Sincerely,

Frank R. Lautenberg

FRL:ted

REPLY TO:
☐ 506 HART SENATE OFFICE BUILDING
WASHINGTON, DC 20510-3002
(202) 224-4744

☐ ONE GATEWAY CENTER SUITE 1011
NEWARK, NEW JERSEY 07102-5311
(201) 645-3030

☐ BARRINGTON COMMONS
208 WHITE HORSE PIKE
SUITES 18-19
BARRINGTON, N.J. 08007-1322
(609) 757-5353

JOHN I. HOGAN

January 20, 1992

Dear Governor Florio,

We are writing to you in an attempt to draw your attention to the **113th Class of State Police Recruits**. As a group, we have successfully completed **ALL** of the pre- Academy testing requirements.

Approximately 8,000 individuals began the selection process which began with a written examination. Following the written was a physical agility test, a psycological screening, an oral interview and a complete medical check as well as a thorough background investigation. From the initial 8,000 people, only 150 of us were ultimately selected to go to the Academy.

The Academy was scheduled to begin on March 8, 1989 but, due to the hiring freeze, we were "put on hold until the freeze is rescinded." Since the freeze, we have recieved three letters and a phone call from Recruiting. The purpose of these letters and phone calls was to have us recruits "maintain a high degree of interest in the State Police and not get discouraged." In the case of the telephone call however, we were all told the same thing,"stay in shape and do not get into any trouble because once the freeze is lifted **you are going in!**"

For most of us these past few years have been a living nightmare. Our employers have lost interest in us as long-term employees because they were contacted by the State Police during our backgroung check and our employers know that we plan on leaving once the Academy opens. Due to this, we have been overlooked during promotion time and even worse, some people have been layed off.

Some of us have passed up other job opportunities because of our loyalty and dedication to the State Police. It has also been nearly impossible for us to further our education because of the minimal amount of time you recieve before reporting to the Academy (two weeks).

Not only have we suffered as individuals, but our families have been affected as well. We have not been able to make long-term investments, such as buying a house, because of the minimal pay you recieve while in the Academy. Even more tragic however, is the fact that we are **READY** and **WILLING** to leave our present jobs or school, but, if for any reason we drop out of the Academy, we come out jobless. Governor Florio this is the risk we are willing to take to become New Jersey State Troopers. If we are not the type of dedicated individuals the State Police wants or the State of New Jersey needs to enforce its laws than we are fighting a lost cause.

On December 26, 1992 the members of the 113th Class recieved a letter stating that our class has been terminated. The reasons were simple, "attrition and the amount of time that has elapsed."

Since receiving this letter, the "original" 113th Recruits have organized as a group. We have decided not to take lying down the decision made by Colonel Justin Dintino that terminated our class. At our meetings we have discussed many things, one of which is litigation.

As Governor of our state, we not only seek your help, but we would also like to hear your opinion on this subject. Sir, we know that you are very busy but, we also know that you are the only one who can help us out of this difficult situation **quickly** and **quietly.**

We can assure you that by helping us you will recieve more of the good publicity and recognition that you truly deserve as Governor of New Jersey.

Sincerely,

The Fighting 113th Recruit Class

On February 3, 1992, we, the members of the Fighting 113th Recruit Class, through our attorney, Francis J. Hartman, officially notified Governor James Florio, the state of New Jersey as a whole, and Colonel Justin Dintino of our plans to formally file a class-action lawsuit. *We were actually going to sue the governor and the colonel of the state police. This was crazy! How did I get involved with this shit?*

THE LAW OFFICES OF

Hartman, Marks & Nugent

FRANCIS J. HARTMAN*
ROBIN G. MARKS*
CHARLES H. NUGENT, JR.*
—
JOY E. MCGINNIS*
STEPHEN H. DUNBAR*

*ALSO A MEMBER OF PENNSYLVANIA BAR

300 CHESTER AVENUE
MOORESTOWN, NJ 08057-0415
—
609-235-0220
—
FAX 609-273-8617
—
OF COUNSEL
W. THOMAS MCGANN

February 3, 1992

Governor James J. Florio
State House
Trenton, N.J. 08625

Re: The 113th State Police Class

Dear Governor Florio:

Enclosed is a copy of a letter to Colonel Justin Dintino. It is my understanding that during a recent appearance in North Jersey, a member of our group made you aware, at a public forum, of the problems these men and women face. You indicated that you would have an aide investigate the matter. As you can see, I represent these men and women and would appreciate your aide speaking to me in this regard.

Governor, these men and women are prepared to do whatever it takes to become state troopers, including seeking public support through the media in order to obtain political support and, at the same time, litigating the matter.

I know you will understand the moral obligation argument better than many people. I am sure also that you are sensitive to any "waste of money" by any agency of the State government.

I recognize that the decision is Colonel Dintino's in the first instance. However, the Attorney General is the head of the Department of Law & Public Safety. Perhaps if we can convince you of the merit of our clients' position, you might support us with the Attorney General.

LAW OFFICES OF

Hartman, Marks & Nugent

Page 2.

Thank you for taking an interest in this matter. I shall wait to hear from someone on your staff.

Very truly yours,

HARTMAN, MARKS & NUGENT

Francis J. Hartman, Esquire

FJH/jtt
Enclosure
bcc: Brice Cote

As a result of our persistence, a special hearing was ordered and held before the assembly's judiciary, Law and Public Safety Committee, on February 27, 1992. At issue was the possible mishandling of the now-infamous Fighting 113th Recruit Class. *We did it! We made enough noise and obtained enough public support to get politicians to listen! Unfreaking believable!*

At this hearing, Francis J. Hartman eloquently detailed our pathetic fight to become troopers before the seated committee. About twenty members of our class joined Brice and me at the hearing, and I sat there glued to my seat, knowing full well that the rest of my life was at stake. My face even appeared in the background of a photograph that was taken of Mr. Hartman during the hearing and printed in the newspaper the following day. *Here, I thought the fame of having my face in the newspaper ended with the glory days of playing sports back in high school. Wow, my picture in the newspaper! How cool is that!*

After our attorney addressed the committee, Colonel Dintino and Attorney General Fred DaVisa, a prick in his own right who was rumored to hate the entire NJSP, were then afforded the opportunity to speak and state their case for "needing to select a new class." To put it mildly, they blundered miserably with their bogus reasons and outrightly lied during their testimony. Fortunately, the committee saw through this as well, and at the conclusion of the hearing, the committee voted unanimously to allow our class to go forward. *We did it! We actually pulled it off! Holy shit!* In just a matter of a few weeks, I went from crying on the front porch of my parents' home to being just inches away from the opportunity of a lifetime!

After this hearing, even the governor James Florio spoke out publicly in support of our class. Yet another spineless move by a politician who now felt the popularity of our cause could help his approval rating! Rumor had it that privately, Florio was furious at Dintino and felt betrayed because he misled Florio into believing we didn't have enough support to move forward. Basically, Florio did what any self-serving politician would do—follow public sentiment—and that was one thing the Fighting 113th had plenty of! *Shit, I better start running and working out again!*

One of the several newspaper articles detailing our fight.

In what most of us thought was a final last-ditch effort to dump our class, Colonel Dintino was successful in one aspect. While outlining his reasons for the need to select new recruits, the colonel pleaded with the committee to at least force our class to go through a battery of tests to make sure there were still enough qualified people to make up the class. They did vote in his favor in this regard, and the members of the 113th class were ordered to go through the following tests a second time:

- physical-agility test
- background investigation
- Minnesota multiphasic personality inventory (MMPI)
- oral-interview board
- medical examination

One at a time, I approached these tests just as I did the first time. From March through June, the various phases were scheduled, and fortunately, I was still in excellent physical condition. In retrospect, I had basically given up my late teens and early twenties from a social standpoint and practically lived for one reason: to become a trooper. Therefore, I had no fear about the background investigation; for I bypassed any wild, crazy drinking parties or activity that may have gotten me into any trouble whatsoever. I was always cautious about where I went and who I hung out with. I would have never forgiven myself if I did one stupid act to get disqualified from acceptance to the NJSP Academy.

As expected, I breezed through the physical, for I no longer looked like a "baby-faced prick!" The background check, MMPI, and medical exam went equally smooth; and the oral board was far less challenging. I was now twenty-two years old—the perfect age for a recruit and a far cry from the wide-eyed youngster who sat there and got besieged with age-oriented questions over three years ago.

On July 31, 1992, I finally received my official letter of acceptance to the New Jersey State Police Academy.

JOHN I. HOGAN

State of New Jersey
DEPARTMENT OF LAW AND PUBLIC SAFETY
DIVISION OF STATE POLICE
POST OFFICE BOX 7068
WEST TRENTON, NEW JERSEY 08628-0068
(609) 882-2000

ROBERT J. DEL TUFO
Attorney General

COLONEL JUSTIN J. DINTINO
Superintendent

July 31, 1992

Mr. John I. Hogan

Dear Mr. Hogan:

Congratulations on being selected for appointment to the New Jersey State Police Academy at <u>Sea Girt</u>, New Jersey, as a recruit in the 113th State Police Class.

You are directed to report to Building #26 on the <u>Sea Girt Academy</u> grounds (see enclosed map) at 1:00 p.m. on <u>Sunday, August 23, 1992</u>. Bring the articles of clothing and equipment detailed to you in the enclosed attachment.

If for any reason you decide not to attend this twenty-one week pre-service training course, kindly contact Lt. Juan Mattos at Division Headquarters, 609-882-2000 extension 2613 as soon as possible. Your cooperation in this regard is requested and will not jeopardize your participation in any future class process.

We wish you continued success in the selection process for a career as a New Jersey State Trooper.

Sincerely,

FOR COL. JUSTIN J. DINTINO
SUPERINTENDENT

Roy D. Bloom, Major
Administration Section Supv.

mc
Encl. (2)

New Jersey Is An Equal Opportunity Employer

With a sincere and special thank you to Brice Cote, Francis J. Hartman, and only by the grace of God, I thought my time had come; and I was finally about to enter the New Jersey State Police Academy. The only thing that made me happier about going into the academy was the realization that I was now forever done with all that political nonsense. I no longer had to worry about a new governor, colonel, or if it was an election year. I would be untouchable to any slime-ball politician once I was a trooper. I could care less if Kermit the Frog was governor now! After enduring all the political bullshit just to get into the academy, I loathed politics and was glad I would never have to be used as a pawn again—or so I thought!

CHAPTER 3

The New Jersey State Police Academy

Sunday, August 23, 1992, was a bright, sunny, picture-perfect summer day. The cloudless blue sky was as delightful as the sun that glared upon the windshield of Brice's white Volkswagen Jetta. We decided to drive to the Sea Girt Military Base, home of the NJSP Academy and situated on the banks of the Atlantic Ocean, together for the first week of our twenty-three-week training regiment. It was an absolutely wonderful beach day; and that's where we were headed except instead of flip-flops, swim trunks, and beer, Brice's vehicle was loaded to the gills with suitcases containing thousands of dollars of military gear and clothing we were directed to report with. Side by side in the front seats of the Jetta, Brice and I sat with completely shaven heads in full business suits. The inner emotions and uncontrollable churning of my stomach were unlike any other that I had experienced in my young life. Though this was always my favorite time of year—great weather, holidays, picnics, and the National Football League's preseason wrapping up—for the first time since I was a kid, I could care less about any of that, especially the Philadelphia Eagles!

We arrived at the opened dual-steel black entrance gates of Sea Girt around noon, about an hour earlier than we were expected. The uniformed trooper standing guard at the gate—a tall skinny red-haired man with a deep, piercing voice—instructed Brice to park, facing outward, on the dirt parking lot just up the road to the right. After asking each of us our names, which were noted on the clipboard he held, the trooper arrogantly said, "Well, well, well, Recruit Cote, we have been waiting for you!" Though we didn't discuss it at length, Brice and I both feared being singled out by instructors because of the hype that surrounded our class. By the time we reported, the entire state police knew full well that

Brice was the main reason that our class was able to proceed, with me being a close second. This fact obviously did not bode well for my mental well-being.

After parking as instructed, we sat in total silence. Sweat began to drip down our faces, but we were too tense to look at each other. From a distance, we could see troopers walking among the various buildings on the grounds, but they all appeared to be headed to the building that was closest to the lot where other recruits had now began to park. It was roughly ninety degrees outside, and it had to be at least one hundred degrees inside the car. My neck was red and irritated from the white dress shirt and tie I wore; my legs and back began to stick the leather interior as sweat seeped through my clothing. My hands and body trembled ever so gently, and admittedly so, I was as nervous as humanly possible.

Not only did we not speak or move a muscle I felt as if neither of us knew the other was even present in the car. I wondered to myself who was more nervous: Brice or me. He had three kids, a mortgage, bills, and was thirty-four, the maximum age to enter the academy. I was single, still lived at home, and had no real responsibilities at aged twenty-two. As the minutes passed, the lot quickly filled, and troopers continued to pack the building closest to us. It was now very close to 1:00 PM—*judgment time*! I had heard tons of academy stories, but nothing, aside from the experience itself, could have prepared me for the next few hours.

Suddenly, a tidal wave of uniformed troopers filed out of the building at 1:00 PM and swarmed the lot where we sat. "Get out! Get Out! Get out of your goddamn cars. Line up and bring your bags with you! Hurry up, you stupid asses!" the instructors yelled. To put it mildly, it was utter chaos. Each recruit, on the average, had two large suitcases and a garment bag. As we all scurried to get in two straight lines as ordered, recruits slipped, tripped, and fell face first onto the dirt parking lot as they stumbled over their luggage. Dust from the sandy, dry lot filled the air as we maneuvered as quickly as possible to do as ordered.

I was smart. I threw my garment bag around my neck and grabbed a suitcase with each hand. Recruits who fell were immediately besieged and circled by troopers who screamed vulgarities and appeared to be purposely kicking dirt and dust upon the fallen recruit. After a few moments of pandemonium, we were assembled in two straight lines, and an eerie silence was now present. The first orderly individual command we received was to place all of our bags on the ground at our feet. *Not hard! No big deal! I can do this!* My heart pounded, sweat dripped into my eyes, and my body quivered, but I knew I could do this first command. No problem!

A minute or so later, a short thin dark-complected sergeant walked up to me and asked, "Were you a paperboy before coming here, jackass?" I had no idea where this odd question originated. I immediately thought he was going to bust my chops about looking young or something. "No, sir!" I responded. "What is your name, stupid?" I replied, "Sir, Recruit Hogan, sir!" He freaked out and screamed, "Then why, RECRUIT HOGAN, do you have that bag around your neck, you idiot?" Here it was, the first command, and I had already screwed up. In pure panic mode, I failed to realize that I left the garment bag around my neck upon placing my suitcases down. This unwanted attention immediately brought three more troopers to me, and I was ordered to drop to the ground and do twenty-five push-ups. Completely surrounded as I quickly did them, I was besieged with generic obscenities by the instructors and continually advised to just quit right now! They continually told me I did not have what it takes to be a trooper and added if I couldn't follow the simplest detail, then how could I ever be responsible enough to be a trooper.

When other recruits who also gained this unwanted attention were collectively back on their feet, a miserable-looking tall trooper, with blond hair and a growl that would make a pit bull run away, took center stage. He immediately greeted us by telling us how slow and stupid we were and introduced himself as Trooper Kilmurray, our class coordinator. *Great!* After commenting on how ugly and sloppy we were in appearance, Trooper Kilmurray ordered us back to our vehicles with our bags. He told us we were too slow and that too many of us had not followed directions. "Back to your cars . . . LET'S GO NOW!"

Sweating profusely and completely disheveled, I ran back to Brice's car, and together, we chucked our bags in as quickly as possible. All the hours and detail given to folding and neatly packing my gear was now for naught! After sitting in the insanely hot car for a few minutes, Trooper Kilmurray bellowed for us to get out and line up. Pandemonium once again ruled! No one wanted to be the last to line up. Everyone again ran to assemble with bags and luggage being pulled, dragged, and lugged into place.

After a quick spiel about military bearing, marching in step and looking straight ahead, Trooper Kilmurray marched us toward the main macadam. Buildings were present on both sides of the neatly manicured lawn. A long straight paved road was ahead of us, and in the distance, you could see where the beach and ocean began. As we proceeded to march, troopers kept a close eye, just hoping to catch a recruit looking around, or perhaps even breathing improperly, just so they could yell at someone. After all, it had been over four years since the last state-police-academy class, and they were as eager as we were, just for different reasons.

With bags in hand, we were steered toward what was soon described as our living quarters: building no. 8. Once in front of this two-storied brick building, Trooper Kilmurray instructed us to place our bags down. Almost instantaneously, we were ordered to get an arm's length away from the person in front and to the sides of us. Once separated, we were ordered into a front-leaning rest position. It was now roughly 2:00 PM on a 90-plus-degree day in late August, and we were in a push-up position in full business attire. With hands placed flatly on the scalding blacktop, I could feel the tips of my spit-shined black dress shoes literally melting into the pavement. As sweat dripped into my eyes, I could not decide what burned more: the salty sweat stinging my eyes or my scorched palms from the blazing blacktop they rested on. By now, though, I was able to block out the bedlam of instructors yelling at recruits who tried lifting their hands from the blistering blacktop. I was focused. I had done push-ups for years in preparation of this day and the weeks of hell that were sure to follow.

After what seemed like an eternity, the recruits of the 113th State Police Class were summoned to their feet. With hands scalded, suits mussed, shoes scraped, and luggage scattered about, we were then ushered into the old brick dormitory and given our room assignments.

Alphabetically by last name, women were assigned bunks on the first floor, men on the second. After lugging my bags up the flights of gray cement steps, I entered my room for the first time and saw eight cots, evenly separated by ugly wooden open-faced lockers that were built into the wall. Each locker had a metal bar for hangers and was divided by roughly five or six shelves. The cots were made of old metal frames and had either a fabric or plastic-covered mattress lying on it. On each cot was one pillow, two white sheets, and one green wool blanket. *Wool blanket in August?*

Instructors were going from room to room, yelling, screaming, and creating havoc wherever possible. Ordered to change into our khakis, set up our lockers per a previously received handout, and make our beds, most of us didn't know what to do first. I was flustered, and my mindset was in sheer panic. Though I had done it for the last fifteen or so years, I forgot how to make a bed, change clothes, and take things from a suitcase and place them on a shelf. *Everyone is yelling and screaming do this and do that. My head is going to explode. I just want to go home! I am never going to make it through twenty-three weeks of this shit!*

After just mere minutes had passed, my bed was partially made, and I had managed to get changed into the "uniform of the day": beige khakis with a matching long-sleeve shirt, black leather military-dress shoes, a blue web belt, blue clip-on tie, and a plain blue baseball cap. My gear, clothes, and suitcases were still scattered about the floor near my bunk, and my new roommates, all seven of them, and I had yet to speak to one another. Too worried about getting our own gear situated, we hadn't introduced ourselves yet. Furthermore, going in, I knew that our class size was believed to be 143 recruits, but only ninety salaries were allocated in the budget. Obviously, some recruits *had* to go! Initially, in my mind, even my own roommates were the enemies to a certain degree.

As we diligently worked to get our own areas situated, instructors repeatedly came into our room to yell at us. Each time they entered, whoever recruit saw him first would yell, "ATTENTION!" at which point everyone had better stop whatever they were doing and snap to attention!

Nowhere near being close to completing the tasks at hand, like cattle, we were shuffled from the dormitory back outside onto the macadam. Roll call was taken, and for the first time, a sense of organization among recruits of the 113th Recruit Class was present. Once the roll call was completed, we were then marched over to building no. 26, which, we quickly learned, would serve as our classroom for the remainder of our training program. Wooden tables with alternating blue and gold plastic chairs lined the interior of building no. 26. A full-sized stage was at the far end of this room, and in the left corner sat an oak podium with a huge NJSP triangle tattooed on it. On the tables in front of each chair, a large white state-police binder and paper name tag were placed. Seated alphabetically in total silence, we awaited our next instruction.

Minutes passed without movement from the 140-plus bald-headed individuals that made up the 113th Recruit Class. Troopers lined the classroom walls, hoping for a reason to scream at someone. Finally, the awkward silence ended as Trooper Kilmurray entered the classroom and took up his position onstage in front of the oak podium. After belittling our collective appearance as a group, Trooper Kilmurray went on to give us a lengthy introduction and detailed topics such as code of conduct, ethics, and academy rules and regulations. Upon completion, Trooper Kilmurray asked if there were any questions, and fortunately, no one was dumb enough to raise his or her hand. This was not a democracy, and stupidity would not be tolerated.

Dinner was the first meal we ate together as a class, but I can't recall what we had. As recruits, we sat four to a table, and no conversation was permitted—not on day one and not on graduation day! Every meal and every item placed upon our trays was scrutinized by the instructors who stood guard at the serving line. "Fat bodies" rarely got to finish their meals and, God forbid, if these overweight recruits were caught taking dessert. Tension was present every second of the day regardless of the activity. When a recruit was lucky enough to finish his meal or upon being ordered out of the mess hall by an instructor, he or she cleaned their plate into the trash and placed it on a metal shelf. Once a group of four recruits had lined up, together, they marched back to the dormitory. No talking, no laughing, no smiling. Only misery was permitted!

Our first night concluded with another session in the classroom. At around 7:00 PM or so, we marched back to our rooms and finished setting up our lockers, making beds, and unpacking our gear. Except for the occasional surprise visit from an instructor, the rest of the night went smoothly. At 10:00 PM, "LIGHTS OUT!" was ordered, and our first day was complete! Before going to bed, my roommates and I decided to wake up at 5:30 AM, which would give us plenty of time to get ready and be outside on the fire line for a roll call, which would be 6:30 AM for the duration of our academy lives.

Fearing I wouldn't be able to sleep due to the unbearable heat that built up in the cement dormitory, I gently lay down on my cot in hopes of not messing up the neatly folded sheets. I closed my eyes but knew I wasn't going to be able to sleep. I wanted a snack, cookies or ice cream perhaps; and I wanted my television, stereo, and king-size water bed. *This sucks!* The only thing that kept me there that night was the knowledge of how disappointed my parents would be if I were to quit. Prior to arriving, I only feared getting dismissed due to injury. I never dreamed that I would actually *want* to quit. But I assure you I was not the only person thinking about resigning.

Amazingly, I was able to fall fast asleep, for I was mentally and physically exhausted. Before I knew it, morning had come, but it felt more like two in the morning instead of five-thirty. All I can recall is hearing loud screams, chaotic yelps, and metal cot frames grinding across the linoleum floor. *Was I dreaming, maybe a bad nightmare?* Our dorm-room light was abruptly flicked on, nearly blinding my sleepy eyes. This was worse than a nightmare, and it sure as hell wasn't the alarm clock that awakened us. Three instructors stood in our doorway and were yelling every curse word known to man for us to get up and get ready. We were ordered to get dressed into our khakis and line up outside on the fire line, which was our assembly point from day one until graduation. I am not sure how long it took us, but we were told we had three minutes! Once dressed, we all ran to the front of the dormitory and lined up. It was pitch-black out, and I overheard someone saying it was around 12:30 AM. *What in the hell is this all about? So much for a good night's sleep!*

Within minutes, our class was completely assembled in front of our dormitory, and Trooper Kilmurray was shouting the roll call. Still dazed and confused, fortunately, I sounded off "Here, sir!" when he bellowed my name aloud.

As he continued through our class alphabetically, the reality of how psychologically trying the first day had been set in. "Recruit Stefanoni, Recruit Stefanoni!" No answer. What happened to my friend Zach? Just more than twenty-four hours ago, he and I went running together at the Florence High track. Did he get hurt? Thrown out already? What could he have possibly done? As we ran around the track together the day before reporting, Zach stated, "They are going to have to pick me up and throw me over the fence to get me out of there!" *Now he was gone?* Chills ran down my spine with the realization that after waiting four years and fighting all the bureaucracy like we did, a total of ten recruits had already resigned or been dismissed within the first twenty-four hours. Yes, it was that psychologically demanding!

Trooper Kilmurray gave us a sarcastic good morning. When some recruits replied back, he said, "Shut up, you idiots!" He was mean, nasty, and flat out condescending. We were given a quick history lesson and advised that we were the first class to train at Sea Girt in many years. (Previous classes were trained at Fort Dix.) Since it had been so long since a class trained at Sea Girt, the instructors stated they were curious if sand still remained on the beach. *WHAT? Are they suggesting what I think they are? Do these guys realize what time it is or how dark it is? This is insane!*

Now the fun really began. We were ordered to run in our khakis and military-dress shoes to the beach and grab two handfuls of sand. The beach, as we quickly learned, was exactly three quarters of a mile from our dorm, and though distance running was not an issue for me, I never tried running in non-cushioned military-dress shoes in the middle of the night. We all knew the purpose of these runs was to weed out those recruits who reported to the academy out of shape. One sure way of forcing people to quit was shin splints, which is guaranteed to happen if you run in these types of shoes. At the conclusion of this mile-and-a-half juggernaut, we stood in formation, and the instructors came around with flashlights to check our handfuls of sand. Though they hinted that we had not brought back enough sand and perhaps we needed to go get more, the games for this evening were complete. After marching back to the entrance of our dorm, we were allowed to retire. Tired, sweaty, sticky, and now sandy, I began to hate this place as I tried unsuccessfully to fall asleep. *Plus my goddamn feet and shins hurt!*

When we assembled a few hours later for our first full day of training, Trooper Kilmurray took great pride in reaffirming that ten individuals had resigned in the first day. *That's freaking crazy, the thousands of dollars spent on purchasing all the gear, shoes, clothing, and necessities gone to waste. Even worse than that, we waited four long and tumultuous years for this, and these individuals just gave up in less than twenty-four hours! Amazing!* As much as I wanted to quit, I figured I had to last at least the first week.

Reveille for my roommates and I came at five-thirty each morning. We dressed, polished our shoes, made our beds, and brushed our teeth. Our day started at the fire line at 6:30 AM with a roll call, and from there, we marched as a class to an adjacent building with a vacant parking lot. It was in this lot where we got to get the "sleepies" from our eyes as we partook in "morning exercises." For roughly thirty minutes, we did jumping jacks and push-ups, ran in place, or did some stretching exercises in our khaki's and dress shoes. The severity and difficulty of the selected exercises were all dependent upon the mood of the instructor that particular morning. *What a freaking way to wake up!*

Once completed with this abysmal task, we then marched to the mess hall for breakfast. The only noise present in the cafeteria was chewing, knives and forks being picked up, and chairs screeching across the cheap linoleum floor as recruits sat or stood up. After breakfast was complete and our foursome assembled at the exit door, we marched back to the dormitory to undertake our second daily chore: cleaning all areas of the academy compound—both inside and out.

Each week, recruits were assigned a different area of responsibility they had to maintain cleanliness of. Whether it was mopping the bathroom or hallway floors, scrubbing the latrines, emptying trash cans, picking up litter, or making the instructors' beds, the next half hour of every morning was spent on these details. At 8:25 AM, we then lined up on the fire line and marched directly to the classroom where we promptly began our studies at eight-thirty each morning.

Because of its affiliation with Seton Hall University, the New Jersey State Police Academy enabled us to receive a total of thirty-two college credits. In addition to the mental and physical torture that we endured, the strict educational standards that were a critical part of our training added more stress to each of us. These mandatory classes were crammed into our twenty-three-week training regiment and were very demanding. Most weekends were spent either studying or at the library, preparing in-depth reports that were required of us. Courses we were obligated to pass were as follows: English, English Composition, sociology, psychology, Report Writing, 2C (Criminal Codes of New Jersey), Title 39 (New Jersey Motor Vehicle Laws), and public speaking. Failure to pass any academic course could result in immediate termination from the academy. Like clockwork, each day, from eight-thirty to noon, was spent in the classroom on these various subjects.

At ten each morning, we would get a break. Finally, we would get fifteen minutes to be human: talk to our classmates or just sit and relax. Most of the time, however, especially in the beginning, we were given "special permission" to leave the classroom and go back to our dorm rooms. Once there, we would find our beds and lockers in total disarray. Our sheets and blankets would be ripped off our bed; our T-shirts, underwear, and gear that were previously folded to perfection were thrown to the floor and mixed in with our roommates' personal gear.

One time, the instructors even went so far as to hurl some of our personal items out the window. Like complete buffoons, we quickly ran outside in our khakis, goofy-looking bald heads, and humbled pride to retrieve the loose articles of clothing, pillows, or other items they humorously chucked out while we were back in the classroom. One of the funniest episodes I can recall was when the instructors completely stripped all of our beds, tied our sheets together, and made one massive pile with our clothes and gear. They then tied this huge mass of clothing into a giant ball and left it in the middle of the floor in our dorm room. Fortunately, the indelible markers we had to personalize all of our gear with upon reporting to the academy prevented us from wearing one another's socks, T-shirts, and underwear!

These ludicrous incidents became common and, eventually, comical. As the weeks passed, my classmates and I realized it was all a mental game, especially when you filed back into the classroom and then got reamed out for being late because we had to rearrange our entire room. Basically, we knew that no matter what we did or how we did it, we were wrong and going to get verbally abused and punished later in the day during physical training (PT) for our actions. Most recruits expected this, and as a group, we accepted it and eventually learned to laugh together about the stressful but humorous events that transpired on a daily basis.

During the morning, while in our classroom setting, I found trying to stay awake and remaining mentally focused on the subject matter at hand became more difficult with each passing day. The chastisement for those who did nod their heads in class once singled out was to run around the outside perimeter of the classroom and shout the lap number each time they passed the main entrance. Just imagine trying to take notes, listen, and concentrate on the instructor when every other minute, you heard some idiot yelling a number from outside as he passed the entrance. You couldn't help but laugh to yourself of course!

Noon was lunchtime. As recruits, we quickly learned to be careful of what to eat and how much to consume because just on the horizon was self-defense class. On the heels of self-defense classes loomed an-hour-and-forty-five-minute session of hard-core physical training. Try getting flipped around on mats for over an hour on a full stomach; it happened, and when it did, recruits were forced to clean up their own vomit as instructors screamed at them for mussing "their" mats.

Self-defense consisted of several weeks of boxing where we actually fought our fellow recruits in a makeshift ring that was centered in the middle of the gymnasium. Just gazing at the boxing ring gave me an uneasy feeling, not knowing who my next opponent would be. The boxing gloves we wore were always soaked with sweat from the previous class as was the headgear we wore for protection. Fortunately, we supplied our own mouthpiece.

Ironically, our boxing regiment was halted halfway through when several members of our class had broken out with ringworm-like symptoms on their hands from the sweaty gloves. Having played sports my entire life, I can say without hesitation that the anxiety and stress of stepping into the boxing ring with instructors looking on and screaming to "punch, punch, punch" was for me the most exhausting and nauseating exercise I had ever experienced. Recruit Rufus Hay and I were roommates and liked each other. After going toe-to-toe, however, I like to think we both had newfound respect for each other following this encounter. We knocked the shit out of each other, and the instructors loved it, and in a sick kind of way, after getting my bell rung a few times and delivering a variety of quality shots myself, I was more confident in my abilities and glad for this occurrence. It was these types of experiences that made us all realize that as much as it sucked and though we hated every minute of it, everything at this hellhole we called home had a purpose. "If you quit here, you will quit out on the road; if you quit out on the road, you DIE" were the words of wisdom instructors bellowed as we took turns punching each other senselessly.

In addition to boxing, we received in-depth training in judo, hand-to-hand combat, weapon retention, and proper and lawful use of the PR-24 nightstick, which we would carry upon graduation from the academy. Flips, holds, defensive positioning, grips, leg kicks, leg sweeps, punching, blocking—you name it— we learned it! By graduation, I felt like a cross between Bruce Lee and Mike Tyson, and call it brainwashing if you will, but the confidence that came with completing each of these daunting phases of training was surreal.

Once the self-defense class concluded, the final "block" of every afternoon consisted of our daily torture session known as PT, two little letters that described hours of endless pain and suffering all designed to make us stronger both mentally and physically. As we dressed identically in either all white shorts and T-shirts or navy blue sweat suits (depending upon the weather), PT always began in the gymnasium where some unlucky recruit would be identified by name (or some ridiculous nickname he or she had dubiously earned) and called to *the Stand*.

Taking the Stand was the most feared event in the academy. The Stand was a three-foot-by-three-foot-by-three-foot navy blue wooden platform that brought fear and anxiety to the heart of every recruit in our class and all previous training-academy classes. It stood ambiguously at the front of the gymnasium. The unlucky recruit whose name was singled out had to immediately get out of formation, sprint as fast as possible, and jump up onto the stand. Once up there, with his or her back facing the rest of the class, he or she then had to do an about-face so he or she was now facing the entire recruit class.

The remainder of our class was neatly lined up in four even columns before him or her. The recruit on the stand would go through an entire procedure, consisting of military steps and cadences, to separate our four rows, thus, giving each row room to begin exercising. The toughest part of this for the individual on the "stand" was that since he or she was facing the class, the commands appeared backward, and trust me, this process got screwed up almost daily. All hell broke loose once the recruit failed to properly "open the ranks"; and this served as the instructors' reason to punish our minds, bodies, and spirits for the next hour and a half.

Sometimes recruits on the stand messed up so badly that they were treated to a free surfing lesson. As they stood there, attempting to open the class, instructors would surround the stand and pick him or her up. They would then shake him or her until the recruit fell haplessly to the ground. It was funny as hell to watch as long as it wasn't you!

Once we were properly spaced, the exercising began. Without exaggeration, it was not uncommon to do jumping jacks for thirty minutes straight. Every muscle in my legs and feet would go numb. As the class was on the verge of passing out—which, to my recollection, happened to two recruits—instructors would yell, "Can you go for one more minute?" Gasping for air and barely audible, we would sound off in an affirmative. The pounding and abuse our bodies took on a daily basis were tremendous. Mentally, though, as you did these exercises and wanted to fall to the ground or give up, instructors would alert us of the dangerous world we were about to enter. They constantly reminded our class that if we gave up in the gym, we would give up on the side of the road as we rolled around with a brazen scumbag who was trying to get our gun!

Our daily physical-training sessions would conclude with a run where we trekked through grass, puddles, cement, blacktop, sand, and water. Once a recruit was identified as "weak" or with a medical ailment, you knew his days were numbered. Instructors mercilessly hounded those recruits, who fell behind in either exercises or running. If they didn't quit, they were soon released for failure to keep up with the class. In my mind, though, I felt anyone who couldn't keep up should be let go. After all, I busted my butt for years to be mentally and physically prepared. Plus, after twenty minutes of push-ups, instructors would ask, "Do you want someone weak, feeble, and who gives up to arrive as your backup if your ass is in a sling?" HELL NO! *Screw those who weren't in shape or became injured and started to fall behind!* Mentally, they were shaping us into hard and callous individuals that despised weakness, even if the weaker person was your bunkmate.

After the physical-training session, we marched in formation back to our dormitory and were afforded the luxury of showering. Unfortunately, we only had an average of five to seven minutes to get changed from our physical-training gear back into our khakis. Most of the time, we showered, but no soap was present. All there was time for was a quick rinse with cold water in hopes of bringing our body temperatures back to normal. We then got dressed and reported back to the fire line, still sweating and out of breath. Once we were in formation, we marched to the mess hall for dinner. Food was shoveled into our mouths at an alarming rate because you never knew when an instructor was going to walk up and kick you out for no reason. Trying to sleep on an empty stomach made a very long night, and to this day, I still feel my sometimes-grotesque eating habits are a result of what I was forced to do in the academy. But make no mistake about it, I loved being there. Knowing that the 113th Recruit Class was enduring the same hardships as all other previous classes is what made being a trooper so special. As each meal passed, we were all one step closer to the graduation, and that was my mental approach. In a place as overwhelmingly challenging as this, you don't look forward to the next day or week. At any minute, something could trip you up and could have you packing your bags and exiting the place we all loved to hate.

After dinner—which, for most of the 113th class, consisted of peanut butter and jelly sandwiches because the food was so bad—we marched directly into the classroom for study hall. From approximately six fifteen to seven thirty each evening, we were able to read or study whatever subject we were currently preparing to be tested in. As usual, no talking was permitted, but for the most part, the mood was light, and only one instructor was present.

After marching back to our rooms, we then had time to shower, do homework, polish our gear, or take care of any personal business. After the first week passed, we were permitted to use the pay phones to call family and friends if we chose to. By the time 10:00 PM rolled around, I couldn't wait for the lights to be ordered off. Every ounce of energy had been depleted, and I needed to recharge. The question that always remained a mystery at lights out was "Are they going to freaking wake us up in a few hours?" Each day in this living hellhole was longer than the next, and as mentioned, I learned to live by taking each hour, not day, one at a time. As I drifted off to sleep, I thanked God for keeping me injury free and for giving me the strength to withstand the stress and pressures that remained constant.

The routine the 113th Recruit Class fell into mirrored a well-oiled, highly polished boot camp. Military bearing ever present, we were, in essence, educated soldiers training for combat. Every day, from five thirty in the morning until ten o'clock at night, became more challenging. The rigors and demands placed on our minds, bodies, and souls were incredible. This was the New Jersey State Police Academy. Renowned across the country as having the toughest, most grueling paramilitary training in the country is what attracted me to the state police in the first place. I hated being there, but in reality, this was my dream, and I was thankful for the opportunity. I knew not just anyone could make it. To finally become a New Jersey state trooper is what served as my sole motivation.

From sunrise to sunset, the recruits of the 113th class drudged through the day's challenges. Hours would pass and eventually turned into days. Reporting back to the academy on Monday mornings was the absolute worst. The thought of having five full days ahead of us totally sucked. By the time Wednesday rolled around, I'd get a second wind and lived for Friday nights, knowing I was going home and another week was completed. I had no girlfriend at home and rarely spoke to anyone when I was home. I wanted no distractions. I was focused, and as each second passed, I knew that January 15, 2003, was that much closer, but I did not dwell on it.

After the first six or eight weeks passed, I had a different perspective. I fell into such a stringent routine that I hated to leave on Friday night. I would have much rather stayed straight through the weekends and graduate sooner. Plus, every Friday night before being dismissed we had to repack every bit of clothing and gear and even bring our stupid wool blanket and pillow home so the bags and luggage we had to carry only became heavier, more numerous, and more cumbersome as the weeks passed.

The weekends were nothing but misery anyway. By the time I got home on Friday night, I barely had the energy to make it up to my bedroom. Saturdays were spent doing wash; ironing; folding underwear, T-shirts, socks, shorts; and taking my khakis to a one-hour dry cleaner to be pressed. At night, I would go to a 5:00 PM mass at Saint Clare's Church with my parents and then catch up on all the sleep and food I didn't get during the week. I would usually fall asleep watching television around ten o'clock as I studied for an exam or wrote one of the several term papers that were also required of us.

With the exception of watching the Eagles, Sunday at the Hogan house was horrific. My friends and family knew not to call or speak to me. The thought of returning to Sea Girt made me sick to my stomach. Yes, it was that bad! I hated that place but had no choice but to return. I believe I was too young to know what true stress was, but I did know that I was a miserable SOB by the time Sunday night rolled around, and I began packing to go back to *hell!*

Brice and I continued to travel together each week just as we did upon reporting back in August. Fall turned into winter, and the Sea Girt ocean breeze quickly became an unwelcome arrival. As my roommates and I became closer, bickering and arguing over the temperature in our room, who farted, who snored, and other small details began to take place. Plain and simple, we were all miserable, tired, and just wanted to get through this training and graduate. My bunkmate and closest friend through the academy was Richard Holmes, an African American from East Orange. We confided in each other and often had "guard duty" together, so we got to spend a lot of time talking.

Guard duty was an egregious scam. It was nothing other than pure physical and mental torture where two sets of two recruits were assigned to patrol the academy grounds on foot in the middle of the night. The shifts were as follows: 9:00 PM to midnight, midnight to 3:00 AM, and 3:00 AM to 6:00 AM. Once a week, each recruit was assigned this duty, and its sole purpose was sleep depravation, or so we all thought. Depending on luck or lack of, there were days when you would wake up at 5:30 AM, have breakfast, go to the Asbury Park YMCA all morning for swimming certifications, go to lunch, have self-defense class followed by PT, have dinner, study hall, then lights out at 10:00 PM only to wake up for guard duty at eleven forty-five to work the midnight to 3:00 AM shift. Attempting to fall asleep at 3:15 AM when you know that at 5:30 AM it starts all over again isn't the easiest thing to do. This was the first time in my life that I was literally aware of the fact that I was sleepwalking.

By December, the mental games had become jokes. The instructors knew our personalities, and we knew theirs. It wasn't that the belittling and humiliation had stopped, but we now knew it wasn't personal and took it all in stride; and though still addressed as recruits until the day we graduated, there was a hint of acceptance as colleagues from the instructors.

In the weeks leading up to graduation, the remaining members of the 113th Recruit Class had now passed all of the required educational and physical requirements. Personally, after being forced to go through remedial firearms training, I conquered my biggest obstacle: qualifying with the issued 9-mm Heckler & Koch firearm that would be mine for the duration of my state-police career. Those closest to me knew I hated guns, hated firing guns, hated loading guns, and hated cleaning guns. Though I was obsessed with the uniform, actually carrying or firing a weapon was the only part of being a trooper I was not fond of. Statistically, though, we learned that the reality of a uniformed police officer ever being forced to utilize deadly force was very slim. I never put much thought or emphasis into the fact that I would now be expected to carry my weapon everywhere I went, whether on duty or not, when traveling within the state of New Jersey. It just came with the territory. I accepted it and assumed that statistics were on my side, and as graduation day approached, I never had second thoughts of my career path.

After being broken down and degraded in every humanly possible way beginning in August, the instructors slowly molded the individuals of the 113th Recruit Class into a unified group who was willing to do anything, including die for one another. Call it brainwashing, but I was willing to do anything for anyone donning the blue and gold uniform of the NJSP. In return, they made me believe that the outfit that I was now a part of would do anything for me. We were a brotherhood, and nobody fucked with New Jersey troopers! Honor, duty, and fidelity are what were preached, and under Trooper Kilmurray's leadership, I knew that if the chips were ever stacked against me, no one in this proud and storied outfit would ever abandon my fellow classmates or me.

As my graduation day approached, the only problem was that I didn't know the first damn thing about being a cop. I could shine shoes, polish brass, whisk toilets, and make a floor look like glass using a mop; but I had no concept of what being a police officer was all about. At the most, we had a few hours of actual hands-on police training such as handcuffing or making motor-vehicle stops. I was in great shape, was confident about not getting my ass kicked, had all my leather uniform gear highly polished; but I didn't know the first thing about being a trooper.

As talk of our commencement began, I was excited but nervous. For nearly five months, my classmates and I had accepted, endured, and passed every challenge thrown at us. None of these tasks, however, really had anything to do with actual hands-on police training. Though it wasn't discussed, I would like to think my fellow classmates felt the same way.

Our Christmas present came in the form of learning what our badge number would be. On our last day at the academy before the Christmas break, I learned that I was to be Trooper John I. Hogan, badge no. 5068. We were informed that no matter what, no other person in history will ever have that number again! I recall Sergeant First Class Bernard telling us, "Even if you quit or get fired, that number is yours for life. No trooper will ever be assigned the same badge number." I remembered thinking to myself, *Fired after what I went through to get here! No way would I ever jeopardize my new career and lifelong dream!* We were also introduced to and given a block of instruction from the NJSP's Employee Assistance Program (EAP). It was during this block that we were all assured that any physical, mental, or other permanent ailment suffered by a trooper during an on-duty altercation (right or wrong in his actions), the state would be responsible for paying that trooper's permanent-disability status if forced to resign as a result. *Whatever! Why are they telling us this bullshit! What's with all the information relating to alcoholism and depression? Do some cops have problems?*

Christmas came and went, as did New Year's Day. On the first morning back to the academy after the New Year, we were treated to a fourth surprise: urine-sample test. We were now just two weeks from graduation, which was slated for January 15, 1993, and the thought of a urine test seemed absurd to me. All I could think about was finally putting on that uniform and marching into the Trenton War Memorial and saluting before Colonel Justin Dintino who would hand me badge no. 5068, which was soon to be mine for life.

The week before graduation came and went, and it was all a matter of routine now. I left on that Friday for the last time, knowing that when I come back to Sea Girt as a recruit on Monday, January 11, 1993, it would be for the last time. The weekend dragged on as I couldn't wait to go back. My class, which had dwindled to ninety-four recruits since arriving that dreadful August afternoon, was ready to take on the world. *Wow, fifty people quit or were forced to resign, and I could probably only name five!*

Monday morning, graduation week, was finally here. The 113th class assembled on the fire line for our last week of training. Instead of the normal "Welcome back, scumbags," Trooper Kilmurray yelled, "Recruit Russano, what's your badge number?" Andrew Russano replied, "Five-zero-nine-four, sir!" "Not anymore, Russano. You are now no. 5-0-9-3. Recruit Maloney post on me!" *What in the hell? How can someone get kicked out five days before graduation?*

With that, Recruit *"Stephen Maloney"* was gone, never to be seen or heard from again. After twenty-two weeks of hell, the former local police officer allegedly tested positive for cocaine on the last urine analysis and was immediately dismissed. That was probably the largest dose of reality I had been hit with in my young life. After the shock of Maloney's dismissal wore off, I settled in for my last week, and before I knew it, Thursday night had arrived. I was going to bed as a civilian for the last time, but sleep was an afterthought for me on this night. The fact that in less than twenty-four hours I was going to be a New Jersey state trooper kept me awake all night. Was I more excited about graduation, or was I more nervous because I knew deep down that I didn't have the faintest idea on *how to be a trooper*?

Friday, January 15, 1993, arrived, and together as one unit, the improbable 113th NJSP Recruit Class marched into the Trenton War Memorial. To say the least, it was the happiest and proudest day of my life. Though the ceremony was a blur, numerous dignitaries and politicians were there and spoke of pride; tradition; and, most importantly, *honor*, *duty*, and *fidelity*. After the ceremony, we were handed our badges, weapons, and bullets. This would be the first time I ever possessed a weapon without supervision as I posed for pictures with my parents, family, and friends who attended.

As I drove home from Trenton in full uniform by myself, with a loaded weapon on my hip, I recalled a million "what if" scenarios popping into my mind. I was truly at a loss as to what I'd do if confronted with a situation during those twenty minutes. I did it! I made it! My high-school-yearbook prophecy had now been fulfilled. I was indeed a New Jersey trooper but only because the certificate and badge said so. What do I do now? Aside from putting on the uniform, I sure as hell don't know how to be a trooper!

CHAPTER 4

Playing a Trooper

"You stay down here, and I'll take the upstairs," the senior trooper whispered to me in a dead-serious tone. With that, he pulled his weapon and entered through the unlocked front door of the large white colonial home we were dispatched to. Mentally, this burglary call just took a real-life twist. Initially, as we sped to the residence, I was excited but nervous. It was roughly 10:30 PM, and the rural roads of Millstone Township were pitch-black as a misty rain fell onto our windshield. I could feel my entire inner-self shaking but needed to prove to my new partner that I was calm; cool; and, above all other things, a trustworthy and reliable colleague. As we neared the property, the senior trooper turned off the lights of our marked New Jersey-trooper car. I assumed we did not want the potential burglars to be aware of our arrival. *Ah, the element of surprise . . . I remember them talking about this tactic in the academy.* Once we parked in front of the totally darkened home, no other cars or persons were visible. We quietly exited the troop car and briskly walked to the front door. The burglar alarm that had sounded, prompting us to respond, was loud and annoying. This deafening high-pitched noise only added to the tension I already felt throughout my entire body. As I watched the senior trooper remove his gun from its holster and approach the house, the reality of what was transpiring smacked me right in the face.

At twenty-three years old and just a few weeks removed from the academy, I was now thrust into real-life action for the first time. To worsen this predicament was the glaring fact that I had no idea what to do or how to act, let alone be a "squared away" trooper. *I wish I were back at the academy, scrubbing toilets.* Following my partner's lead, I too grabbed my weapon. The black metal was cold and intimidating. With my left thumb, I wearily unsnapped the button that secured my gun to my holster. I then hesitantly removed my Heckler & Koch 9-mm semiautomatic pistol with my left hand. My body and hands trembled. *Shit, did I remember to fully load my ammunition clip? Is there a live round in the chamber?* My palms were sweaty. My breathing was erratic. It was early February, very damp and cold; but my body temperature was overheating from nervousness, anxiety, and anticipation.

In the academy, instructors advised that if we were lucky, we would never have to draw our weapons throughout our career. Statistically, I recall them telling us a very, very slim percentage of police officers across the country ever have to use deadly force. Ironically, the probability of the same officer using deadly force twice in his career is very improbable. *Great! Here I am with less than a fucking month on the job, and already, I am put into a situation where I am drawing my weapon.*

A possible burglary in progress was the call received from dispatch minutes ago. The thoughts and ideas that ran rampant in my mind were endless and incomplete as the senior trooper drove to the scene. *How great would it be to catch the burglar in action,* I thought to myself. Personally, this was what I had waited a lifetime for. To be "on the job" as a New Jersey state trooper was my sole dream, but as this scenario unfolded before me, I was now unexpectedly confronted with numerous circumstances I never gave much thought to.

Could I really shoot somebody? Would I panic or overreact? Will my actions get my partner shot, even killed? Will the burglar overpower me and take my weapon, then kill my partner and me with my own weapon? What if I shoot an innocent person or the homeowner? Even worse, what if a little kid comes running around the corner, and I shoot him or her? Mentally, I was at a loss and realized I had never given much thought to the seriousness and irreversible impact my actions could have. *This is it. I just know I am going to screw something up, and someone will get hurt because of my actions.*

Once we were on the porch, no sign of forced entry was visible as I stood behind my partner. We quietly entered the unlocked home, and straight ahead of us was a beautiful hardwood staircase that wrapped around to the left. My partner went straight up the steps and immediately disappeared. I was alone, confused and at a total loss at what to do next. *What in God's name do I do now?* My weapon was in my left hand, but it was far from steady. I stood frozen in time for the next few seconds. It was eerily quiet.

As I struggled internally to regain confidence and composure, I leaned up against a wall and slowly peeked left into the living-room area. Barely able to control my breathing, I exhaled deeply when I saw no one was present. As I hesitantly went from room to room, no sign of forced entry or theft was present. The tension and anxiety that controlled my body slowly ceased. Gradually, I began to regain my poise as I checked the home farther, room by room. Within minutes, my partner and I were reunited on the first floor and concluded that the call was a false alarm. Once back in the troop car, we notified dispatch of our findings, and I immediately handwrote the operations report. Much to my disliking and embarrassment, my hands were still shaking, but I did my best to conceal it from the senior trooper, who appeared completely unfazed by what just transpired. I already loved being a trooper, but as I sat there, writing the report, I prayed that would be the last time I ever had to draw my weapon in a real-life scenario.

While most may not admit it, I feel every police officer, at some point in their career, will second-guess themselves and their abilities. Taking someone's life or being confronted with a situation that could result in your own death is not something that was ever discussed at the barracks. We all knew the dangers of being a police officer. It's been my experience that most cops enjoy living on the edge. The adrenaline rush we get maybe five, six, or even seven times a day is, to say the least, extremely addictive. The power and prestige that are bestowed on New Jersey troopers is overwhelming, especially to a impressionable new, young recruit who waited a lifetime to don the blue and gold. To put it bluntly, John I. Hogan #5068 ate, slept, and breathed the culture of the New Jersey State Police.

In retrospect, our preparation to the realities of being a trooper is hard-core: mentally and physically exhaustive. The body, mind, and soul are transformed during this insanely intense training. You leave the academy with a sense of invincibility. With credentials in his or her hand, its then up to each individual trooper to withstand the daily unknowns that confront every police officer across the country. Only the individual officer knows, deep down, if he or she has what it takes to adapt, interpret, and react in a split second to any given situation.

What weighed most heavily in my mind on a daily basis was whether I could rise to the top if I had to. If I failed, I would ruin what the instructors ingrained in us to be the only and most important thing we had going for us upon graduating from the academy: **our reputation.** Repeatedly during our training, instructors alluded to the importance of not getting "labeled" because once a junior trooper was in bad standing, life at the barracks could be miserable for that individual. Hopefully, statistics will be on my side, and I won't ever be in that miniscule percentage who will ever be confronted with a deadly-force situation or other critical incident, but what if I'm not so lucky?

Over the course of the next few months, I settled in and learned what being a trooper was really about while at my first assigned post: the Hightstown Station. Situated on the southbound side of Route 130 in Middlesex County, this barracks was older and run-down in appearance. Surprisingly and most upsetting to me, however, was, unlike what was preached in the academy, the most palpable observation was the lack of camaraderie at the barracks. Prior to exiting the academy, Trooper Kilmurray assured us every trooper would have our back, be our "brother," and give their life for one another but, apparently, not at this barracks.

Needless to say, from an outsider's perspective, there were kinks in the armor at the Hightstown Station. Unexpectedly, the "brotherhood" at this barracks I was now a part of was more equivalent to a halfway house. Among our eight-person squad were unique personalities who refused to ride with one another, barely spoke to certain squad members, and definitely didn't party or hang out after work ended as I hoped. I was fortunate, however, to have a very good "trooper coach" named Leslie "Rob" Bice. At five foot eight and around one hundred and fifty pounds, Trooper Bice was far from the mean, nasty-dispositioned individual I assumed would be my mentor. A very mellow and soft-spoken gentleman, Trooper Bice's biggest accomplishment was to never have had an Internal Affairs Bureau (IAB) complaint during his fifteen-year career. He taught me the correct way to speak to motorists and the importance of avoiding verbal confrontations that could only escalate into more problematic situations. His motto was simple—"The power of the pen"—meaning, write your ticket and send the motorists on their way without disputing the issue.

Trooper Coach was an eight-week crash course in how to actually be a trooper. During this time, I continuously rode with Trooper Bice or other senior troopers and experienced arrests for driving while intoxicated (DWI); investigated motor-vehicle accidents; and handled various complaints such as alarms, trespassing, and other minor infractions. While working the midnight shift on the coach program, I was also fortunate enough to make an arrest for what I really wanted to concentrate on and practiced so often in my parents' basement: *drug possession*! Admittedly, though, after completing the volumes of paperwork and required reports that came with these arrests over the course of several hours, I swore I never wanted to make another criminal arrest again.

With a decent foundation to now work with, I almost felt like I knew what to do as my two-month "trooper coach" orientation concluded. In mid-March 1993, I set out on duty for the first time by myself. I arrived to the barracks an hour early, as was customary, to do the dishes, empty the trash cans, and maintain the overall cleanliness of the barracks, as was every junior trooper's job. Once dressed, I inspected the interior and exterior of my assigned marked troop car, loaded the shotgun, tested my radar, and pulled out of the Hightstown Station. Alone in the troop car for the first time, I was the happiest and proudest human being alive. Each time the dispatcher came over the airwaves, I was hoping to be detailed to a serious crime or traumatic situation so I could prove that I could handle anything. Even if they didn't like one another, my peers' opinion of me was paramount in my mind. Being "squared away" was what I strived for, and I refused to become one of those guys that other troopers didn't want to ride with. Now that I had the uniform, the car, the badge, and the mentality, everything else was up to me; and I strived to become the most squared-away trooper I could be.

As was tradition with new-recruit classes, our first assignment was short-lived and, we rotated stations as a class, according to troops. The state police was divided into three areas: Troop A (south), Troop B (north), and Troop C (central). Graduated recruits were disseminated among the stations that made up these three troops. The other (2) troops that comprised the state police were Troop D (New Jersey Turnpike) and Troop E (Garden State Parkway).

My second assignment landed me at Troop C's most notorious barracks: Fort Dix. Located in Wrightstown, just outside of the Fort Dix and Maguire Air Force military installations, this barracks was the exact opposite of Hightstown. From day one, Sgt. Billy Vowell spoke of squad loyalty, unity, and *insisted* that we have squad outings that came to include fishing expeditions, overnight stays in Atlantic City, picnics and parties, lots of parties, where drinking, joking and having fun were rampant.

This was the trooper lifestyle I always heard stories about and couldn't wait to live. Work hard and play even harder—this was the mentality at Troop C's busiest barracks. Fort Dix was synonymous with, and often called, the Wild West. This well-deserved reputation was not because of the disgusting walls, floors, lockers, or fact that the water was not consumable or even suitable for showering. Instead, it was dubiously named so because of its proximity to the military bases, where several section 8 housing complexes were situated, and trust me, the inhabitants of these "projects" were always up to no good. At Dix, drunk driving and warrant arrests were very easy to come by, and they quickly lost their luster to me. Even more importantly, I almost felt hypocritical arresting "DUIs," knowing I was guilty of this offense from time to time.

As a trooper, the "system" stated locking up drunks was just something we had to do (on the average, one a month), but to separate yourself and be considered a "squared away" trooper, you had to make drug arrests, and despite the volumes of paperwork it entailed, this was my burning desire and true reason for wanting to be a trooper.

While at Dix, in hopes of garnering and solidifying my reputation to my peers, I began to quiz the minds of senior troopers assigned there, many of whom I respected and looked up to because they had already done the ultimate "time on the Big Road," also known as Troop D—the New Jersey Turnpike.

Just as I had been instructed to do in the academy, I tried to learn something—good or bad—from every trooper I came in contact with. For example, while at Hightstown, I learned *not* to "hawk bars" in hopes of making DWI arrests because the douche-bag trooper, who was infamous for having a "heavy thumb," was disliked by everyone for this inexcusable activity. At Fort Dix though, the troopers were all great guys and talked from experience. Jerk-offs were not permitted at Dix; and if they surfaced, they were quickly identified, singled out, and sent packing! Through conversations with experienced senior troopers, I learned little tips like observing a subject's body and eye movements when being questioned; finding the places either in a vehicle or on a person where contraband may be concealed; and knowing *everyone*, no matter what or why, lies to the police.

With each passing day, my confidence and abilities in becoming a good trooper increased. My level of awareness to my surroundings and the subjects I was now dealing with on a daily basis was at an all-time high. Making good, quality narcotic arrests and the paperwork that came with it quickly became second nature as everyone on the squad chipped in, and then once the "perp" was dropped off at the county jail, our squad would most often go to a local bar or hang in the rear of the barracks for hours of "debriefing."

After spending nearly a year at my second assignment, prior to leaving Fort Dix, I had made the largest seizure in recent memory: two pounds of marijuana. Though the issue of "profiling" had never surfaced either in the academy or at my first two assignments, I did learn the equivalent to "reverse profiling." Much like in Camden City, North Philadelphia, or other predominant minority areas, I was subjected to an area known as Sunbury Village in Pemberton Township, Burling County. It was in this area where Caucasian motorists were often singled out and stopped if motor-vehicle infractions were observed and questioned about their presence in this area. These routine stops often lead to arrest for narcotics, weapons, or other contraband. *So much for common stereotypes!* I was no longer naive and felt ready for the place I dreamed of patrolling since I was a child: the New Jersey Turnpike. Unfortunately, due to the dangers and complexity of incidents that occurred on the turnpike, only troopers with a minimum of sixteen months' service could be assigned to "the Big Road." Though I was willing, eager, and ready, the turnpike would have to wait, and the third and final rotation for the 113th Recruit Class landed me at the Wilburtha Station in West Trenton.

Situated at the base of the hill leading up to Division Headquarters, the Wilburtha Station, with its fresh and friendly atmosphere, was unlike any other barracks I had stepped into. Complete with an actual jail cell as opposed to the normal "handcuff locked to a bench" that served as a cell at most stations, Wilburtha was neat, clean, and properly outfitted with all basic necessities.

Unfortunately, even though we were "state" troopers, we were forbidden by our superiors to patrol Trenton City, so there was no use for any of this great equipment. In a nutshell, my time at Wilburtha was an abysmal tour.

Upon meeting my new sergeant for the first time, I was poignantly advised to steer clear of Trenton. I was further informed that if I chose to go into the city and got involved in something, I was on my own. *What a pussy this guy was!* With one of the highest crime rates in New Jersey, I was incensed that we were not allowed to patrol Trenton. Personally, I thought the superiors who ran the station were cowards for not insisting we go into the city and aggressively patrol for criminal activity as was the case when Colonel Pagano was empowered to lead the ranks.

Instead, day shifts were wasted with junior troopers, like myself, acting as overpaid delivery persons. At least twice a day—if not more, we did "package relays" between the Division Headquarters and Troop C headquarters, which was located on the southbound side of Route 1 in Princeton. With no specific area of responsibility, troopers from Wilburtha patrolled Interstate Highways 95, 195, and 295. As known by most New Jerseans, these roads are mainly comprised of business commuters. The mundane, daily practice of writing speeding tickets to decent, hardworking citizens going to work bored the hell out of me. I did not join the state police to write tickets to commuters who would then be forced to pay the ridiculous insurance surcharges that New Jersey is nationally infamous for.

To put it mildly, I couldn't wait to leave Wilburtha. With the exception of occasionally "sneaking" into the inner city streets of Trenton on midnights with K.C., time stood still, and each day brought more bullshit as we served as gophers for the pompous division personnel. Finally, my sixteen months of service arrived, and I was now permitted to request a transfer. Without hesitation and despite the lecturing of my boy K.C., who nearly got jammed up on the 'Pike years previously, I submitted my paperwork requesting an immediate transfer to Troop D. I couldn't wait to be identified as a "turnpike trooper"!

Forever resentful of the fact we weren't permitted to patrol Stuyvesant, Oakland, Perry, or other "mean streets" of Trenton, once on the 'Pike, I could do what I truly joined the state police for and be a real "trooper." In December 1994, my transfer request was granted, and with just less than two years of active duty, along with my classmate Joe Sansone, we were the first troopers from the 113th Recruit Class to be assigned to the enigma known as the New Jersey Turnpike.

CHAPTER 5

The Black Dragon

Reporting to the storied New Brunswick Barracks for my first day of duty was more intimidating than day one at the academy. Decades of state police lore; stories of wild chases, shootings, murders, massive contraband seizures and pandemonious, theatrical-like events gave the infamous New Jersey Turnpike its well-deserved reputation. This roadway is commonly known by most motorists as Interstate 95 or "the road that connects New York City to Philadelphia," but throughout the Division of State Police, because of its aerial structure and demonic reputation it is referred to as the Black Dragon.

At first glance, the circular-shaped barracks located within the Turnpike Authority Building on the southbound side of exit # 9 gives off an unassuming persona to the millions of motorists who pass it daily. Nestled back on a hilltop and barely noticeable from the roadway, most passer-bys probably had no idea this structure doubled as a state-police barracks.

For me, however, in addition to the fears and apprehension I already had for the potential dangers that lie ahead, after hearing numerous gut-wrenching stories of the unbelievable and tragic incidents that previously occurred on the Big Road, I had chills as I approached the legendary barracks for the first time.

Once inside, my eyes shifted quickly, and I tried to take in as much as possible but was fearful that one of the senior troopers who was present may chastise me. As I looked around, I couldn't help but to mentally relive the numerous dramatic events that transpired within the confines of this infamous building.

Dingy walls and less-than-desirable flooring covered the small outdated dispatch area that sat to the left. On the opposite side of this wall was a single warped wooden bench with (2) sets of handcuffs locked to it. Next to this "cell" was a fingerprinting station; and I immediately wondered if Joanne Chesimard, Yu Kikumura, or other high-profile criminals were processed on the same fingerprinting board I now hoped to use.

Mentally, I was overcome with an eerie feeling of "if these walls could talk"! On the backside of the main corridor was a prisoner cell, and I was disappointed to see that it was empty during my initial venture into the barracks. Peering around and trying to remain unnoticed, I could sense the high level of activity that this station was notorious for. During this brief encounter, the phones were constantly ringing, the trooper who was serving as the dispatcher barked details over the radio, and I could sense the likelihood of utter chaos braking out at any given minute.

After all, this was the very place where Trooper Werner Forrester was stationed when he was murdered by the members of the Black Panthers, including the most sought-after fugitive to date in New Jersey: the aforementioned Joanne Chesimard.

Even more menacing than the structure and aura of the New Brunswick Barracks were the troopers I initially encountered. As I carried the mounds of uniforms and gear I had down the spiral staircase that led to the "round room" where our lockers were located, each trooper I passed seemed more muscular, intimidating, and unapproachable. My "How are you, sir?" was continuously ignored by senior troopers, and in most cases, I was given a dirty look for even speaking to a turnpike trooper. Rumored as being a little meaner and crazier than the rest, troopers assigned to the 'Pike received a certain distinction throughout the Division of State Police. It was deliberated that no trooper's career was complete unless he or she did time on the Big Road, but as we all knew, there were a certain percentage of troopers who would never consider doing turnpike time.

Fitting in and being accepted by the likes of Billy Klimek, Dave Maruca, Sean Boero, and Kevin Goldberg was my ultimate goal. These guys were notorious throughout the division as the top "lock up" guys, and unbeknownst to them, I strived to join them at the top. Fortunately, I was assigned to squad #6, the same squad that Trooper Klimek was on. This, or so I thought, was my in. All I had to do was ride with and observe Trooper Klimek in action, and I too could soon become revered throughout the division for drug interdiction. The problem was, Klimek—like all the other squared-away troopers who I wanted to be like—wouldn't even acknowledge my existence let alone trust me enough to go on patrol with them.

My first three days on the turnpike were spent working day shifts and riding with Trooper Russ Gutter. With nothing other than mile markers and U-turns to learn, the only tricky part was determining what township you were in when making a motor vehicle stop. Trooper Gutter was extremely knowledgeable regarding turnpike policy and also served as our union representative. Unfortunately, Russ was the last person I should ride with if I were to be criminally active. He knew that and never pretended to be anything other than a good guy who liked to challenge the system. Russ was a great resource for everything except investigative questions and was one of the few senior troopers who were friendly to me from the start.

After my customary three days of authorized duty leave (ADL), I returned to work and was assigned my own car, equipment, and area of responsibility by Sgt. Jeff Suarez. When I pulled out of the barracks to go on patrol alone for the first time, I was alarmed at the speed in which traffic flowed. Previous to this assignment, I had only been on the turnpike in my personal car a few times, and now, here I was, in charge of an entire assigned area of the busiest roadway in all of New Jersey, perhaps the nation. Regardless of what happened in my area, I had to handle it—alone; "One job, one trooper" was the motto on the Big Road. I knew the only way to impress my new squad mates and prove that I was squared away was to handle all jobs quickly, efficiently, and without help. Keeping traffic moving was the underlying responsibility for troopers on the turnpike. If the traffic stopped, so did the toll revenues. With the exception of fatal accidents, *nothing* stopped traffic from flowing on the turnpike. Using high visibility with both marked and unmarked trooper cruisers, we tried to control the speed of traffic, but regardless of the number of troopers assigned to this roadway, the average speed at which the traffic flowed was still roughly seventy-five miles per hour on any given day despite all signs indicated the limit at 55 MPH.

With the traffic flowing continuously, troopers who were criminally active could then concentrate on what the Big Road was notorious for: guns, drugs, money, and bad-guys!

As my first few weeks of assignment on the 'Pike passed, frustration set in as I persistently tried to make an arrest. *I had to prove myself!* Then, to make matters worse, while alone on patrol, my classmate Joe Sansone made a narcotic arrest, and the razzing began. "Hey, boot, when are you going to be like your classmate and start bringing in some weight [referring to narcotics]?" or "Hey, troop, isn't it about time you stop being dead weight around here [referring to my lack of arrests]?" As hard as I tried to show my squad and other members at the barracks that I was going to be a "lock up" guy, I continued to fail. In reality, I was shy, timid, and even intimidated by the persons, mostly out of staters, I was stopping during the course of my shift. I quickly realized I was not confident, and I did not know the first thing about highway drug interdiction. *It all seemed so easy in my parents' basement!*

In the meantime, I handled my jobs, cleared accidents as quickly as possible, and did everything I could to try and fit in. None of this, however, was going to help get me noticed by the troopers I envied; then the unthinkable happened and forever changed my life and career path.

Part II

Deadly Force

Its pitch-black outside, and I'm awakened by my alarm clock blasting rap music from Power 99 FM. Outside of my covers, I could feel the brisk, cold air that swirled from the combination of the ceiling fan centered above my bed and the preset thermostat temperature in my house being kept at sixty-two degrees, even in the winter. *I have to be cold when I sleep!* The only heat I felt was from the internal heater of my king-size water bed as I lay there, struggling to prevent myself from falling back to sleep. It's 4:35 AM, and I had to be out of the house by five. *Day shifts suck!* From 6:00 AM to 4:00 PM on this day, March 23, 1995, a section of the New Jersey Turnpike would belong to me. With slightly more than two months of experience on the 'Pike, I was still struggling to fit in; make my first individual arrest; and, most importantly, earn the respect of the senior troopers assigned to the New Brunswick Barracks.

As usual, I got to the station around 5:30 AM so I could take out the trash, clean the dishes, make coffee, etc. At twenty-four years old, I was the youngest and, along with Sansone, the most junior guy on the turnpike. If I am labeled "salty," my reputation—as well as my entire locker, uniforms, gear, and even my personal vehicle—could have been destroyed by the infamous Phantom. (Part of state-police folklore, the phantom routinely preyed upon any trooper believed to be too salty or for failure to adhere to the numerous unwritten rules or codes of conduct at any given barracks.)

When I completed those menial duties, most of which I split with Sansone, together, we trekked down the spiral staircase and entered the circular locker room. Lined with aging dark brown cabinets that served as lockers, a massive weight room anchored the middle portion of this room and was frequently used by the numerous muscle-heads that were currently assigned to New Brunswick.

As we began to dress in our class A winter uniform, Sergeant Jeff Suarez arrived and promptly advised that I would "have the book" or serve as the administrative trooper for the day. Additional responsibilities for the "bookman" consisted of doing computer checks, logging motor-vehicle stops, and running criminal-history or background checks of any prisoners that were locked up during our shift. I immediately advised Sgt Suarez that I had a grand jury at 10:00 AM for an arrest that was "TOTed" to me (turned over to) by Trooper Mark Wondrack because, as everyone knew and constantly reminded me, I had yet to make a solo arrest! Upon learning this, Sgt. Suarez told me to disregard and assigned this duty to my classmate Joe Sansone.

After our squad briefing, I was assigned to patrol the "south," which was from milepost 61 to 73 or exits 7A to 8A. Since this area was closest to my residence, I was more familiar with this territory and, for obvious reasons, preferred this assignment. Plus, being further south meant less traffic which was critical as I was still adjusting to the unbelievable speed and volume of traffic that flowed daily on the 'Pike. Because seniority ruled on the Big Road, I became very familiar with the southern area since Troopers Busz, Gutter, Klimek, and Vona always had first preference and consistently selected the more northern territories that made up the New Brunswick Station.

Upon completing my equipment and vehicle inspections, I departed the parking lot of the barracks at roughly 6:20 AM. I immediately headed southbound and drove around in a sleepy funk for most of the morning. After stopping for breakfast and doing a final "loop" of my assigned area, I headed off Interchange No. 9 en route to Middlesex County Courthouse for a grand jury, which was a formal hearing where a prosecutor walked you through the events that led up the arrest. The civilians that made up the "jury" then voted whether or not to indict the arrested individual.

This particular hearing was for an arrest made on the midnight shift while riding with Trooper Wondrack. A routine motor-vehicle stop of a rental car from North Carolina was conducted, and though he assumed the role of the lead during this stop, he was good enough to give me credit for finding the loaded 9-mm pistol that led to this arrest. This, or so I hoped, would lessen the ridicule I currently faced from other station personnel for my lack of criminal activity.

Once I finished testifying before the grand jury, which took roughly ten minutes, I drove through the center of New Brunswick and headed back to the turnpike where I resumed my area of responsibility. Mentally, I wasn't in the mood to work, and before I realized it, lunchtime was quickly approaching, and I hadn't done a freaking thing all day. Once at Interchange 7A (milepost 61), I turned around at the toll plaza and headed northbound. Still in a sleepy funk, I observed no motor-vehicle infractions to enforce and was now growing concerned because I had absolutely no activity written on my daily patrol log.

Within minutes, I swiftly reached and entered the milepost 75 U-turn, which is a service ramp that crosses over the entire turnpike and is off-limits to the public. As I headed down the ramp to travel southbound, I encountered a white Volkswagen Jetta that was occupied by two black males sitting in their car, just at the base of the ramp. Identical to the Volkswagen I drove in to the academy with Brice for twenty-three weeks, it was facing northbound and had come to a stop. *No big deal. They're probably just lost or perhaps contemplating making an illegal U-turn.*

Facing opposite their vehicle, I pulled my marked troop car next to the driver's side window of the Volkswagen. As I hit the automatic window button to put mine down, I motioned to the driver to roll his window down. It was a bright, sunny, crisp, and cold day; and the sky was cloudless. As the sun's glare pierced my eyes, I asked the driver what he was doing. Without looking at me, he immediately stated that he was lost and needed to turn around. His breath dissipated in the cold March air, and I could tell he was very nervous for some reason.

Less than five feet apart and face-to-face while seated in our vehicles, I advised him that it was illegal for him to utilize this ramp. Sensing his heightened sense of nervousness, I asked the driver, a black male in his late twenties with close-cropped hair, if he had his driver's license. Almost as if he purposely ignored my question, he hesitantly replied, "It's not my car!" With this response, a lump began to form in my throat, and an uneasy feeling overcame my body. My sixth sense, which I started to question because of my lack of arrests, told me this guy wasn't your ordinary knucklehead.

As this encounter unfolded, the passenger, a thin, black male in his late twenties, remained motionless, looking straight ahead the entire time and never once acknowledging my presence. Lastly, I could tell the driver was extremely jittery and at times even observed his hands shaking. *This dude looks like me the first time I had to draw my weapon, shaking like a crackbaby!* I ordered the operator to stay put and cautiously turned the troop car around to pull behind the white Volkswagen. Keeping a close eye on the car and its occupants the entire time, I then called the stop in to the bookman at the New Brunswick Station, Trooper J. Sansone.

Once completing this standard operating procedure (SOP), I exited the troop car and briskly walked up to the driver and asked for his license, registration, and insurance. After erratically explaining to me that the car was his uncle's and he didn't have any identification or paperwork for the car, I asked the operator to step out. With my trooper hat pulled down over my eyes, the driver—who was about six feet three, dark skinned, and appeared to have a muscular build hidden by the brown leather bomber jacket he was wearing—towered over me. *Oh Christ, I don't like this.* Fighting my own fears and emotions, I attempted to maintain control of the scene as he immediately began rambling on about being lost and just needing to turn around. In my best command voice, I directed the driver, "Just chill out, relax, and hang on a second!"

A quick pat down for weapons revealed a glass crackpipe on the inside-jacket pocket of this individual, who now identified himself as "John Smith." (If that doesn't set off bells, you shouldn't be working in law enforcement!) The transparent pipe was shrouded in a dirty white paper towel and gave the impression of frequent use. Burn marks covered the entire length of the glass pipe, and the operator immediately stated, "Man, that shit ain't mine! I don't fuck wit da rock!" As I further patted down this subject, I continued to question him as to where he was coming from and where he was headed in addition to whose vehicle it was. During this encounter, John Smith constantly fidgeted and refused to look at me as his head appeared to be on a swivel. Aside from realizing the obvious—that this guy had a suspended license and maybe a stolen car, I had no idea what was about to happen. Growing up in quaint little Florence Township just didn't prepare me for this, and I had no idea of just how "green" I truly was.

As much as I wanted to, I knew I couldn't lock up this scumbag for just a crack-pipe. The guys at the station would hound me mercilessly. It was an unwritten rule that you never arrest a "2B" (black male) unless you had at least an ounce of coke; bullet of heroin; loaded weapon; or, at the minimal, a pound of marijuana. Sadly, white folks, on the other hand, got locked up for anything more than a roach. Pathetically, it was a numbers game that we were all aware of, and as unfair as it was, we had to play along to keep the stats even-keeled. These unwritten policies were never explained to me, nor did I understand or question them; it was all just a part of being a turnpike trooper!

When no further contraband was found, I immediately focused my attention to the passenger. Prior to approaching the passenger's side of the vehicle, I ordered John Smith to sit on the hood of my troop car and not move. He had a jagged, glazed look in his eyes and continued to peer everywhere but at me. Reluctantly, he leaned back on the hood of my troop car as ordered, but I was far from convinced that the remainder of this encounter was going to go smoothly.

The ill feeling I had in the pit of my stomach just kept getting worse by the second. Being new and trying to prove my mettle, as much as I wanted to, I just couldn't call for backup! I had no choice—one job, one trooper!

I now quickly attempted to walk up to the individual seated in the front right passenger's seat. As I turned my back, John Smith immediately got up and began to walk hesitantly back toward the driver's side of his car. I screamed for him to stop and sit back down. After bouncing left and right on his feet a few times, he obeyed my command. The same exact scenario played out as I again tried to reach the passenger. "Move again, motherfucker, and I will lock you up for obstructing! I'm not playing with you, asshole! Sit down! Don't move or talk!"

I was hoping this idle threat would at least keep John Smith seated momentarily. I was now caught in a cat-and-mouse game, and the bad guy was getting to me. I had to maintain control of the scene! I was in a zone, and the chatter that blared from the portable radio that was connected to my side was inaudible to me. I was focused but scared. Nothing else in life mattered at this point except finding a way to keep these thugs from overpowering me. I knew shit was fucked up, but I didn't know to what extent. *Goddamn it! Why didn't I have the balls to call for backup? Screw pride! This was my life!*

On my third attempt, I finally reached the passenger's window, and just as I did, John Smith leaped from the hood of the troop car and bolted directly to his door. Before I knew it, he was inside the Volkswagen, which had been running the entire time. In less than a few seconds' time, he was seated, the door was shut, and the car was in gear. I heard the engine roar as he accelerated rapidly in first gear. *What in the fuck do I do now?*

I was caught flat-footed between the Volkswagen and troop car. Instinctively, I chased the driver and reached his window just as he began to accelerate. Running alongside the Volkswagen, on impulse, I reached through the partially opened window, attempting to grab the keys and turn off the car's ignition. As long as the passenger, who I never got to pat down, didn't have a gun and blow my freaking head off, I figured this was the logical split-second thing to do.

My breathing had all but stopped. The next few seconds were a blur. I didn't hear anything and only saw the driver's entire body leaning forward as if to make the car go faster. Both his hands were on the wheel, and I could see his knuckles turning white from the death grip he had on the steering wheel. At last glance, the passenger appeared to be screaming, his mouth was wide open, but all sounds evaded me. As he banged his hands on the dashboard, everything appeared to be in slow motion. Fear left my body and was replaced by a desire to live.

Everything was happening so quickly but yet appeared to be occurring in fragmented intervals, step by step. Would I rise to the top or fall flat on my face? Concerns over reputation and doing the right thing gave way to sheer primal instinct.

At this point, I was running alongside the Volkswagen with my right arm inside the window. The driver was attempting to hit my hand away as I reached for the ignition keys. Suddenly, due to the speed at which I was running as I tried to keep up, I lost my balance. Falling straight down, my right arm clutched the interior of driver's door, and my right tricep and armpit banged down on the window. Supporting all of my weight with this one arm, both legs were now being dragged along the ground. As I held on for dear life solely with my right arm, I struggled to regain my footing.

As the milliseconds passed, my right leg was under the car as my left shoe dragged on the blacktop. I screamed for him to stop the vehicle. Instinctively, without thought, I grabbed my gun. With my left hand, I removed my weapon from its holster and pointed it directly at the head of John Smith as I held on to prevent myself from falling underneath the car. "Stop the fucking car or I am going to blow your fucking head off!" is what I think I screamed from this most precarious position.

The last thing I recall seeing was John Smith's right hand come off the steering wheel and grab the barrel of my weapon. *Fuck!* I thought to myself. Not only am I holding on for dear life here, now this cocksucker is attempting to steal my weapon and possibly use it against me. I knew my only other option was to let go and sacrifice the possibility of allowing my legs and lower extremities to be run over by the Volkswagen. At all cost, I had to retain possession of my weapon.

As we fought for control of my weapon, his right hand tugged at, twisted, and turned the barrel of my gun, hoping to pry it from my death grip. Getting run over just wasn't how I wanted this day to end. *Christ, I wasn't even supposed to be out on the road today! All this shit because of stupid grand jury for an arrest that wasn't even mine!*

Could I really shoot someone if I had to? Was it the right thing to do? What if the driver was truly a good guy and just panicked? Does he have children, a wife, and parents? What are the repercussions if I fire? Can I lose my job? Will I go to jail if I am wrong? What if he gains control of my weapon? Does the passenger have a gun? Is there a gun under the driver's seat? Would these guys be able to shoot me, a police officer in full uniform? Why is he attempting to flee?

In the academy, we were instructed that if you are in a situation and have the luxury to ask yourself, "Should I shoot?" then the answer is no. Dangling precariously from their vehicle and within inches of losing my weapon and possibly my life, I did not have to ask myself or the Lord for forgiveness of the inevitable. My will to survive took over.

I have no recollection of seeing or hearing the rounds go off or where they went. When I fell off and rolled backward, I knew I had shot the driver, banged the hell out of my head, and somehow avoided being run over. Uncertain if the adrenaline was preventing me from feeling any serious injuries, I recall just lying on the ground with weapon in-hand, unaware of how many shots I fired and what was now transpiring around me. I had no idea how or what stopped the fleeing Volkswagen, but up ahead in the distance, I observed it at a standstill. Having yet moved a muscle, I recalled seeing a pair of feet exit the passenger's side of the Volkswagen; and a black male ran right past me, down the ramp, and toward the southbound lanes of the turnpike.

Before I knew it, troopers were everywhere. Trooper Justin McCarthy helped me to my feet and positioned me upright in a seated fashion on the silver, metal guardrail. I recall hearing someone say that backup was en route because the car came back a "signal 18" or stolen motor vehicle. Before paramedics arrived, I just had to walk up to the Volkswagen and see for myself what just occurred. Not knowing the consequences of what I was about to see, as I approached the Volkswagen, I observed the operator, John Smith, still seated in the driver's chair. His upper torso had fallen to the right, near the area where the passenger was previously seated. Blood filled the entire center's console area and was splattered about the passenger's seat and floor area. I remember hearing him gurgle from all the blood he was swallowing. Mentally, I was overcome with anxiety and emotion, and I immediately began to dry heave. Almost in tears and nearly vomiting, I couldn't help but to think that the man who, seconds ago was trying to get my gun, now begged for help. I wanted to help him. I needed to save his life! A group of troopers wisely removed me from the area as other troopers and a local policeman from Medford Township who witnessed the entire tragedy began lifesaving first-aid treatment on John Smith.

One second, you are fighting for your own life; the next, you are trying to save someone else's—this is just one example of the immense and traumatic adrenaline swings a police officer must endure. As they all sped to my assistance, the troopers probably could care less about the occupants of the stolen vehicle; now they were administering medical treatment to save the life of an individual who, quite possibly, could have taken the life of one of their own. This mentality, I believe, is why it takes a special person—a rare, unique breed of human being—to wear a law-enforcement uniform.

Seated again on the cold guardrail, I continued to dry heave. *Would he die? Did I just kill someone? How many rounds did I fire? Was I justified? Am I going to jail for murder? I'm going to lose my job and go to prison!* Unknown to me, these "thoughts" were being said aloud in-between my attempts to throw up.

Trooper McCarthy grabbed me and shouted, "John, I saw the whole thing! You didn't do anything wrong! Stop talking like that!" As this transpired, I observed the passenger, who was now handcuffed and surrounded by troopers, being walked back to the scene. As he stood approximately ten yards away, he repeatedly screamed, "I'm shot! I'm shot!" *How in the hell did he get shot?* I wondered to myself.

In an instant, the scene became movielike. Helicopters from both the State police and local news stations were flying overhead. Detectives and troopers were everywhere, setting up a crime-scene perimeter. Ambulances, with sirens blaring loudly, raced to the scene. Traffic had slowed, and witnesses came to a stop on the shoulder. Within minutes, a simple motor-vehicle stop was turned into what appeared to be a multimillion-dollar movie production, only this wasn't Hollywood or New York City; this was the New Jersey Turnpike!

Within minutes, I was whisked from the scene by superior officers and taken back to the New Brunswick Barracks. Before going to the hospital, I gave a brief statement of the incident to investigators from the NJSP's Major Crimes Unit. Once at Saint Peter's Hospital in Edison, I was treated for overall body soreness and deep bruises on my right arm and triceps. I also had a bad bump on the back of my head, a sore left ankle, and a damaged shoulder, which would eventually require surgery as a result of being dragged.

Once released from the hospital after refusing to be admitted for further observation, I was transported back to the New Brunswick Station. As I entered, it appeared as if everyone was just staring at me. Two turnpike-authority workers were present, wearing full-bodied wet suits, and a strong bleach-like odor permeated the barracks.

Led into a private room by members from Major Crimes, I was informed that in addition to not having a driver's license and possessing a stolen motor vehicle, John Smith and his counterpart were both fugitives. From the passenger, it was learned that they met earlier in the day in Jersey City where they both resided. After smoking crack cocaine together, they reportedly committed a burglary in the Jamesburg area. While traveling back to Jersey City on the turnpike, they realized they were headed in the wrong direction and were trying to turn around when our most unfortunate encounter unraveled. *How's that for timing?* As it was then explained to me, the turnpike workers wearing the chemical suits were cleaning the station's cell because to top it all off, both subjects were believed to be HIV-positive. As a result of being exposed to their blood, I then underwent two years of continuous HIV testing to ensure I had not been infected. *Talk about a burdensome cross to bear at twenty-four years of age!*

Most people probably think this type of thing can't happen in broad daylight. Something this unbelievable can only take place in a big city or in the middle of the night. The truth is, the general public has no clue as to the dangers that exist on the New Jersey Turnpike or the unrealistic volumes of weapons, drugs, and contraband that flow daily. The mystique of the Black Dragon is what separated turnpike troopers from the rest of the Division. Those of us who worked on the Big Road did so by choice. We didn't get paid more or have special privileges. As turnpike troopers, we just took more pride in "doing the job and making the big grab."

The day following the shooting, a member of the NJSP's Employee's Assistance Program visited me at my residence. I was asked about the incident and if I felt the need to drink alcohol, stay with family as opposed to remain home alone, and a bunch of other routine, generic questions by the counselor. Fearful of opening up my true emotions from this incident, I foolishly downplayed the totality of this tragedy and the repercussions I was currently enduring, both physically and psychologically. Before leaving, I was deemed "fit for duty" by the counselor and he offered me two tickets to the Philadelphia 76'ers' basketball game that night. Though appreciative, I declined the offer, and we mutually agreed to remain in contact to address the possibility of me suffering posttraumatic stress syndrome.

Two days later, like a good soldier, I suited up and reunited myself with Squad Six. Patrolling the Big Road was where I wanted to be, and no one tried to hold me back. Oblivious to what was really going on internally, I just assumed the repetitious nightmares and flashbacks of the incident were a normal reaction. Eventually, they would stop! After all, I was a turnpike trooper—fearless and unflappable. I wanted everyone to respect and like me. I couldn't show weakness! *What would my peers or, even worse, my class-coordinator Trooper Kilmurray think of me if I stated I wasn't mentally prepared to return to full duty? Troopers are hard! No emotions allowed! Plus, like Kilmurray said, troopers never let one another down, and if I didn't return to work, my squad would be short-staffed.* In my mind, it was my only option.

In exchange for all the emotional and physical trauma of nearly taking a life and perhaps giving my own, I was awarded with a plaque during a luncheon hosted by the Middlesex County 200 Club Award, a small consolation for the lifelong psychological scars this incident left me with.

1995
Valor Award

TROOPER JOHN HOGAN
New Jersey State Police

On March 22, 1995, Trooper John Hogan, while patrolling the New Jersey Turnpike, stopped a vehicle for making an illegal u-turn at M.P. 75, South Brunswick Township, Middlesex County. Upon approaching the vehicle, occupied by two men, the Trooper requested the driver's license and vehicle registration, which he failed to produce. The Trooper then asked the driver to step from the vehicle and during a pat down search found a crack pipe. He ordered the driver to the rear of the car and then approached the passenger. During his approach, the driver disregarded his orders and re-entered the vehicle and attempted to depart the scene. Trooper Hogan ran to the driver's door and reached in the window to stop the driver from fleeing. With Trooper Hogan hanging on the driver's door, the suspect accelerated, dragging the Trooper, who was able to draw his weapon. At this point, the driver grabbed the Trooper's handgun. Fearing for his life, the Trooper discharged three rounds, striking both the driver and the passenger. The suspect vehicle then collided with an arriving back-up Troop car, thus ending this life threatening encounter.

Trooper Hogan's professional action and display of courage reflects great credit upon himself and is in keeping with the highest traditions of the New Jersey State Police.

CHAPTER 6

Just Another Day

Reporting back to work after this critical incident brought newfound attention from the troopers who I wanted to emulate. "Hoge's" was the nickname Trooper Klimek now addressed me with each day. As for the other troopers who used to ignore me, they now passed by and stated, "Good Job, Troop!" I had made it. I was now a respected turnpike trooper. Within the next few months, I had been honored with a Valor Award from the Middlesex County 200 Club; and the road that, for me, initially seemed chaotic, turbulent, and overwhelming now began to slow down. Just as I had longed to do, from listening and observing, I began to learn the patterns that drug couriers or "mules" used to transport narcotics. With each passing shift, I had newfound confidence in my abilities to become a "lock up" guy.

I was young, single, muscular, confident, and cocky—but always respectful. At twenty-five years of age, I had tons of friends and a great family, owned my own home, traveled, partied, and could purchase any basic necessities I wanted. Most important to me, however, was my passion and love affair with my job. I reached the point in my career where I felt on any given day, I was capable of making sizable weapon, narcotic, or currency seizures. After all, the Black Dragon is the nation's most traveled highway. To ordinary civilians, it is simply Interstate 95. To aggressive young troopers looking to make a name for themselves, however, it is the most drug—and weapon-infested roadway in the country, and for the select few of us who chose to, we took great pride in our personal "war on drugs."

Each day of my assignment on the turnpike brought new and exciting adventures. Troopers assigned to the Big Road knew that within the millions of motorists that traveled this "city on wheels," a certain percentage was involved in criminal activity unparalleled to that which existed at regular road stations. Nestled between the metropolis of New York City and Philadelphia, the New Jersey Turnpike was identified by the federal government as a major "pipeline" for illicit activity at the height of the war on drugs. To further boast this claim, the Feds personally trained and provided New Jersey troopers with information, bulletins, and other tactics to permeate the flow of drugs through New Jersey's borders.

Having just being involved in a shooting didn't deter me from being criminally active. In fact, it left me with a burning desire to remove this type of character and element from the roadways of New Jersey. Trooper John Hogan, no. 5068, was now part of the legacy of the Black Dragon, and in my mind, I had to keep the reputation of the turnpike troopers going by making more arrests. Tainted with HIV or not, my blood flowed the blue and gold colors of the NJSP, and making high-profile criminal arrests was now forever embedded in me as a result of this tragic incident. Regardless of the shift that our squad worked, a new day meant a new adventure!

Part I

No Longer Naive

It's Saturday morning, about 7:30 AM, and I've been awake since my alarm clock blared at four thirty. After a quick shower, I jumped into my POV (personal vehicle) and headed northbound after gaining entry to the New Jersey Turnpike via the Pennsylvania Extension in Florence, where my town house adjacently sat. Still groggy on this cold, desolate, and dark morning, I bitched to myself that day shifts should start at 8:00 AM so we didn't have to get up so early.

As a matter of procedure, I arrived at the barracks for my ten-hour tour of duty at 5:30 AM. By six fifteen, the sun began to peek through the gray clouds, and I was now donning the historic and charismatic French blue uniform of the New Jersey State Police. As I fought to keep my mind and body awake, the realization that I was about to begin patrolling the most feared stretch of highway in the nation began to set in.

All the joking, ball busting, and horseplay that routinely took place during our squad briefings ended as members of Squad Six exited the barracks after being issued our patrol cars, shotguns, portable radios, and other patrol-related necessities. Alone on patrol and essentially acting as your own boss, however, did have numerous perks. *Do I want to go eat, get coffee, hang out in the barracks, or take a quick nap? Why did I go out with my friends and drink last night?* My head was pounding, eyes burning from improper sleep, and the sun's glare was beaming in from the troop car's windshield, only adding to my misery. Despite a total lack of motivation, I said to myself, *Screw it! I'm gonna go lock somebody up and spend the rest of the day at the barracks doing paperwork.*

After a quick loop of my assigned area to ensure there were no "13s" (distressed motorists), I was now traveling southbound in the truck lanes of the New Jersey Turnpike. My marked New Jersey State Police trooper cruiser was clean and shiny. My uniform was tight fitting, muscles (hopefully) bulging through the wool blouse that signified our winter—Class A uniform. My brass nameplate, buttons, and hat badge glistened from the hours spent at home, polishing them. My black leather shoes, belt, handcuff case, ammunition pouch, and holster were polished to perfection, almost mirror-like. In my mind, I epitomized what I thought a New Jersey trooper should be.

I began pacing, (traveling along with a suspect car at the same speed), a vehicle that was in the left lane of the inner or Cars-Only portion of the highway. At roughly seventy-seven miles per hour, I looked over to see what appeared to be two Hispanic male subjects in a Pennsylvania-registered vehicle. Training, experience, and loose stereotyping now had me thinking that this motor-vehicle stop could be anything but ordinary. Assuming that everyone heading southbound was coming from New York City, I began to ponder why these two young men were up so early; what they did and where they slept last night; and, lastly, were they legitimate citizens. Fortunately, because they were speeding, I had the probable cause to stop them and find out the answers to these questions that ran rampant in my mind upon seeing any violation regardless of the occupant's gender or race.

My heart began pounding, and my hands started to sweat as my white-knuckle grip on the steering wheel further tensed. If they are up to no good, I anticipate they will use the old "No hablo Ingles!" trick on me. After I established the basis for the stop—in this case, blatant speeding—I maneuvered my trooper car from the outer roadway to the Cars Only inner roadway, utilizing a Z-turn. I saw the two males beginning to speak, so I quickly activated my overhead lights, hoping to cut off their conversation. Their vehicle—which I noted to be very new and shiny, "probably rented"—immediately pulled to the right shoulder and came to a complete stop.

I grabbed my trooper hat and positioned it as low as possible over my eyes as I exited the cruiser. The shiny black brim on the hat nearly touched my nose as I briskly—but cautiously—walked up to the passenger's side window and asked the operator for his license and registration. The driver, a Hispanic male in his midtwenties, was wearing a bright blue "NYPD" T-shirt. *SHIT! It's not a homerun after all,* I thought to myself. When they failed to produce any identification and said the vehicle was rented, bells immediately started going off in my mind. I then asked the driver to exit the vehicle so I could separate the two subjects for further questioning. *What's the deal with the New York Police Department T-shirt?* I wondered to myself.

We eyed each other up as he walked toward me. Being tactful, I kept close watch on the only thing he had that could kill me: his hands. As a matter of practice, I positioned myself between his vehicle and my marked troop car, enabling me to see the other occupant as well. This also permitted me to be that much closer to the troop car in the event this asshole decides to jump me. Plus, if I get shot or injured, hopefully, I can always crawl to the troop car for cover.

As he walked back toward me, the driver was half smiling and appeared cool and calm. *The game has begun!* This was how and where troopers and good cops distinguish themselves. *Was I going to allow him to outsmart me and beat me at my own game? Would I be intimidated by him wearing an NYPD T-shirt? Just how far do I take the questioning? I don't want to piss him off or let him know I think he may be involved with a particular criminal offense. What if he runs or refuses to answer my questions? If he does refuse, then I have even tougher and more difficult decisions to make. Do I call for a drug dog or secure the car in hopes of getting a search warrant from a judge?*

These thoughts and questions run steady in a good cop's mind. But if you let yourself get so wrapped up in conversation, you may forget your "distance rule," and before you know it, the scumbag is on top of you, grabbing for your weapon. Another permanent danger is the traffic: cars and trucks whizzing by at seventy, eighty, and even ninety miles per hour as you stand a mere three or four feet from the right lane of traffic. I'd bet the bank a civilian would shit his pants if, while approaching a car or speaking to a subject, out of nowhere, a TT's (tractor trailer) horn blows, causing his asshole to pucker like nothing else in life could. With all this going on both in and out of his mind and body, a trooper must always remain focused and, above all else, maintain control of any given situation.

"Hablo Ingles?" I asked. "Yes, sir!" was the response. Reaching for a neutral ground to put his mind at ease, I asked where he got that "really sharp

NYPD T-shirt." After learning that his uncle, who was supposedly a cop in the Bronx, gave it to him, I asked what precinct his uncle worked at. Upon stuttering over his own words, he advised me that he couldn't recall what precinct or even his uncle's name! With each shuffle of his feet, "Julio's" eyes now continually avoided making eye contact with me. Wide-eyed and becoming pale before my eyes, I could almost see Julio's heart pumping through his shirt as he constantly looked rearward into his vehicle, where all that was visible was the back of his friend's head. I started to wonder if maybe he was attempting to get his friend's attention. *Do they already have a plan to jump me?* I realized I wanted to quickly wrap up my questioning and stay safe. The longer I stayed back there, the more time the passenger had to debate what he was going to do and say. For all I know, the passenger could have picked up an uzi from under the seat after I walked away and was waiting to blow my freaking head off. Just before I instructed him to stand at the front of his vehicle, I asked Julio where he was going. The cool and calm individual from a few moments ago was now no longer smiling as he said he was going to Philadelphia to visit family for a few days.

If it were a game, he and I both knew that I won round one. He failed to answer the most basic of questions and was more nervous than a virgin on her wedding night. Before I even approached the passenger, I was certain he would give me completely conflicting information, thus, forming probable cause for a consensual search of their vehicle.

Seated straight up in the passenger seat and looking forward, the passenger didn't flinch or look at me when I asked his name. Julio, who was cooperative and standing as directed at the front of his vehicle, turned to me and said—*you guessed it*—"No hablo Ingles!" *I've been here before. No big deal.* I briefly held a conversation with the passenger, Rafael, to the best of my ability. I knew enough Spanish to obtain the essential information I needed during a roadside motor-vehicle stop. After just two or three questions, I realized these guys were undoubtedly attempting to hide what had become obvious. With that said, I now had developed my probable cause, and I asked Julio if he would sign a New Jersey State Police consent-to-search form.

I fed him some bullshit as to why I wanted to search, like needing to get the vehicle's identification number off the dashboard since he didn't have the registration. By doing this, I was hoping he would just think I was a stupid cop, a good guy just looking for the registration information. In reality, however, I had already pegged these two as drug couriers. With that said, as a matter of personal preference, I never once allowed the word "narcotics" to ever come into the conversation even though I knew in my heart these knuckleheads were transporting dope. *My only questions were was he going to sign this form, or was I going to have to decide to call a drug dog if he refused consent, and just how much dope is in the car!*

Believe it or not, like 95 percent of individuals, the driver tentatively but with no hesitation signed the form; and without even realizing it, his actions alone just told me that somewhere in that car, there had to be drugs, weapons, or contraband of some type.

By now, I am convinced that this motor-vehicle stop is going to result in arrest. I alerted dispatch that I was "Okay, checking further." This alerted my squad mates, who already knew of my aggressive nature, to start heading toward me because it's not often that I indiscreetly call for backup unless I had something legitimate.

As backup arrived, the nervousness of possibly being ambushed turned to excited energy because I knew from the attitude and demeanor of these two, there was probably a decent amount of drugs here—two Hispanic males in their twenties, a rental car, no identification, no idea as to where they are going or how long they are staying. Furthermore, both men were now extremely nervous after putting up an initial cool facade; they made no eye contact; and most telling, they were traveling *southbound* on the New Jersey Turnpike.

Now, all that's left was finding it. Is there a hidden compartment, a trapdoor, a secret trigger switch? Is it hidden in the door panels, heating vents, seat cushions, under the dashboard; or are these two dumb enough to leave it in plain view?

After canvassing the interior of the car very quickly, I popped the trunk. Like magic, there it was: a box with four brick-sized packages that were sealed with duct tape. Undoubtedly, this was a controlled dangerous substance (CDS), but was it cocaine or heroin? The only difference to me was the dollar value I could take on my statistics for yearly seizures. The individuals were immediately given their Miranda rights, handcuffed, and transported separately back to the Cranbury Barracks, which had, in the past year, replaced the aging and defunct New Brunswick Barracks.

Ironically, back at the station, the subjects' bags were searched, and we learned that these two males had entered the country via San Juan, Puerto Rico the previous night. The vehicle had been rented for them by a subject using a fake name, which was very common for drug mules. After admitting to purchasing the NYPD T-shirt at LaGuardia International Airport upon landing to "hopefully fool any cop that stops him," Julio and his friend Rafael were committed to the county jail in default of one-hundred-thousand-dollar bail.

The CDS turned out to be four kilograms (almost nine pounds) of cocaine valued at roughly one hundred thousand dollars. Julio and Rafael were set to fly out of Philadelphia International Airport the next morning. To this day, I believe their plane tickets remain stapled to the inside flap of the official-case jacket at the Cranbury Barracks. As predicted, I spent the rest of the day in the station doing paperwork, and it was just another typical day on the Big Road.

Day after day, scenes like this became the norm during my tenure at Troop D—the New Jersey Turnpike. Every report I did, as well as every report done by another trooper, was read and initialed by a supervisor. These reports were then forwarded up the chain of command. Every arrest report detailed the race, gender, age, and other pertinent information for statistical analysis. Ultimately, these reports were forwarded, or at least the statistics were, to the only individual who superceded the colonel of the New Jersey State Police: the Office of the Attorney General. Though there were rumors about the federal government looking at the statistics from State Police arrests, racial profiling accusations never surfaced. Furthermore, never once did my superiors in the NJSP or any member from the attorney general's office ever officially question me or my colleagues about this alleged law-enforcement practice. To our knowledge, the war on drugs was paramount, and there was no other place in the world to fight this war than the New Jersey Turnpike. Road troopers were the state's foot soldiers in this war, and since our practices and policies were never questioned, we assumed we had full support of our elected officials. Even more importantly, with each arrest came a personalized letter of recognition from the top political officials in the entire state of New Jersey. Almost daily, during the height of our aggressive campaign to rid the roadways of drugs, guns, and other illicit contraband, I would receive a letter of praise from none other than the governor herself, Christine Todd Whitman, and Attorney General Peter Verniero which was signed by the colonel of the State Police, Carl A. Williams (official copy of one of the more than sixty letters I received):

State of New Jersey
DEPARTMENT OF LAW AND PUBLIC SAFETY
DIVISION OF STATE POLICE
POST OFFICE BOX 7068
WEST TRENTON NJ 08628-0068

CHRISTINE TODD WHITMAN
Governor

PETER VERNIERO
Attorney General

August 21, 1997

COLONEL CARL A. WILLIAMS
Superintendent
TELEPHONE: (609) 882-2000
FAX: (609) 882-6920

Trooper John Hogan #5068

Dear Trooper Hogan:

I would like to take this opportunity to recognize your efforts on August 9, 1997, in Middlesex County, which resulted in the apprehension of two subjects for possession of 4 kilos of cocaine valued at $92,000.00.

Your actions bring great credit to the Division of State Police and yourself as a sworn member. I congratulate you on a job well done. A copy of this letter has been forwarded to the Personnel Bureau to be made a permanent part of your personnel file.

Sincerely,

Carl A. Williams
Colonel
Superintendent

ec

c: Personnel Bureau
      Troop D Hdqtrs.

New Jersey Is An Equal Opportunity Employer • Printed on Recycled Paper and Recyclable

Part II

Not Always Routine

Not all arrests were so neat and clean unfortunately. From one second to the next, the tension that could be felt when the troop-car radio was quiet almost felt eerie. Would the next transmission be a fatal motor-vehicle accident or a five-car pileup with serious injuries? Maybe some jackass felt like sneaking in the back gate of the 10S service area to commit an armed robbery at Roy Roger's. Perhaps a passerby on his cell phone would report a domestic in progress as boyfriend and girlfriend, gay male lovers, or husband and wife attempted to beat the shit out of each other as they drove to their destination. Better yet, maybe a frantic woman would call in to identify a man driving next to her masturbating, or a vehicle in which a girl would be performing a sex act on the male driver. My point is, the New Jersey Turnpike truly was the city on wheels it was renowned for, and after a few months of patrolling it, you learned to take everything in stride and expect the unexpected.

While counting the minutes down till the end of my shift one weekday afternoon, I started to head southbound. I was in a bitchy mood all day because I was assigned to patrol the north end of our station area, which I hated. The farther north you go means more traffic. More traffic means more idiots. More idiots mean more accidents. I hated the north, and everyone on the squad knew it. Accidents, traffic, and tickets were pointless to me. I was a "lock up" guy! I despised writing tickets and being detailed to minor incidents or accidents. Those things just kept me from doing what I loved: making arrests!

Mentally, the day was over. Traveling at about seventy miles per hour, I planned on taking a slow ride south to the station, refill the troop car's gas tank, and then I could call it a day. The members from the squad that relieved ours had just begun signing on, and once they did, they resumed control of the respective station area.

Suddenly, out of nowhere, a beat-up-looking blue Honda whizzed passed my marked troop car. I was in the outer truck lanes, the Honda in the left lane of the inner roadway. *What in the hell are they thinking? You don't pass a marked troop car!* From behind, the car appeared old, raggedy, and dirty, a far cry from the normal rented vehicle a mule would use. As I paced the speeding vehicle, I noted the two male subjects seated in the front and one female passenger seated alone in the rear. Though I didn't prescribe to this theory, a senior trooper once explained that a perfect drug-related motor vehicle stop would have three persons: (1) person to make the transaction, (1) subject to serve as the lookout, and (1) subject to remain with the vehicle so a quick exit could be made following the illegal transaction. Additionally, experience taught me you could never go wrong with a Virginia-registered vehicle, especially southbound like these subjects were traveling. *Screw it! I still have a few minutes to waste! As much as I despised doing it, if nothing else, I'll get a quick ticket then rush back to the station and go home.*

I crossed over to the inner roadway, got behind the Honda, and activated the overhead lights. I immediately saw all three occupants turn and look at me. The driver immediately made a furtive movement and appeared to reach under his seat or behind his back. I wasn't exactly sure what he was reaching for—or where—but I did know these actions caused a lump to begin forming in my throat. My heart started palpitating, and I clenched the steering wheel a little tighter. Initially, based on the poor condition of the car alone, I thought there was no way this could be a potentially high-risk stop. As their evasive actions intensified however, my opinion and gut-feelings began to change.

As they slowed down, my instinct told me to call the stop in before approaching, an NJSP standard operating procedure that was seldom followed and rarely enforced. As I notified dispatch of the stop, our vehicles pulled to the right shoulder and came to a complete stop.

Dirty, nasty, and a total hoodlum were the only adjectives I could think of when I peered into the driver's eyes. He was sweating and looked like a typical base-head. Now I was thinking that this may be a stolen car, or maybe he was a fugitive. *This motherfucker was scary looking.* The car stunk, clothes and food were thrown about, and as I reached the passenger's window, I got a very uneasy feeling about these thugs. Before I even asked for his credentials, the driver, in a Jamaican accent, asked why he had been stopped. Unjustified thoughts and unsubstantiated stereotypes such as gang-bangers; Jamaican Posse members; ruthless and violent criminals; murderous felons; and callous, cold-blooded villains quickly overtook my mindset. Every negative perception I had ever heard, read, or seen about Jamaicans immediately ran through my mind; and worse of all, I had three of them staring at me. I was the enemy. *I wish I didn't stop this car!* These people had "bad ass" written on their foreheads, and I sensed chaos.

I had learned to trust my instincts, and thank God, I did. I advised the driver to stay put, and without saying another word, overcome with a total sense of fear, I returned to my troop car and radioed for backup. This was very, very uncommon for me to do!

Knowing backup would soon arrive, I walked back up to the car. All three occupants were stone-faced. Their eyes had death in them. I could tell they were not fans of the police. The stares and looks from the three of them penetrated my bulletproof vest, and I felt vulnerable. My hands were sweaty, and I was, admittedly, scared. I had read, seen, and heard so much about the violent tendencies of Jamaicans that I was now letting it affect my duty and responsibilities. But still, this was one motley-looking crew. The golden rule is, no matter what, a trooper goes *home* at the end of his shift, and I honestly thought this rule was in jeopardy as I stood alone on the shoulder confronting these occupants.

After failing to produce the credentials, the driver exited as ordered. As he did, however, out of the corner of my eye, I saw him toss what appeared to be a belt or rope to the female passenger that was seating in the rear seat area. I had no clue what it was or why he would do this. The long thin shiny contraband that he tossed was unidentifiable, but I just sensed it was something bad.

Now I'm caught! If I overreact, he may panic, and we could end up rolling around on the ground directly into the right lane of traffic. Or worse, one of the passengers could get out and shoot me or bash my head in with whatever weapons, tools, or hammers that may have been inside that vehicle.

As calmly as I could, I began to speak with the driver, ignoring what I just witnessed. *This is how quickly things happen and decisions, life threatening decisions, are made on the fly!* No matter what, I could not let him sense my uncertainty! Traffic was soaring by, it's noisy, and a warm breeze was blowing. It's a beautiful day, and I just wanted to go home! As I talked to him, I did a quick pat down for weapons. He's clean, thank God! Free of weapons, I then felt comfortable in asking him about the item he tossed to the female, who was seated in the rear. I expected to hear that it was a belt or rope or some article of clothing. Instead, he vehemently denied tossing anything, and as this conversation unfolded, I observed the female leaning forward, almost sitting up in her seat. It appeared as if she were attempting to conceal whatever the driver tossed to her. FUCK! *All hell is about to break loose, and backup has not yet arrived.*

Now he knew I was aware that something is going down. My eyes continuously shifted from him, to the occupants, and back to him. Apprehension filled the air as the driver and I quickly exchanged glances at each other. He knew I knew, and I knew he knew, but how would the rest of this scenario unfold? I was in a very, very bad situation. Three on one, contraband, and only God knew what else was inside this vehicle. What in the hell was I going to do now?

Before I could make a decision, the driver immediately pushed me and bolted for his door. I ran to the backseat and ripped the female, who was hunched over, attempting to stuff this long ropelike package down her person from the car just as the driver sped away. In my mind, I was thankful to have safely parted ways with the two male subjects. Once cuffed, the "package," which was partially sticking out from her midsection, was removed. When asked about the content of the package, she stated, "I think it's coke!" As she was still lying on the shoulder of the roadway where she was cuffed, I quickly advised the station that the vehicle and two male occupants have fled. I further advised dispatch that I had recovered the CDS and placed one occupant under arrest.

Once this information was transmitted, I quickly helped the prisoner to her feet, positioned her in the rear seat of my troop car, and gave chase (completely against SOP). Maniacally, in and out of traffic, I pursued the Honda as she screamed obscenities at me from the rear seat of the troop car. Lights and siren blaring, driving on the shoulder, cutting other cars off—whatever it took, I was going to catch these bastards. Every uniformed trooper from the barracks was now in a car, giving chase as well.

Just a few miles north of the Cranbury Station—which is located on the southbound side of the turnpike, just beyond the Molly Pitcher Service Area—I caught up with the blue Honda. In fact, I passed it. The scumbags crossed over from the inner to the outer roadway, but fortunately, the piece of shit they were driving began to overheat.

Their vehicle was now smoking, and the Honda's maximum speed was roughly twenty miles per hour. As they drove on the right shoulder of the outer roadway, three marked troop cars were about to besiege their location. Seeing the approaching troop cars, the bad guys appeared to give the Honda one last attempt to accelerate from the angrily approaching troopers. Black smoke bellowed from the Honda's hood, and the engine sputtered. During this last-ditch effort to flee, I drove parallel to them on the inner roadway, separated by the metal guardrail. Fortunately, traffic on both roadways was now beginning to slow down as motorists watched the event unfold.

With the Honda still somehow able to go forward, I then witnessed the impossible. Just as troopers converged, the operator jumped from the moving car and fled on foot. Miraculously, he ran across all twelve lanes of traffic without getting struck by a car or truck. With each horn that shrieked, I was certain this chase would end with the operator being a road pizza. After scaling a ten-foot fence that separated the turnpike from a private property, troopers gave chase and eventually captured the fleeing suspect.

The passenger also leapt from the car and nearly ran into oncoming traffic as he tried to evade the soon-to-be arresting troopers. I distinctly remember him rolling toward the roadway and nearly being decapitated by a slow-moving tractor trailer. "Clink, Clink, sounded the metal handcuffs placed on this subject—let's go asshole! Two down, one to go!"

"Soaries" probably wished he never ran. Not only did he got caught and resist arrest, but I think about eight troopers needed a new can of Pepper Mace by the time this dirt bag was subdued and handcuffed. We had to let him air out for about two hours before he could even be fingerprinted because of all the Mace he had been sprayed with. The "rope" turned out to be fifteen ounces of high-purity cocaine apparently packaged as such because it was flown in from Jamaica, most likely taped to the midsection area of the mule.

Back at the station, we learned that Soaries was a badass from Virginia and had a criminal rap sheet that would impress Jessie James. In his trunk was a photo album containing numerous pictures of weapons, parties, thugs flashing gang signs, and even dead bodies. Apparently, several of his "home boys" had been murdered in one fashion or another, and they took pictures of the crime scenes as well as photos of them lying in their caskets.

The three subjects were processed and eventually committed to the Middlesex County Jail in default of bail. Life on the New Jersey Turnpike was fast, dangerous, and chaotic. While it takes a special person to become a New Jersey trooper, it was suspected that those of us that requested assignment to the 'Pike were a unique breed (or maybe we were just a little crazier than the rest). To date, thirteen troopers have paid the ultimate sacrifice while assigned to Troop D, the most of any state-police troop. Vicariously, through their spirit, reputations and courage, I tried my best to uphold the traditions of the NJSP and this rare breed of individual known as, "Turnpike Troopers".

CHAPTER 7

King of the Big Road

Now that I achieved status as a lock up guy, doors pertaining to my future career path within the state police began to open for me. At the advice of others, I started submitting my career résumé for various jobs of interest. I knew it was just a matter of time before I would leave the road and achieve special assignment to one of the numerous investigative bureaus that the Division of State Police offered.

From a career standpoint, I had earned the respect of my peers, was well-liked by my superiors, did a brief stint on a Tactical Patrol Unit (TPU), and received numerous awards and commendations for diligent patrol-related arrests. In addition to serving time in Troop C, I had now worked at the storied New Brunswick Barracks; the Moorestown Barracks, from my residence while on TPU; and was part of the Cranbury Station's grand opening.

I had now replaced the troopers I most admired—Klimek, Boero, and Marucca—who, like most, used their reputation and career on the turnpike as a stepping stone to obtain jobs as a detective, investigator, or instructor. Just as I had been three years previous, inexperienced troopers who now reported to the turnpike wanting to be criminally active hoped to be assigned to my squad and learn just as history had allowed me to do.

I was enthralled that junior troopers looked up to me. Knowing that the turnpike was recognized by top law-enforcement officials throughout the country due to its significance in the drug trade made me even prouder to be a part of the turnpike's stigma. From criminal investigations and interviews, it became evident that the reputation of turnpike troopers was not only historic in New

Jersey, but even high-level drug dealers were responsive to the tenacity at which drug interdiction was exercised on the New Jersey Turnpike.

For example, while working day shifts (6:00 AM to 4:00 PM) one day in mid-January, I signed on to begin patrol at 6:15 AM. Minutes later, I received a call via dispatch of a signal 11 (motor-vehicle accident) just north of exit 7A in Mercer County. Upon arrival at the scene, I observed that a single motor vehicle had driven off the side of the road and crashed into the tree line while traveling northbound. The driver was standing outside of the vehicle and was uninjured, but his car was not drivable. After a quick conversation with the operator, it was blatant that he was still intoxicated from an all-night drinking binge. Since no medical attention was needed, I transported this subject back to the station where a breathalyzer test confirmed my suspicions, and the operator was formally charged with DWI. Now I had to do an accident report and a DWI report. My day was over, and I wasn't real happy about it! I hated doing drunk driving and accident reports!

While at the station, my squad mates, who knew of my dislike for doing anything other than investigation reports, called to bust my balls. They had all stopped to have breakfast together, which was customary. In the next few minutes, I allowed them to coax me into coming up to 8N, the Joyce Kilmer Service Area, to eat breakfast with them at Bob's Big Boy. Reluctantly, I did join them. *What the hell! My day is over, so I might as well go eat.*

During breakfast, Troopers Nini and Emer joked sarcastically that since I was "in the house" for the rest of the day, they would have to be the ones to get the bad guys off the road. After eating, we walked outside as a group to where our troop cars were neatly lined up in the rear of the service area. When I departed, they were still standing around, talking outside their respective troop car. In a pissed-off tone, I said I had to go back and get started on the paperwork and reports that awaited me. Plus, I had to get the drunk out of the station before Sergeant Gasior kills me. Apparently, while I was gone, the guy became very annoyed at being left alone in the cell and repeatedly disturbed Sergeant Gasior by hitting the safety alert that was embedded in the walls of each cell at the new state-of-the-art Cranbury Station.

As I headed back, a light, wet snow was falling; and I had no desire to go back to the barracks and do paperwork. Continuing southbound and searching for any reason not to go back to the station, I began to pace a bright red Pontiac with New Jersey tags. *Why would anyone wash their car on a day like this? No one's car is this clean in mid-January! It's a little slick out to be speeding.*

Traffic was light, and the operator was traveling roughly seventy miles per hour in the right lane. By turnpike standards, this was pretty slow, but still, it was fifteen miles faster than the posted limit. Furthermore, the light, wet snow caused the road conditions to become slick. As I got closer, I noted the vehicle contain only one male occupant. After substantiating the operator's speed, I now had a reason to put off going back to the station for at least a few minutes. A routine motor-vehicle stop was then initiated.

Once our vehicles came to rest on the right shoulder, I called the stop in and approached the passenger's side of the vehicle. The driver, a wide-eyed male in his mid thirties, had "mule" tattooed on his forehead. In broken English, the driver advised that a friend had rented the car for him and that he did not have a driver's license. When asked where he was headed, the operator stated he was not sure and added that he had to go to someplace in Pennsylvania.

The driver was very nice, soft-spoken, and in my heart, before I asked my next question, I couldn't help but to feel bad for this individual. I knew what was coming next, and by now, the driver had all but surrendered to me. Experience taught me that whatever contraband he had in this vehicle definitely did not belong to him. He was simply being paid to drive this car from point A to point B so that the scumbag who truly owned the contraband did not get arrested. This poor guy was as nervous as he was clueless.

At first glance, the car was immaculate and had a strong perfume smell. This was a common trick used by couriers to conceal the identity of drugs. After our brief conversation, the operator agreed to sign an NJSP consent-to-search form, and the rest was academic.

Because the interior was so pristine, I went right to the trunk, expecting to find something huge. As predicted, the trunk was filled to capacity with two massive-sized black duffel bags. Scattered about the trunk were perfumed dryer sheets and a few other canisters of various-smelling gels. Inside the duffle bags were tightly wrapped bundles of marijuana that ended up weighing in excess of seventy pounds. *How many joints can you make with seventy pounds of marijuana?*

While en route back to the station, the subject admitted to being paid three hundred dollars to transport the marijuana. Ironically, his instructions were to simply follow the black Ford that was just a few tenths of a mile ahead of him when he was stopped. His lone instruction was to transport the drugs from New York City to the Pennsylvania border (exit no. 6), and then he could go back to New York City and return the rental car. He advised that the men who paid him this money stated they were too afraid of being stopped by troopers on the New Jersey Turnpike because of our reputation. This poor guy said he needed the money that bad, so he figured he could make one hundred and fifty dollars an hour for the two-hour trip. Attempts to locate the black Ford were unsuccessful, so as usual, and as sad as it was, only the mule was arrested. As you can imagine, my squad mates, who quickly arrived as backup, were fuming because of the fierce but friendly competition we had in comparing arrests and seizures.

Since joining the state police, my underlying goal was twofold: (1) fit in with my peers and (2) ultimately become Trooper of the Year. While in Troop C, I went through the motions, played the game, and learned as much as I could just so I would be the best trooper possible. Every story I heard from senior troopers seemed to center around guys like Cazzuppee, Sullivan, Caffrey, and Mastella—all former Trooper of the Year awardees who gained their prominence by making incredible drug seizures either on the turnpike or in Cocaine Alley (the southern tip of New Jersey where the mouth of the turnpike meets State Highways 295 and Route 130). Cocaine Alley is where troopers assigned to the Moorestown Barracks, the Troop A Barracks of Bridgeton, and the DITU (Drug Interdiction Unit) teams would congregate and make a majority of their spectacular seizures as vehicles either entered or exited New Jersey.

Through my travels and experiences on the turnpike, I had now worked directly with each of the aforementioned Trooper of the Year awardees in one capacity or another. As my arrests became routine, chatter throughout the division began regarding who would be the next Trooper of the Year. Sergeant First Class (SFC) Brian Caffrey, who was my assistant station commander at Cranbury, began referring to me as "TOY." As the spring of 1998 approached, he reminded daily that I had to keep pace with other troopers if I were to obtain this cherished feat. Statistically, I was the leading arrest trooper on the turnpike, and this distinction earned whoever this trooper was the title "King of the Big Road," and in all honesty, I relished this classification.

Each day, I set out to implement the variety of tactics, stereotypes, and training methods I learned from my senior counterparts in hopes of making an arrest. A ten-hour tour of duty without an arrest was considered a failure by me and Sergeant First Class Caffrey. When he wasn't chasing me out of the station, Sergeant First Class Caffrey was painting a rosy picture of us working together, wearing our Trooper of the Year red ribbons pinned to our uniforms in a newly formed drug-interdiction unit he was rumored to be petitioning the Division to reinitiate.

Under Caffrey's guidance, I began to turn down opportunities to get off the road, knowing it would prevent me from obtaining my final career goal. Regardless of the shift I was working, I was focused and patrolled the turnpike at a feverous pitch. Many days, I foolishly went without eating and allowed my pending reports to back up just so I could be out on patrol. Engulfed in the pressure I felt to win this award, I bypassed taking days off, volunteered to work overtime details in hopes making more arrests, and did all of my reports at home on my personal computer so as to not lose patrol time.

What started out so innocently with the seizure of a loaded 9-mm handgun back in late 1994, making arrests became my drug, and I was as much an addict as the people I was arresting. For no other reason than to illustrate the type of activity that exists on the New Jersey Turnpike, the following is a recap of my three-plus years of patrolling the Big Road. I can only hope this information could once again justify a police officer's right to search or ask someone for consent to search. Sadly, as a result of the racial-profiling controversy, this right has been suspended, thus, allowing criminals, drugs, and contraband to flow freely through New Jersey and its neighboring states.

YEAR 1: 1995

As previously mentioned, my first arrest came during my third week of patrolling the New Jersey Turnpike. A group of individuals traveling southbound back to North Carolina deemed it necessary to carry a concealed deadly weapon loaded with hollow-point ammunition up to New York for "protection" as they shopped. The odor of the marijuana they were smoking when stopped was what led to our search that located the loaded 9-mm handgun.

Less than a week later, I finally initiated my first solo arrest after stopping two individuals carrying four ounces of crack cocaine and roughly two hundred dollars' worth of marijuana. The open container of E&J Brandy led to the seizure of the estimated four thousand dollars' worth of crack cocaine, which was mildly concealed in the glove box.

A month or so later, two Rutgers University students were arrested for DUI and possession of angel dust after playing Ping-Pong with their car and using the turnpike's cement medians as the paddles. Unknown to them and completely whacked out of their minds as they drove back from New York City, the two had been slipped "dusted" marijuana while looking to score the weed.

A week later, March 23, 1995, my first shooting incident occurred; and as earlier referenced, these were the absolute "best" that society had to offer. Charged with aggravated assault on a trooper, possession of a stolen motor vehicle, burglary tools, and various other criminal offenses, the driver later pleaded guilty and was sentenced to seven to ten years in state prison. I, on the other hand, had to endure shoulder surgery, undetected posttraumatic stress syndrome, and two years of AIDS testing.

My first arrest upon returning to work after the shooting found me alone and confronted with three individuals who had an estimated thirteen thousand dollars' worth of "pancake" crack cocaine (thirteen ounces). Also found was a small amount of marijuana, a butane torch, and crackpipe.

A few weeks later, a "consent to search" authorized by the driver led to the finding of twenty thousand dollars' worth of cocaine. This was also the first time someone actually took the time to try and hide their "stash" as it was concealed under the spare tire in the trunk.

This was followed by a motor-vehicle stop that revealed a stolen car being operated by an individual who was in possession of an ounce (estimated one thousand dollars' worth) of crack cocaine.

Two days later, twenty thousand dollars' worth of heroin was recovered along with four thousand dollars' worth of cocaine. The courier utilized coffee grinds in an attempt to conceal the smell.

Almost a month passed before my next sizable seizure, which was an estimated fourteen thousand dollars' worth of cocaine.

A week later, a recently discharged serviceman was arrested for possession of a loaded handgun and four thousand dollars' worth of cocaine. His inability to find a job upon being discharged had admittedly forced him to make a quick buck selling drugs back in North Carolina.

Nine days later, two juveniles driving erratically in a stolen motor vehicle were arrested and charged with this offense.

During the last month of 1995, my first year on the Big Road concluded with investigations that led to the seizure of two kilograms (2.2 pounds per kilo) of cocaine valued at forty-six thousand dollars as well as a smaller "grab" of fifteen hundred dollars' worth of cocaine to end the year.

YEAR 2: 1996

This year started out strong when on the third day January, a consent to search recovered an estimated one hundred sixty thousand dollars' worth of heroin.

Soon thereafter, a high-speed chase led to charges of possession of cocaine and destruction of evidence against the driver who turned out to be a wanted fugitive.

Three weeks later, a consent to search led to the finding of two loaded handguns and twenty-three thousand dollars' worth of cocaine.

The next arrest came when I observed the largest bong of my life. I swear this thing was nearly three feet long, and the operator was arrested for minor possession of marijuana as well as various items of paraphernalia he had with him.

A reverse sting operation conducted at an area hotel led to the arrest of three individuals for possession of roughly twenty-five hundred dollars' worth of crack cocaine.

A week later, a routine stop led to the seizure of a pound of marijuana—for personal use, of course.

Also within this same month, another consent to search led to the recovery of an estimated three thousand dollars' worth of crack cocaine.

My last substantial arrest of 1996 was the seizure of three pounds of cocaine valued at roughly thirty-nine thousand dollars.

YEAR 3: 1997

I started the year by seizing twenty-four ounces of cocaine followed by another ten thousand dollars' worth of crack cocaine three weeks later.

After seizing fifty pounds of marijuana in February and nine ounces of cocaine in March, my classmate Joe Sansone and I let one get away in late March. Together, we estimated about four kilos of cocaine were dumped by the passenger during a high-speed chase that took us into Philadelphia and back into New Jersey with the bad guys eventually getting away on foot.

Within the next few months, sixty-six thousand dollars of cocaine were seized in addition to thirty pounds of marijuana as I prepared to make my run at becoming king of the Big Road.

Statistics for the Trooper of the Year Award ran much like the state's fiscal year.

July 1, 1997, to June 30, 1998, was to be my run at Trooper of the Year, and nothing could stop me. My tactics, approach, and demeanor were flawless. Up to this point, I had *never* received one motorist complaint citing race, misconduct, unlawful search, etc. I felt that I was doing everything properly and by the book. After all, I was not doing anything different than any other trooper who I worked with. The only difference was I was more proficient at making arrests. Even the superiors I respected most told me I was gifted; I had the "sixth sense" that police officers were notorious for. In fact, I was so good that I didn't even need a whole year's statistics to solidify my Trooper of the Year Award.

The following is a ten-month total of arrest statistics up to April 22, 1998, as submitted by my immediate supervisor Sgt. Fred Gasior to the Division of State Police in recognition of my activity (exact copy):

NOMINATION OF TROOPER JOHN HOGAN FOR
TROOPER OF THE YEAR

During a ten-month period culminating on May 1, 1998 Trooper John I. Hogan #5068 initiated thirty seven (37) patrol related investigations, which started as routine motor vehicle stops. These stops occurred while Tpr. Hogan was assigned as a General Road Duty Trooper at the Troop "D" Cranbury Barracks. During the course of these thirty seven investigations, criminal charges were filed for Possession of CDS, Possession with Intent to Distribute, Possession of CDW, Possession of Pirated Video's, Receiving Stolen Property, Eluding, Theft of Services, Possession of Narcotic Paraphernalia (including hidden compartments), and Money Laundering. A total of one hundred thirty two criminal charges were filed by Tpr. Hogan during this period and resulted in the arrest of sixty six (66) persons.

Confiscated during these investigations was an estimated two hundred twelve (212) pounds of marijuana valued at $424,000.00. Also seized was an estimated twenty three (23) pounds of cocaine valued at $320,000.00, approximately two (2) pounds of heroin valued at $128, 000.00, US Currency in the amount of $95,000.00, and one hundred seventy pirated videos valued at $17, 600.00. The total confiscated amount for these investigations is in excess of $984,000.00. Furthermore, Trooper Hogan confiscated six (6) concealed deadly weapons which included four (4) assault style weapons containing high capacity magazines and hollow point ammunition. A subject wanted for Homicide out of Philadelphia, PA was also arrested by Tpr. Hogan and is now being prosecuted for the drug related murder.

During the course of some of these investigations Tpr. Hogan has worked closely with the Drug Enforcement Agency, New York and Philadelphia Police Departments as well as the NJSP's PRS and Intelligence Units. Two of these cases have led Tpr. Hogan to develop confidential informants, which in one instance, he has turned the informant over to the DEA. This informant is still working with the DEA and Cranbury Station Detectives and to date has delivered in excess of $150,000.00 of heroin. Also seized as a result of this informant have been two motor vehicles and to date, two subjects have been arrested. The second informant is also still working and to date has been in contact with the NJSP's Narcotics Unit who have assumed responsibility for furthering this investigation. Both of these informants were cultivated by Tpr. Hogan during the course of his extreme courteous conduct in dealing with these subjects once they were placed under arrest.

On April 23, 1998 Tpr. Hogan was involved in an on duty incident during which time he was struck in the right leg by a motor vehicle and injured his lower back and leg areas. He has since been on sick leave recuperating but due to the facts listed above, feel he is extremely deserving of being the New Jersey State Police's **1998 TROOPER OF THE YEAR.**

CHAPTER 8

Final Patrol: The "Turnpike Shooting"

I didn't have any strange premonitions—no weird feelings in my stomach. I am neither a superstitious person nor did any subliminal messages tell me not to go to work this evening. Just was the case when I worked any midnight shift (9:00 PM to 7:00 AM), I left the house at exactly 8:00 PM. Prior to leaving, I worked out in the gym I had assembled in my basement. I ate a healthy dinner, showered, and departed. My strict regiment had everything timed perfectly, and I always arrived at the Cranbury Station at least a half hour before my shift started. Tonight would be no different. As I drove northbound on the New Jersey Turnpike after getting on in Florence via Interchange No. 6, nothing seemed or felt awkward. The forecast called for light rain, but for now, it was dry though the rain that was to come could be felt in the cold, damp air.

The bass of my Bose stereo system in my metallic green 1998 Mustang GT was thumping. The volume was cranked up. A Nas compact disc blared, and as usual, I attempted to sing along with the lyrics, but I had no clue what the words were. Rap was always my music of choice. The stories these songs tell are phenomenal. The lyrics to Nas's "Affirmative Action" always got me hyped for duty. Listening to songs from Notorious Big, Little Kim, and Eminem gave me a different perspective on life and helped when I dealt with suspected bad guys, drug couriers, and straight-up thugs.

These songs portrayed a life of lost hope. The artists speak of growing up with no food on the table; having to sell drugs; or stealing just to get money so shoes, clothing, and other basic necessities could be purchased. Additionally, rap lyrics also commonly referenced methods used to transport weapons, money, and drugs. Biggie rapped about "sittin' on top of fifty grand in the Nautica van" and spoke about "niggas who hate Dominicans"; anyone who's familiar with the drug business knows that because of their rival factions and turf wars, this tends to be true. Nas, on the other hand, in his song "Street Dreams," says, "A drug dealer's destiny is reaching a ki" (kilogram)." My all-time favorite is Biggie's "Ten Crack Commandments," which is a rap that lays out the ten basic rules for being a successful drug dealer. A close second is NWA's (Niggas wit Attitude) "Fuck da Police."

As strange as it may sound for me—a white police officer to listen to rap music—the truth is I liked the beat and loved the stories these songs tell. I often wondered if life in "the hood" or ghetto was as poor, negative, and inescapable as these musicians portrayed it to be. From these songs, I also gained knowledge and a basic understanding as to how and why someone may choose to get involved in selling or transporting drugs and the need to carry weapons for protection. While I was as far removed as possible from living a life similar to those in the ghetto, I knew the street terms and lingo for the different types of drugs, weapons, and paraphernalia used by those involved in this illicit business.

I knew that Puerto Ricans and Dominicans disliked each other, and a Mexican would get upset if you call him Puerto Rican and vise versa. Because I chose to get involved in drug interdiction, I figured any edge I gained could only help when I am dealing with a suspect. Staying cool, composed, and speaking to individuals in a language they understood, and even began to trust, helped me be successful in seizing drug money and narcotics while avoiding physical confrontation—most of the time!

Like most troopers, I drove exclusively in the left lane at about eighty miles per hour. Tapping my hands on the leather steering wheel, I attempted to verbally keep up with Nas as I relaxed in the soft gray leather driver's seat of my Mustang as a juicy big ball of Red Man chewing tobacco was in my mouth. My weapon rested—unholstered—next to me on the passenger's seat. The huge green plastic cup that I used as a spittoon was wedged between my seat and the center console. With dried spit and tobacco clinging to the sides of this cup, a stale odor of old tobacco permeated from it and gave the otherwise immaculate interior a foul lingering odor. At around 8:25 PM, I entered the parking lot of the Cranbury Barracks, my second home!

After gaining entry to the barracks through the rear doors, via our sophisticated card-reader entry system, I went right to the locker room. I then placed my gun in my locker, which was never secured. *If you can't trust your fellow troopers, who can you trust?* My routine once at the station was just as anal as prior to leaving! I then said, "What's up!" to anyone in the locker room and headed straight for the DB (detective bureau) to see if anyone was "in the house" with an arrest. If not, I would go up on the "hard deck," where the working squad's sergeant and bookman sat. This was also where all the dispatch equipment and ledgers for accidents, investigations, and operations reports were kept.

As a matter of habit, I then checked to see if any arrests were made during the course of the day. *I loved the competition!* From there, I would walk back to the kitchen and grab a cup of coffee that I would drink as I got dressed into the uniform of the day.

The Cranbury Barracks was very new; clean; and, by state-police standards, beautiful. We had a professional-size weight room complete with stereo and more machines than most high schools and probably some college football programs. The locker room and showers were neatly maintained and sanitary. The kitchen was clean and always had coffee, juices, and other necessities. The detective bureau was huge. Each of the "dicks" (detective) had their own desk, typewriter, and telephone. A separate computer station was also set up for the purpose of doing criminal-history or other background checks on any suspect who was under investigation. The far wall was lined with windows that overlooked the southbound lanes of the turnpike. Opposite this wall were massive filing cabinets that contained years of investigation reports from some of the most notorious crimes ever committed on the 'Pike, which I often read when delegated to administrative duties by my squad supervisor.

The radio room or "hard deck" was state of the art. Situated at the main entrance, it was the nerve center for the entire barracks. The lobby was separated from the hard deck by large bulletproof windows, and ever present in the lobby area were the photographs of each trooper who paid the ultimate sacrifice while on patrol in Troop D.

Inside the radio room were cameras, phones, keys, logs, and a television complete with on-demand cable. This is where the duty sergeant and bookman spent the majority of their shift. Just down the hall to the right was the breathalyzer room, and next to it were two separate holding cells: one for the male and one for the female. Complete with metal sinks and toilets, cement beds, and the aforementioned security buzzers, this would be the first station I ever worked at that had real prisoner cells. After being assigned to Cranbury, I couldn't imagine ever going back to a "normal" barracks as a road-duty trooper. Even the walls were white, clean, freshly painted, and well maintained by the Turnpike Authority's maintenance staff.

Once back in the locker room with my coffee, I started getting dressed into my uniform. Aside from our weapons, which we were expected to carry at all times when within the boundaries of New Jersey, all of our uniforms and gear were kept at the barracks. As troopers, we were not permitted to be in uniform while driving our personal car. Just as I began to put Brasso on my belt buckle, nameplate, hat badge, sand brown buckle, and ammo-pouch buttons, my squad sergeant arrived. I heard him but could not see him. My locker sat all the way to the left rear of the room, and unintentionally, just three lockers away to my left was Trooper John Emer, my squad mate and one of the best people I have ever met in life. As was the norm for this "salty" boot, he had yet to arrive for duty, and it was quickly nearing 9:00 PM.

Within a minute or so, my sergeant had made his way over to my locker. "And what is on your agenda for tonight?" Sergeant Fred Gasior asked me in his usual smiling, sarcastic manner. He knew, as did the entire squad, that if I were out on patrol, I'd be looking to bring him some "company." Ninety-nine percent of the time, Sergeant Gasior stayed in the station doing administrative work. "Bringing him company" meant going out and locking somebody up and returning to the station to do the required paperwork.

As I wiped off the dried Brasso to reveal gleaming buttons, Freddie then deflated my balloon. He stated that he wanted me to ride with Trooper James Kenna tonight. He said, "It's near the end of the month, and Jimmy is the only one who doesn't have a body!" Subliminally, I knew he wanted me to go out with Jimmy in hopes that we would make an arrest, but theoretically, because we rotated partners daily, I guess it was just my turn to ride with Trooper Kenna.

Ironically, Jimmy was just getting back into the groove after being involved in a shooting about three weeks previously. In that incident, while alone and placing a suspect under arrest for possessing a pound of cocaine, a physical altercation erupted. Able to flee, the suspect stole Jimmy's troop car and, while escaping, nearly ran Trooper Kenna over with his own troop car. In defense of his life, Jimmy fired at the suspect who was captured a few miles later.

It wasn't that I didn't like or want to ride with Jimmy Kenna; I was just much closer and trusted the instincts and actions of guys like Mike Nini, Gary Vona, Ricky Hatrak, or my boy John Emer more because of the familiarity I had in patrolling with these troopers. As a squad, though, we all got along great. Scott Busz was the senior man, and Chuck "Don't Call me Charles" Allen was a squared-away junior trooper who had recently came to our squad. Squad Six was the shit; and as a unit, we prided ourselves in always leading the station in investigations, arrests, seized drugs, weapons, and money on a monthly basis.

Fred was great to work for too. We always got an extra day off for making an arrest, and he never busted our balls for leaving early or not writing a certain amount of tickets. As a squad, we went to dinners both with and without our significant others, had "squad meetings" at the Jester's Court in Hightstown, and even spent holidays at one another's homes for parties. As a group, we worked diligently, laughed at the dangers we faced daily, and took our duties in the war on drugs seriously and personally. Despite the various personalities, we al blended extremely well, and the camaraderie was phenomenal.

If I had to choose, I'd say I had the least in common with Jimmy Kenna. He was smart, having graduated from Trenton State College, and yearned to be a "lock up" guy. Rumor had it that he asked to be transferred to our squad after allegedly being told by superiors that he needed to be more active and aggressive in his criminal program. Many thought that because his father was a captain in the state police, Jimmy had "Daddy" pull the strings for him, and many resented him for this perception, whether legitimate or not. Personally, I liked his father. In fact, I first met Captain Kenna at Jimmy's son's baptismal party in 1997. Mr. Kenna approached me and expressed how excited Jimmy was to be working with me. The captain said he hoped that his son could learn as much as possible from me because he had heard how successful I had been at making arrests. *Wow, this was great! To have a captain come to me while at his son's home and say these things was fantastic. My career was only going upward!*

Overall, Jimmy Kenna is a really nice, sincere, and caring person with a great family. He was always pleasant and willing to do whatever was asked of him. His reputation as a trooper, unfortunately, was less than desirable. Most guys felt he was a nervous Nellie and wasn't "turnpike material." Most thought he was very high-strung and always had a blank stare on his face, which some troopers misconstrued as arrogance.

When he first arrived at Cranbury and worked on a squad, which we rarely saw because of the rotation, admittedly, I didn't care about or like him either. In my mind, this was Squad Six's station and wanted everyone to be like Emer, Nini, and me. When a "boot" or junior trooper arrives at a new station, the first time he comes in contact with other troopers, it is an unwritten rule that you call them sir and at least offer to shake hands. From what I heard and witnessed, Jimmy didn't do this, and it did not sit well with most of the guys at the barracks, especially the senior members at the Cranbury Station. "He's a salty jerkoff who thinks because his dad is a captain he can do what he wants!" From what I had heard, he did have a rough beginning on the Big Road, but I can't substantiate whether or not the Phantom struck.

My opinion of Jimmy Kenna changed once he came to our squad and I dealt with him on a daily basis. He was eager, genuine, and somewhat knowledgeable but far from the cocky and arrogant person his reputation had misled us to believe. He and I were just different, and despite being a great guy, we just didn't have a whole lot in common. He was married, had just had a beautiful baby boy, and Jimmy rarely came out drinking with the guys. He was far quieter and more reserved than the rest of us, and though we all got along great, he was perceived as an outcast for the wacky and wild bunch commonly known as Squad Six.

I, on the other hand, was all jacked up on creatine, protein, and EAS sports drinks. I lived to work out and kept fit just to look better in my uniform. When I wasn't working or lifting, I was jet-setting to South Beach, Vegas, or Cancun, or touring the coast of California. As much as I loved my job, when I was on ADL (authorized duty leave), no bar, city, state, or country was safe. My classmate Kenny Franco and I traveled extensively and played just as hard as we had worked in the academy to become troopers—chicks, tattoos, nightclubs, beaches, and muscles! In my mind, I was living the American dream, and it just didn't get any better than this!

Growing up and seeing my father go to work at a warehouse for his entire life made me realize at a young age that I better choose something I liked. To love my job to the point that I didn't consider it work was tremendous. Furthermore, it gave me financial freedom, and I took full advantage of it. As far as I was concerned, I was just getting back all of the years I spent waiting to become a trooper.

Before going out on patrol, our squad always gathered in the briefing room. We would tell jokes, bust one another's balls, and exchange stories from the weekends. My weekend escapades in Philly, New York, or wherever else I ended up always were the highlights for the married guys. They often joked of living vicariously through me, and as a newspaper article suggested following the April 23, 1998, incident: "Trooper Hogan had it all going for him!" *Man, did I!*

A huge television complete with a satellite dish and "NFL ticket" sat at the head table in the briefing room. Sergeant Gasior always sat at that table facing us. A bulletin board for overtime details and STFA (State Troopers Fraternal Association, the union that represents all road troopers) union notices were posted on it. Shotgun lockers occupied the left side of the room while flashlights and portable radio chargers were lined up on the back wall. By nine fifteen, the briefing had concluded, and Trooper Kenna and I were ready to go on patrol.

I told Jimmy we would take troop car no. 823. Trooper Emer and I had the same car the previous night. Initially, I was hesitant because there was a short in the troop-car radio. On two or three occasions the previous night, I was forced to shut off the car to reset the radio. Without doing that, we were unable to make radio contact with dispatch. *No big deal. The car ran good, so we can work around a tiny radio problem!*

Completely unknown to us, together, we walked out the rear doors of the Cranbury Station for the last time as uniformed New Jersey State Troopers. Jimmy carried his briefcase, and I had mine. The brown leather case contained tickets, warnings, three extra sets of handcuffs, a digital drug scale, a few copies of any report we may have to complete, and my chewing tobacco. We each carried our own flashlight, and our portable radios were clipped to our sides. Prior to getting into the marked troop car, Jimmy loaded the shotgun and placed it in the rack that sat centered on the floor of the front-seat compartment. I got in the driver's seat, and Jimmy sat next to me in the bucket seat of the brand-new white 1998 Ford Crown Victoria marked with all the insignia of a New Jersey State Police trooper cruiser.

We did our normal vehicle inspection—which consisted of checking the overhead lights, tires, and spotlight—and made sure we had road flares and a fire extinguisher. Once this was completed, we officially signed on with dispatch. "One com from 823, signal 21." The dispatch responded, "Loud and clear, 823, 9:21 PM." We were now ready for patrol!

A light drizzle began to fall as we pulled out of the Cranbury Station. After cutting through 7S, the Molly Pitcher Service Area, we headed southbound. Traffic density was normal for a weeknight. Nothing at all seemed odd or different about this evening. From the time I left, all indications appeared that it was just going to be a typical midnight shift. Traffic would eventually thin out, and then we would go sit in the Pit and run radar and observe passing traffic. For now, though, the first order of business was to do a "loop" of our assigned area, which was from exits 7A to 8A: (The Pit was a small paved enclave that was nestled beneath the ramp into Interchange 8A. Positioned on the southbound's Cars Only roadway, the Pit was notorious and quite often utilized by troopers who wanted to sit, observe, and be selective in which vehicles they chose to stop.)

Doing a loop simply meant checking your assigned area to make sure no cars were broken down or accidents had occurred. It was amazing to see how dumb some people were. Pitch-black out and they would be resting on the left shoulder with no lights on or flares lit as they attempted to change a tire. It's pretty incredible to me that more fatalities don't occur as a result of flat-out stupidity on the 'Pike.

As we drove southbound in the left lane, Jimmy "lit up" cars we passed with the right-alley light. This was done in an attempt to see the number of occupants as well as other critical data such as sex, approximate age, race, and overall physical appearance. Never once was I informed or lectured about this most common practice, and to my knowledge, just about everyone exercised it. Personally, I felt it gave us a tactical edge. The element of surprise often allowed us to observe a driver's body language when he or she was "lit up," and if doing this gave us an advantage, I couldn't see how it could be construed as wrong.

Furthermore, since our superiors never addressed it, as troopers, we assumed it was acceptable and never saw any harm in utilizing this tool.

Once we got to 7A, I exited the main line, turned around at the toll plaza, and promptly headed northbound. As we drove, I promised Jimmy that unless we got an incredibly huge drug seizure (like two kilos or more), he could take credit for whatever arrest we made tonight. The only other condition was, if we arrested white people, *I had to take it.* I wanted the real-large seizure because it would add to my ever-growing totals for the Trooper of the Year crusade, and the "buzz" around the station and Division was that I was the hands-down favorite, with only May and June remaining. Having made so many arrests, though, I needed to be aware of my stats. That is why I also needed to arrest white people no matter how small an amount of drugs or contraband they possessed. It was a pathetic numbers game, but trust me, it was played. The proof is in the pudding, and the investigations ledger from any year prior to 1999 would back this claim.

After passing the station, which sat just south of exit 8A, we were now close to completing our loop and could start concentrating on making some stops that would hopefully lead to an arrest.

Upon reaching the northbound "split" where the car and truck lanes separated just south of Interchange 8A, I decided to stay right and entered the truck lanes. I was going between seventy-five and eighty miles per hour, the normal speed at which most troopers patrolled. Out of nowhere, on the inner roadway in the right lane, was a car that appeared to be stuck in wet tar. I quickly slowed down, and both Jimmy and I began to observe the operation of this vehicle. Within seconds, the operator drifted slowly from the right lane, halfway into the center lane, then back to the right; and was going roughly forty-five miles per hour. At the next Z cut, I crossed over onto the inner roadway, and we then tailed this vehicle for a quarter mile or so.

The driver's speed of forty-five miles per hour stayed the same, and so did his awful attempt to maintain control of his vehicle. Suspecting a possible DWI, I got closer and activated the overheard lights. Initially, no description could be obtained, and the driver immediately pulled to the right shoulder. In doing so, though, the operator leaned forward and appeared to be reaching toward the lower right-front passenger's area. Observing this, Jimmy quickly exited as I called the stop in to dispatch. Having no idea what race the operator was, especially now that he had ducked out of view, I notified the dispatch of the stop, gave them our location and the vehicle's New York registration number, and stated that it was a white male operator. Without explanation aside from that damn "consent decree" the state police was under, from the day I reported to the turnpike, I learned from senior troopers that, when in doubt, it's always a white male! I jotted the stop on our patrol chart, and to not conflict with what I had called in to dispatch, I also noted "w/m" for white male as the operator. (Though this was not mandatory, I did it at the suggestion of certain supervisors who told me because of my arrest statistics, I needed to be cognizant of how many whites and nonwhites I was stopping on a daily basis.)

Trooper Kenna was already at the passenger's side of the vehicle. I quickly exited and took my normal strategic position at the right rear of the suspect car. I overheard Jimmy ask the operator—now identified as a young black male— why he didn't have his driver's license with him. A few seconds later, the dispatch blurted, "Car no. 823, is your mike clear?" This meant they needed to relay a message to us and did not want the suspect to be made aware of this. Upon hearing this, Jimmy turned off his portable radio, and I advised dispatch that my microphone was clear of the suspect. They alerted us that the car was an NCIC (National Crime Information Center) "hit," meaning the car was reported stolen. Within the bat of an eye, we went from a subject with no driver's license to a felonious motor-vehicle stop! Rather than rip him from the car and handcuff him like we were now supposed to, Jimmy calmly spoke to the driver who, because of the coded language Jimmy and I were now using, was still unaware of our new revelation.

As we probed further, oddly, the car was registered to a woman with the same last name as the operator. *Had he stolen it from her? It's unlikely, but it has happened to me before!* After a few minutes, we learned that this subject was a student at Temple University in Philadelphia. While he was at Temple, the car had been stolen a few months back. After being recovered, though, it was never properly removed from the NCIC computer by the recovering agency (the Philadelphia Police Department) and, therefore, still showed as "stolen" in the computer when the registration was entered. The operator apologized for his driving demeanor and agreed to pay more attention to the road. Ironically, in the front right passenger's area sat a beautiful new puppy he had just bought for his girlfriend. He was taking the puppy to New York as a surprise for her. Apparently, he was attempting to pet the crying puppy as he drove, causing him to slow down and drift from his lane. After explaining to the driver what he needed to do to get his car properly removed from the NCIC computer, Jimmy issued the operator a warning, and he was released. It really felt good to help someone out. We advised him that in a crime-ridden city like Philadelphia, they may just lock him up and ask questions later, especially in the area of Temple University.

After clearing this stop, we drove a little farther north and turned around at the 75U to head south. It was probably around ten thirty or so. An annoying light drizzle continued to fall, and as usual for this time of night, traffic began thinning out.

As we headed southbound, making an arrest was undoubtedly the foremost—but unspoken—thought on our minds. We knew what we were looking for. From training, experience, and flat-out knowledge, we knew to concentrate on stopping out of state-, particularly southern state, registered vehicles once an infraction was observed. Pennsylvania-, Maryland-, District of Columbia-, Virginia-, and North Carolina-registered vehicles always got more attention. The perfect drug-interdiction stop in my own mind was a newer-model Dodge, Pontiac, or Ford compact car, which, 95 percent of the time, was rented. From personal experience, I learned that the biggest seizures came when a subject was by himself or sometimes with a second occupant. Mules were just that. They were paid a prearranged dollar figure by a higher-level dealer to go pick up the drugs and bring them back—no questions asked. These dealers were smart enough not to transport the drugs themselves because they could get serious prison time if stopped and arrested. Aside from all the personal experiences I had with drug interdiction, coupled with the knowledge I gained from elder Troopers and superiors-alike, I also received specialized training from the state police at a seminar entitled "Narcotic-Trafficking Trends." Adversaries would probably say that this was just a politically correct term for "racial profiling," but this training class addressed methods used to transport narcotics as well as the various members of all races who were involved in this illegal activity.

As we headed southbound the night of April 23, Jimmy was mentioning his son and how much he loved being a new father. The mood in our car was light as we chatted casually. When we observed a vehicle with an out-of-state tag, I would pace it to determine its speed or if they were violating any other motor-vehicle violations. As we passed other motor vehicles, Jimmy again used the right-alley light of the light bar to look in cars for an instant and determine the number of occupants as well as gender, race, and physical characteristics. As a matter of practice, I never stopped a car unless a motor-vehicle infraction was observed and could be verbally substantiated to the driver. I also tried to avoid stopping New Jersey-registered cars because in all likelihood, the occupants would be the family of or friends of a fellow police officer. Additionally, because infractions were so abundant on the turnpike, I didn't feel it was right to "crush out" the motorists who, in reality, paid our salaries.

As Jimmy and I continued conversing, we were quickly nearing the end of our assigned area: Interchange 7A. A group of vehicles were pretty far ahead of us, and I accelerated to catch up to them in a last ditch effort to make a stop. Amid the talk of hearing how proud of his son Jimmy was, we decided we better make a stop because nearly an hour has passed since an entry had been made on our patrol chart. It was an unwritten rule that an entry should be made at least every hour. As we approached the small pack of cars, one in particular appeared to be traveling slightly faster that the rest. From a distance, it appeared to be a minivan, and I began to pace it at speeds ranging from sixty-seven to seventy-one miles per hour as it slightly pulled away from the rest of the pack. Nothing was excessive about this speed, but with the wet conditions and the fact that we had not done anything in nearly an hour, we decided to make the stop. I said to Jimmy that unless the driver was a total jerk, I would write the operator a quick warning, and then we would go get coffee at Dunkin Donuts on Route 130 as we routinely did on midnight shift. This way, we would have each written a warning, and then we could go sit in the Pit and try to lock someone up. We were currently at milepost 63 in Hamilton Township, Mercer County, where it was taboo to make arrests because of the difficult procedures at the county jail, the paperwork this county required, and the fact that an arraignment was mandatory for every felony arrest. *Plain and simple, you don't look for or make arrests in Mercer County!*

I accelerated to roughly seventy-seven miles per hour and got directly behind the gold-colored New York-registered Dodge Caravan, which was traveling in the center lane. The windows appeared tinted, and I immediately activated the overhead lights. The operator, for some unknown reason, slammed on his brakes, and I was forced to maneuver the troop car to the left to avoid striking the rear of the van. *What a fucking asshole! Though uncommon, it wasn't the first time some idiot had done this to me!*

The driver then slowed to a crawl, but failed to pull over or even change lanes, indicating that he intended to pull over and stop. With a careful watch on the van, I leaned forward to the right and grabbed the troop car's microphone and pushed the PA (public address) button. I intended to scream at this dope over the PA system. When I keyed the microphone, I heard three quick beeps, which meant it was a live microphone that went directly to, and was recorded by the dispatch. *Thank God I didn't yell what I wanted to!* I glanced down and realized that the troop car's radio was malfunctioning just as it had the previous night. As a result, I was unable to switch to the PA system. "SHIT!"

I then attempted to illuminate the interior of the van with the spotlight and takedown lights of the troop car. I also blasted the siren in hopes of getting the driver to pull over. Through the tinted glass, silhouettes were now visible; and there appeared to be at least three, four, or maybe even five people inside. They all appeared to be moving around hastily and in a panic-like fashion. Though cliché, it looked exactly like, "a Chinese fire drill", whatever that really is! *Are they grabbing and loading guns, uzis, mac 9s, AK-47s? Maybe they are concealing drugs and are planning to just start shooting at us. Why are they not pulling over? Goddamn it! All I wanted was a freaking warning!*

My heart was in my throat, my stomach churned, and already white-knuckled, I squeezed the soft blue steering wheel even tighter. I told Jimmy to be ready because they were either going to take off; pull over and bail; or, worse, immediately open fire! The occupants' actions left us with no other thoughts or choices. They were gearing up for something, but what it was remained a tense mystery. My heart felt as if it were pounding through my bulletproof vest. Sweat beaded on my brow, my breathing was erratic, and my eyes were fixated on the deliberate movements of the silhouettes that jumped around, unprovoked, inside of the van.

Was this it? Were Trooper Kenna and I meant to go down in a blaze of gunfire? The actions of the operator and occupants warranted all the anxiety and fear that now overtook my body. "Pull the fuck over!" I shouted. The useless microphone was still in my hand. I was in a trance—just waiting, wondering, and mentally playing out what could well be the last few seconds of my life. It never even entered my mind to call the stop in or advise the station of what was going on. I was too focused or, truthfully put, frozen from fear and anticipation. In my mind, we were sitting ducks, just waiting for the inevitable. No one jumps around or panics like this unless something catastrophic is going to be the end result. I was convinced this could be the end for me and my partner. Never before had I been so certain that something tragic was about to happen!

In the next few seconds, which seemed like a lifetime, the operator abruptly pulled from the center lane to the right shoulder and abruptly stopped. Even before the troop car came to a complete stop on the right shoulder, Jimmy leaped from our vehicle and ran directly to the passenger's side of the van with his weapon drawn. As he jumped from our car, I pleaded with him to be careful and brought the troop car to a complete stop roughly ten feet behind the van. I hurriedly slammed the cars gear shift into park with my right hand, while trying to keep all of our exterior lights illuminated on the interior of the van.

I swiftly exited the troop car to assist Trooper Kenna. I immediately heard screaming from both the inside and outside of the van. It sounded as if Jimmy was urging the occupants to keep quiet, put their hands in the air, and roll the window down. Ever present was a loud banging sound: metal on glass. Amid the screaming, it appeared that Jimmy was hitting the passenger's window, possibly with his metal flashlight, trying to get the occupant in the passenger's seat to roll down the window. It was abnormal chaos.

I ran up to the front of the troop car in hopes of taking up my normal strategic position at the rear passenger's side of the suspect vehicle. As I attempted to run between our car and the van, I noticed the van's brake lights were on. My left hand grasped my still-holstered weapon. In my right hand was my issued black Maglite flashlight. I held it upward, shining it into the rear window and hoping not to further startle the occupants.

Just as I was centered between our vehicles, I made contact with the driver's eyes in the rearview mirror. I observed his right hand on the column gear shift. At this instant, I saw the operator's arm move downward vigorously on the gear shift. All indications were that he was purposely putting the van in reverse. I heard the engine roar, and suddenly, the van came rearward at me. I dove to the left to avoid being struck. My portable radio broke away from its clip on my belt and went flying into the air, then crashed onto the slick blacktop. The van struck me in the right lower-leg area as it accelerated in reverse, striking the troop car. Gunshots rang out, but I didn't know how many or by whom. I knew it! A firefight was in progress. Is Jimmy shot? All I could hear were screams and yelps, but they all ran together into one chaotic series of horrifying noises that I could not even begin to identify or comprehend. I needed to assist my partner!

Where was Trooper Kenna? Is he alive? Where is he shot, and how many times did he get blasted? All this for a fucking warning!

Upon being struck, I was able to quickly regain my balance. I staggered, shuffling my feet in a left rearward direction. My upper body was still partially crouched. As I looked up, I saw that the van's brake lights were now illuminated again. *That motherfucker just tried to run me over!*

Just as I began to recompose myself, the van again came at me in reverse. Uncertain of my exact location, I knew I had been knocked backward and to the left, I now stood either very near or worse yet, partially in the right lane of traffic. Observing the vans movements, I immediately unholstered my weapon and quickly fired two rounds into the rear of the van, aimed at the driver in hopes of preventing him from striking me again. *Bang! Bang!* Double tap—just as I was trained to do in a life threatening situation! I was 100 percent positive the operator was trying to run me over.

I hastily retreated as the van came back and struck the front end of the troop car for the second time. Completely oblivious to my surroundings, I was still standing in or very close to the right lane of traffic and, in hindsight, knew it was just a matter of time before I got whacked by a tractor trailer or other passing vehicle. *I had to get out of traffic's way as well as the asshole trying to run me over with his van. Is Kenna dead, wounded? Where is he, and how many guns do they have? How long do I have before they fire at him or me again?*

After the van struck the troop car the second time, the van appeared to move forward. In reality, I would later learn it was actually the troop car moving in reverse.

I had gotten out so quickly that the gear shift did not fully go into park, and therefore, once struck, it slipped down into neutral, allowing it to be pushed rearward.

Approximately eight or ten seconds of spine-chilling inactivity then took place. Screaming and chaos were ever present, but everything seemed to slow down. Now order could be restored! Because of the impact between the van and troop car, which rolled rearward, I was now able to move in-between the two vehicles and out of harm's way from traffic. Everyone had stopped firing. I had no idea if Jimmy was shot, alive, or dead. I heard screams, but nothing was clear, as if hundreds of people were shouting at the same time. Loud and garbled, everything ran together. Inside the van, people were still jumping around. I too joined in the shouting, "Sit still and put your hands up!"

Then, out of nowhere, the van came at me again in reverse. Unbelievable! How could this be happening? I scurried backward. Shots rang out. *Here we go again! Where are these shots coming from? Are they aimed at me, Jimmy—both of us?* I instantly fired three rounds at the driver and was able to get out of the way just before it struck me again. The van then hit the troop car yet again.

This time, however, the van didn't stop. After smashing into the troop car, the van pushed the troop car in reverse for approximately forty feet before losing contact. Amazingly, the van, almost on a ninety-degree angle in reverse, then went straight back, perpendicular to the roadway.

As it entered the main line, traveling in reverse, the van then slammed into a small Honda that was traveling in the center lane. Upon the deafening impact, the Honda veered left, crashed into the center cement barrier, and instantly burst into flames. *At any second, I was expecting to wake up in a cold sweat—this had to be a bad dream!*

The van, due to its perpendicular position on the roadway, now sat motionless and in complete darkness as approaching traffic veered helplessly left or right to avoid striking the van.

Fortunately, traffic quickly came to a complete stop as I heard a tractor trailer's horn blaring and tires screeching to a halt to prevent t-boning the van and its occupants, almost certain to cause multiple fatalities if struck.

With the front end of the van facing west and the rear completely smashed in from the collision with the Honda, the van now sat haplessly across the middle lanes of traffic. Not sure how or what happened, I took a position of cover near the troop car for fear of what may occur next.

Ahead in the distance on the right shoulder, I saw a figure half-running toward me from the direction where the stop originally occurred. It was Trooper Kenna. *Awesome! He is alive!* I thought to myself. "Are you okay?" I shouted out to him.

Prior to reaching my position, however, the once-still van suddenly appeared to move forward. Barely crawling, it came straight toward me at a snail's pace. As I stood in front of the troop car, the van rolled by my position and I could hear the occupants shouting as it left the roadway, tumbling down the embankment and coming to a final rest in a drainage ditch. *If this goddamn van moves again—* I thought.

Instinctively, not knowing what else could possibly happen, I dropped my ammunition magazine to the ground and reloaded. I had no idea how many rounds I had fired but needed to be fully prepared. *Obviously, these guys and their means of transportation are not going down without a fight!*

Fully loaded and ready for anything, I stood at the top of the embankment and covered Jimmy as he cautiously went down to the van. Everyone was yelling and screaming. From the top of the embankment, I shouted, "Shut the fuck up and get your hands in the air!" At this point, I had no idea if Jimmy had been fired at or what truly transpired from his vantage point. One by one, the subjects were removed from the van and handcuffed.

In my mind, it was just a matter of time before we would learn how much drugs, guns, and other contraband were present in the van. After all, why would anyone act like this if they didn't have anything to hide? I was confident and convinced that the "mother load" was inside this van even though the characteristics of the occupants—four black males in their early twenties—was never what I would stereotype for a quality drug-interdiction stop. *Wow, this fucking warning wasn't worth it; that's for sure!*

Sgt. Donnie Reid was the first to arrive on the scene. As I stood at the top of the embankment, I heard one of the van's occupants yelling, "Sorry" and "It was an accident." I angrily told Sergeant Reid, "That motherfucker tried to kill me and now he is apologizing!" I wanted Sergeant Reid to hear, witness, and document this cock-suckers' apologies! Within minutes, troopers from every barracks on the turnpike and Troop C appeared to be on the scene.

Fire trucks, helicopters, ambulances, unmarked cars, and "blue lighters" pulled up by the droves. Everyone—from troopers, firemen, Emergency Medical Technicians (EMT's), and even civilians—were haphazardly running through the crime scene.

I recall leaning on my troop car, gazing outward in a bewildered funk, staring at the Honda which had by now burned completely down to its frame on the left shoulder. As I gathered myself, I witnessed shell casings being kicked or stepped on by arriving medical personnel. Some casings and other evidence was even run over or blown away by passing cars. *So much for a secure and uncontaminated crime scene! Johnny Cochran would have a field day with this circus!*

Everyone that arrived came up to me and asked what happened. I was dazed, confused, and disoriented. To put it bluntly, aside from knowing the driver tried to run me over, I really wasn't sure what happened, how it happened and most importantly, why it happened.

Just how many times did the troop car get hit? Was Jimmy shot at, and if not, what did he see that caused him to fire his weapon? How did the troop car go in reverse if it was in park? How fast was the van going when it hit me? How many times did it come in reverse? Were the wheels spinning loudly in reverse as the van came back at me? They had to be because every vehicle's tires will spin in reverse on wet blacktop. How many shots did I fire? Was I shot at? Why am I standing here and not being removed from the scene and isolated like my first shooting? I wish all these people would leave me alone and stop asking so many freaking questions.

As I stood there, angry and pissed off, every trooper on the scene theorized about what must have happened. No one told me what to say or how to say it, but in listening to the repeated hypotheses, my own recollection of what transpired was convoluted by what I was hearing. As troopers, we were just trying to piece everything together in hopes of making sense of all of this madness. Additionally and most important, aside from the occupants' well-being, even though they tried to kill me, I knew soon enough detectives would search the van; and we would find the reason—the drugs, the guns, or whatever it was that made these men react the way they did instead of just pulling over.

The occupants of the van were immediately given medical treatment and placed in ambulances. To my knowledge, one or two subjects were flown by helicopter to area hospitals. The scene was total chaos. The Honda, completely scorched and now down to its melted tires, sat alone on the left shoulder, and the van remained face first down in the drainage ditch. Fortunately, our troop car ended up rolling to a stop on the edge of the embankment. Another foot or so and it too may have tumbled down the embankment. Evidence was scattered everywhere, and the crime scene was disastrously contaminated by now.

To this day, I have no idea how long I remained at the scene. I would approximate that I told my version of what happened to at least twenty-five people. In turn, I then listened to them, along with another twenty or so people, tell me what they thought happened and why. I was eventually removed from the scene after demanding that I be taken to the hospital. My lower back and right leg had begun to throb, and I wanted to get away from everyone.

Unlike my first incident, where control of the scene was immediately taken, this was a cluster fuck—no other way to describe it. Trooper John Ogg drove me to St. Francis Hospital in Trenton. As we drove there, I thought how weird it was that I almost died tonight, and now I was being taken to the same hospital where I was born.

Once at the hospital, I was given muscle relaxing medication and some pain relievers followed by a full body examination of my outer extremities. I had a red contusion on my lower right leg, and my lower back was stiff and tight. Stupidly, I declined to be admitted, and Trooper Ogg drove me back to the Cranbury Barracks. As we passed by the shooting scene on the northbound side, I wondered if they recovered the guns and drugs yet. I was pissed off and upset. I truly felt that the operator purposely tried to run me over, and I hated him for it. My stomach was nauseous, and I had never felt this internal rage before. I sat quietly the entire ride back, and I pondered my future. As much as I loved my job, I started to wonder if it was worth giving my life for. At the pace I was going, I was destined to be the next trooper killed on the Black Dragon.

Before I even got back to the Cranbury Station to give my formal interview, I decided that I would never go back to active patrol. Having a red ribbon to pin on my uniform was not a fair trade for my life. Regardless of how much cocaine, heroin, marijuana, or guns these individuals possessed to make them react in this fashion, I was convinced that April 23, 1998 would be my final night of patrol, and that was *my* decision.

The aftermath, April 23, 1998

The trauma, suffering and flashbacks from my first shooting were certain to be mild in comparison to this event. I no longer had the desire to carry a gun, wear the uniform or continue my career as a trooper. As promised, to both my family and myself, I never returned to work following this harrowing and traumatic event. I endured more physical suffering and mental anguish than a barracks-full of troopers; I knew when to say-enough was enough.

Apparently, the Division of State Police felt the same way too. Within a few weeks time, my class coordinator, Robert Kilmurray, who was now a Sergeant First Class (SFC) and in charge of the Medical Services Unit, asked me to meet with him. During this meeting I was all but asked to submit my application that would allow me to retire from the Division of State Police based on the trauma I endured over the course of my short career.

In return for the psychological and physical damage I endured, I was all but guaranteed to receive sixty-six percent of my current pay and continued medical benefits from the State. The only thing that stood in the way was the completion of the investigation into the April 23, 1998 tragedy. SFC. Kilmurray seemed to feel that the process should take roughly three months and that by summer, 1998, I should begin receiving my disability pension.

CHAPTER 9

The Investigation

(Note: To the best of my ability, the following is a true recollection using the facts as they were learned or relayed to me. Utilizing a personal journal which I maintained daily, this is how the events of the investigation unfolded before me.)

"Danny was driving! I can't drive; my license is suspended!" said Keshon Moore when questioned by the detectives at the scene, just minutes after his actions caused chaos to erupt on the New Jersey Turnpike. Just prior to being carted off in an ambulance for observation, the van's operator asked the detective who was leaning over him. "I'm in real trouble, right? How long can I go to jail for this?"

After being released from the hospital a few hours later, Keshon Moore gave a formal statement to NJSP Major Crime's investigators at the Cranbury Station. He concluded this interview by saying (verbatim), "I'd like to apologize for the incident. Apologize to my friends, to the police officers. **I can't blame anybody but myself; it was a mistake.**" While under oath during this interview, Mr. Moore swore to not being under the influence of alcohol or drugs and further claimed to have had the cruise control set at fifty-five miles per hour since entering the New Jersey Turnpike via the Lincoln Tunnel.

Weeks later, however, laboratory and expert reports revealed that Mr. Moore was under the influence of marijuana, and the vehicle's cruise-control mechanism was never engaged. (Consequently, he was *never* charged with driving under the influence.) Also, using the turnpike toll ticket found inside the van, they had determined that Mr. Moore's minimum average speed was at least sixty-two miles per hour during the duration of his trip. The turnpike at this time was still marked with speed-limit signs reading *55 mph*. Given the fact that it was raining harder up north, one can only assume their vehicle was traveling at a slower speed during the heavier rain and sped up well beyond the posted speed limit to balance this average.

After a series of interviews, Mr. Moore finally admitted to investigators that he and the front right-seat passenger Danny Reyes conspired and attempted to switch seats upon realizing they were being stopped. This admission explains the "Chinese fire drill" and amount of time it took for them to finally pull over on this tragic evening.

Eventually, Keshon Moore recanted his original statement to investigators that it was him and not Danny Reyes who was driving the van. Furthermore and admirably so, Keshon Moore, in his formal statement accepted full responsibility for causing the entire catastrophe.

To recap this tragedy, here is a list of undisputable facts: Keshon Moore was speeding well beyond the posted fifty-five miles per hour speed limit, had refused to pull over for a marked police cruiser, struck (accidentally or not) a police officer with a deadly weapon (a four-thousand-pound vehicle), was driving with a suspended license while under the influence of marijuana, and lastly, initiated a second major accident that caused the Honda he collided with to explode.

In his own defense, Mr. Keshon Moore simply, and rightfully so, blamed himself. He claimed that his unfamiliarity with the rented vehicle (which he should not have been driving in the first place) caused him to panic, knowing full well that he had a suspended license. In essence, as opposed to just pulling over as directed, Keshon Moore concocted a plan to switch seats with front right passenger Danny Reyes, ultimately leading to the tragic and historic events that transpired the night of April 23, 1998.

With these admissions by Mr. Moore, common sense alone would have any normal person thinking, **"Case Closed!"** right?

When I completed giving my formal statement to investigators, twelve long, grueling, and mentally exhaustive hours had passed. The previous night's drizzle had given way to a bright, blue, and eye-piercing sunny sky. I was groggy, sore, in a mental funk, and hungry. In the interim, I had *repeatedly* told my version of the events, listened to other troopers depict what they assumed happened, and even spoke with Trooper Kenna on several occasions about the chaos that occurred. Though I had complete access to it, I refused to look at the van that nearly took my life that was now parked, unsecured, in the carport of the Cranbury Station.

As a whole, the barracks now appeared more like a museum. Troopers and investigators came and went; made contact with Kenna and me; and, if they chose to, went and viewed the van as well as the charred remains of the Honda, which was also now at the Cranbury "Museum." There was no order, no security, and no privacy. All of the restrictions, formalities, and guidelines that were supposed to be adhered to during an investigation did not exist, and nothing but uncertainty took control. Who was in charge of this fiasco was anyone's guess!

Even the Colonel, Carl A. Williams, gave a formal and inaccurate statement to the swarm of media that now congregated in the main parking area of the Cranbury Station. Trucks from ESPN, CNN, Fox, and every local affiliate besieged the barracks. For starters, the colonel read a press release, stating that Kenna and me had clocked the van using the troop car's radar when, in reality, our troop car, as was the case with most turnpike cruisers, did not even have a radar unit installed. I should have realized right then and there I was in trouble!

Prior to going on ADL at around 12:30 PM, my last official order from Major Crimes was to issue the driver, Keshon Moore, a summons for speeding and driving while on the suspended list. While doing this, I casually asked Lieutenant Carpenter what the driver of the van was charged with. I wasn't sure if they charged him with attempted murder or aggravated assault on a trooper. The lieutenant immediately pulled me into a room by myself and stated that due to the complexity of the investigation, all the facts needed to be gathered, and instead of the state police filing charges, he stated that a grand jury would decide what charges should be filed **against the driver.**

Throughout the course of the night, I had seen faces, badges, and groups of people who I knew were not affiliated with the state police. As the hours passed, troopers and detectives alike whispered to me that Jimmy Kenna may have overreacted, but everyone present agreed, no matter what, I was justified in reverting to deadly force because the van had been used as a weapon against me. Though I was very hesitant to give a formal statement because of everything I witnessed and heard around me, I knew I was justified in firing my weapon. Furthermore, since I had not been read my Miranda rights, I never thought in a million years *I* was being investigated for possible criminal charges. *I got run over for Christ's sake!*

The most important thing for me to do was not to answer questions regarding when and why Kenna fired his weapon, a fact that I was still unclear about to begin with. I had absolutely nothing to hide, so why shouldn't I give my statement? In retrospect, where was my union, the State Troopers Fraternal Association (STFA) and my union delegate? Why was I not being represented or advised by anyone what to do? Unbeknownst to me, from day one, I was on my own!

After learning that the driver—who was now escorted, almost celebrity-like, around the Cranbury Barracks with a blue New Jersey Turnpike Authority jumpsuit on, drinking our juice and eating our food—was not going to be criminally charged, I was furious. Left alone to drive home in my POV, I listened to the various news radio accounts of the incident in my personal car. As I tried to put all the activities, new faces, badges, and events leading up to my departure in perspective, I had a bad feeling and wondered if giving a formal statement was the right thing to do, especially since I was far from certain about what really did occur. I was still confused about how, why, and what exactly happened. The only thing I was certain about was that I was justified in firing. The totality of what happened—or, more importantly, who it happened to—had not sunk in yet.

Subconsciously, I quickly began to realize something was wrong. The SP *always* investigates there own major incidents. Who were all those people, and why were they there? Why did some of my friends tell me not to give a formal statement? What in the hell took almost twelve hours for me to even give my statement? How can they not charge that bastard who ran me over?

After getting a couple hours of sleep—which was constantly interrupted by flashbacks, phone calls, and unwelcome visitors who stopped by to check on me—I turned on the television. Every channel I tuned in to had accounts of the shooting. The incident, however, was not the focus on their reporting. What the media thought most important was; two white New Jersey state troopers shot four minority males! *OH SHIT! They are going to turn this into a racial incident!*

Within forty-eight hours, every minority activist—from Reverend Al Sharpton to ministers from local churches—was claiming that race was to blame for the shooting. Once it was made public that the troopers were white and the occupants were minorities, the likes of Cochran, Scheck, and other high-profile attorneys who attach themselves to cases where large settlements are guaranteed came out of the woodwork. Instead of combating the negative onslaught by divulging Keshon Moore's statement where he took full responsibility for this tragedy, the STFA, the NJSP, the state of New Jersey, and every other facet of internal support that Trooper Kenna and I **thought we had** sat quietly, allowing our reputations and actions to be judged and immediately tarnished by these individuals as well as the mass media. No one came to our defense—*no one*!

Claims and allegations of racial profiling exploded. This issue quickly became national news, and for months and, eventually, years, every major news channel and print publication reported on this alleged policing tactic. Minority activists immediately began demanding that the governor of New Jersey, Christine Todd Whitman, personally get involved in the prosecution, and as you will see, she did whatever they said. Their initial demand was to make certain that the state police did not have authority over the April 23 shooting investigation.

Once these demands were made, the governor appeased her critics and announced that she was removing authority of the investigation from the NJSP's

Major Crimes Unit. The investigation was immediately turned over to a "specially appointed" prosecutor. Her handpicked selection for this newly established title was James Gerrow, a prosecutor from my home county of Burlington. Gerrow was instantly ordained with the title of "special deputy attorney general" and assumed complete control over the investigation. Rumored to be a fair, honest, and diligent prosecutor who always gave law enforcement the benefit of the doubt, James Gerrow immediately went from a small-time county prosecutor to reporting directly to the State Attorney General, Peter Verniero.

Quite a big jump, but deep down, given his reputation, I felt at ease with Mr. Gerrow's selection, not that my opinion mattered in the least bit. Serving as colead in the investigation was Charles Grinnell, a deputy attorney general, also hand-picked by Whitman and Verniero. This action would mark the first time in state-police history that an investigation involving an on-duty trooper would be conducted by an outside agency.

To further appease the mounting pressure she felt, the governor also announced that the State Attorney General's Office would be given maximum control over the investigation. She then insisted that the grand-jury proceedings be switched from the normal county jurisdiction to a state jurisdiction.

A *Star-Ledger* article printed on May 18, 1998 stated, "The change of the grand jury from county jurisdiction to state jurisdiction will give Verniero a closer supervisory role over the investigation." Comments by John McDonald—a criminal-defense lawyer in Somerville, New Jersey—seemed to echo most sentiment with regard to the change in the jurisdiction of the grand jury. McDonald said, "Using the state's grand jury in this case is unusual. Typically, they are reserved for complicated cases involving many defendants such as organized crime, white-collar crime, or public-corruption cases."

The stage was set! Whitman handpicked Gerrow, and he reported directly to her lifelong friend, Peter Verniero, whom she personally appointed as the Attorney General once elected governor. I said it before, but I should have realized right then and there I was in real trouble!

As politicians began to take over the investigation, here is what was known and factual: Trooper Kenna fired six rounds, and I fired five. Three of the four men inside the van were wounded, and *one occupant believed he was shot after the van had come to a complete stop down the embankment they had crashed into*. The driver, Keshon Moore, recanted on his initial claim that he was not driving and admitted to be driving with a suspended license. He and the front right passenger Danny Reyes acknowledged they had unsuccessfully attempted to switch seats. Mr. Moore also claimed that he inadvertently stepped on the gas pedal and had a hard time getting the van into park. Therefore, the van lunged into reverse (a few times), and he knew he struck the police cruiser but claimed he did not hit or see the officer at the rear of his vehicle.

What followed was the most slanted, comprehensive, costly, and time-consuming investigation in the history of New Jersey. Over two hundred and fifty "characters" would be involved in the investigation. Rumor had it that the "Lindberg kidnapping looked like a misdemeanor" compared to this investigation.

Every step of the way, the state's personally selected team of investigators would concur with the van's occupants' attorneys; none other than Johnny Cochran, Barry Scheck, Wayne Greenfeeder, and Peter Nuefield, just to name a few. I, on the other hand, called my union president at the STFA Thomas Iszricki who said, "Don't worry, kid. I was talking to some people I know, and they said you're gonna be fine!"

As much as I would love to defend them, the truth is; my union offered no support, no legal advice, and no guidance. They never even told me I should seek an attorney on my own. The van's occupants had Cochran, and I have Iszricki telling me I am going to be all right!

Days went by and the headlines remained the same: MINORITIES DEMAND JUSTICE, RACIAL PROFILING PREVALENT IN NJSP, 4 UNARMED MINORITIES SHOT BY 2 WHITE TROOPERS! With the exception of my close friends and family, no one from the NJSP or the union that supposedly represented me even called. When it came time to return to work, Trooper Kenna and I were issued new weapons and given the opportunity to return to duty. Jimmy went back and was assigned to administrative tasks, but I still felt the same as I did the night of the incident and had no desire to ever go back; thus, I remained out on sick leave collecting my full pay.

Apparently, no legal-defense system or formal policy as to handling a trooper who gets involved with an on-duty, traumatic incident was ever implemented by the STFA who I relentlessly called for help. I did not know what else to do. Obviously, I needed an attorney! The norm was to have our "sister" agency, the Office of the Attorney General, assign an attorney to represent a trooper. But in this case, rumor had it that the attorney general was out to make examples of us; and to further support this, I received a letter, advising that the State Attorney General's Office was not going to defend me, as was the case in my initial shooting, upon preparing for grand jury.

Not even the attorney who represents the STFA called me! On several occasions, I called down to their Manasquan office, hoping to get advice or guidance after being pounded mercilessly in the media, but it was always the same old "Stop worrying, kid. You're gonna be fine!" Most of my other calls went unreturned.

For the next two weeks, the only updates I heard about the investigation came from newspapers and nightly news reports. Field searches and mock reenactments were taking place, but unlike the attorneys representing the van's occupants, we were not privy to any of the findings.

Though never formally substantiated, I learned that the lead prosecutor in the case, James Gerrow, somehow—miraculously, personally found a copper projectile bullet fragment in the same cement drainage culvert where the van came to rest during a field search. This fragment was found just north of where the van ended its collision course, and ballistic reports determined that this fragment was fired from my weapon. *Why was the lead prosecutor participating in a field search during a multimillion-dollar investigation? What are the odds that he finds this needle in a haystack? Other field searches were previously conducted and even metal detectors were utilized, but on this day, he somehow was the one to "plant"—I mean find this evidence? Even more incredible was the fact that this crucial piece of evidence was allegedly found only seven minutes into the field search.* Ironically and entirely unknown to me, from this day on, the state would attempt to prove that I fired at the van's occupants **after** their vehicle had come to a complete stop and were sitting helpless down in the culvert.

Still unrepresented by an attorney or having received any verbal support or guidance from the STFA or NJSP, my first interaction with the investigation came on May 4, 1998. I was called at home and *ordered* to come to the Cranbury Barracks the following morning at 10:00 AM to participate in a live reenactment of the shooting. Like the good soldier, I did as told, and without legal representation or having been advised of my Miranda rights, I reported as directed and gave a detailed account of the shooting to the best of my recollection.

Though he later denied it, this emotional morning ended with Mr. Gerrow placing his arm around me as we stood together in the kitchen of the Cranbury Station. With false compassion, Mr. Gerrow told me I had a very trying day, reliving the experience of the shooting for their benefit, and that in the end, I will be fine. He then stated I should head home so it doesn't appear that I am being given special treatment by him or the scores of other investigators that were present.

What struck me most odd about this day, since I was unaware of his miraculous "fragment find" from a few days prior, was the multitude of questions surrounding whether or not I fired my weapon *after* the van had passed me and came to a final rest down the embankment. No video or photographs were taken of this reenactment, and the State would later attempt to say that this reenactment never even took place. At the time, I had absolutely no clue that the state's main objective was to *prove* that I fired after the van came to a complete rest.

Why would I ever shoot at the van or its occupants then? Why did Gerrow repeatedly ask me about this? I had no reason to shoot, and there was no threat to me at that point, so I would not have been justified in shooting. It just never happened!

Gerrow and state investigators knew it was a gross violation of my civil rights to have me do this reenactment, especially without being mirandized and afforded the right to have an attorney present, but yet, they trampled away, fully shielded from any wrongdoing by Verniero and Whitman. *As a cop, you would have thought I should have known better! Though now ashamed, the truth is, mentally—I was a wreck—and just wanted to be included in their investigation!*

Later that same day, the state, who had now hired famed criminologist Dr. Henry Lee (from the O. J. Simpson trial), conducted their own reenactment of the shooting for Dr. Lee. Henry Lee was called upon to reconstruct the scene, even though everyone had already determined this to be impossible due to the serious breaches in properly securing the crime scene the night of the incident. For beginners, only six of the eleven bullet casings were found, and important items such as glass from the van had been discarded.

During the months of May and June, the reconstruction team, led by Dr. Henry Lee went to work. In the meantime, weekly meetings were held by the state's investigative team, and often and oddly, these meetings were held in the New York City office of Johnny Cochran, who, of course, worked side-by-side with Dr. Lee during the O. J. Simpson trial. Every finding and detail related to the investigation was reported to the new "dream team" by state investigators, yet the only information I could obtain was through secret phone calls from friends who "heard this or that." Most information I learned came from the ever-increasing media coverage that dominated the front pages as momentum in the anti-racial-profiling campaign mounted.

Since money was no object in this investigation, the state found it necessary to purchase a 1997 Dodge Caravan, identical to the one used as a weapon against me. Even the color was duplicated! With each passing day, I learned more details concerning the case from "friends" who were close to the investigation. They advised me they didn't like the way the entire investigation was being conducted. I quickly learned that everything appeared one-sided and that Kenna's and my formal statements were being shredded by the lead prosecutor. From the very few troopers who were concerned about me, I was advised to go out and get my own attorney as quickly as humanly possible.

Naturally, I called my union. After all, they hadn't stopped taking union dues from my paycheck. I needed support and advice; that is what a union does, right? In a panic, I called the STFA office yet again and informed them of what my fellow troopers were telling me. Assuming they too would be taken aback and pissed off by hearing this, I knew they would finally offer some sort of resolution.

Instead, they again downplayed the issue and stated that they could be no help, and if I chose to hire an attorney, their policy was to not offer any financial support. *What in the hell were my dues for?* When I asked this, the helpless pricks, who were on a speakerphone, responded, "We are a contract-negotiations union." Wow, I wish they would have told us this in the academy where they came off as the proudest and most supportive group since the teamsters! I was alone—on an island—and the circling sharks were named Whitman, Verniero, Gerrow, Cochran, and Scheck. It was only a matter of time before I became chum!

By the end of May, I had contacted a few attorneys on my own. With the help of my sister Mary, who was familiar with several area firms from her years as a stenographer, I called and met with some reputable attorneys. But like most cops, I didn't like defense attorneys, and regardless of whom I met with, I was not comfortable enough to hire anyone. Furthermore, their retaining fees were astronomical. I was at a loss. I didn't know what to do!

On the final Saturday of May 1998, I was awakened very early by my pager going off. The number was not familiar to me, and the area code was a 2-0-1 number, which I knew was North Jersey. I immediately called the number, and strangely, it was the Hackensack Police Department. *What the hell did I do now?* I had a brief conversation with the captain who answered the phone, and I learned that this individual was friendly with an academy classmate of mine who provided my number to him. As our conversation concluded, he stated that, "based on the beating I was taking in the media, I better find a qualified attorney." The captain then referred me to a Hackensack-based attorney named Robert L. Galantucci. Pathetically, this was the first friendly advice I received via a law-enforcement member, and it came from someone not affiliated with the NJSP or the STFA!

The following Monday, I called the office of Robert Galantucci and much to my surprise, was patched through to him by the secretary who answered. *How good of an attorney can this guy be if I am able to get right through to him, I thought!*

After a brief conversation, Mr. Galantucci appeared to be knowledgeable about my case and we agreed to meet the following morning. After securing directions from him directly (as opposed to transferring me back to his secretary like the others had), I hung up with a really good feeling about this man whom I never heard of or knew nothing about. That Tuesday, I made the ninety-minute drive to 55 State Street and entered the city Hackensack, New Jersey, for the first time in my life. Located just one block from the Bergen County Courthouse, the office environment at Galantucci & Patuto was friendly with a certain air of class surrounding it. *I can just imagine how much this guy is going to cost me!*

To date, most attorneys I met with wanted to first discuss their hourly rates and retainer fees, which had ranged from $2500 to $10,000. and their hourly rates were averaging $250. per hour. Once this topic was addressed, they then asked me about the incident and why I needed to meet with them.

From the onset, Robert L. Galantucci was different. He appeared caring and compassionate. What I liked most about him was that he just sat back and listened to me. I addressed my fears and concerns, and he made me feel like a real person. My comfort level with this stranger, aside from the fact that he was a *defense attorney*, was astounding. Though I knew nothing about his reputation, credentials, or experience level, I knew from the start he was the attorney I wanted defending me. Unlike the others, money wasn't discussed. Upon leaving his office during our initial meeting, I asked about his retainer fee and hourly rates. Surprisingly, he shrugged this question off and said that I had enough to worry about—and that we would address finances at the proper time. Wow, it was if an angel had just come into my life.

Throughout the course of our initial meeting, I quickly learned that Robert Galantucci had vast experience in dealing with officer-involved shootings and had already been through the mill with the likes of Reverend Al Sharpton and other community activists. As I sat there, I began to realize how privileged I was to even be seated in his office, let alone be fortunate enough to have one of the state's most respected and renowned attorneys willing to defend me. In my mind, there was no one else more qualified to fight the state on my behalf than Mr Robert L. Galantucci.

I'll never forget our first meeting when I detailed the events of April 23, 1998, for him. When I completed my uninterrupted account of the events leading up to the shooting, he stated, "It sounds like you did nothing wrong! You don't need an attorney, unless,—and he pointed his finger at me—"politics get involved!" *Need I say more?*

Our first meeting ended with "Mr. G" stating, "From this day on, I am your best friend. You speak to no one without calling me first." A lifelong friendship was immediately forged, and Robert L. Galantucci quickly became my second father!

Though it was on page 20 of the Newark *Star-Ledger*, unlike the normal front-page headlines my name had started to become accustomed to, retaining Mr. Galantucci brought the first of very few positive news articles (excerpts from the lengthy article):

Trooper in Pike Case Hires Noted Attorney

One of two state troopers involved in last months shooting on the Turnpike has hired Robert L. Galantucci, a Hackensack criminal lawyer who has made a high-profile career out of defending police officers. "He was just troubled about the slander that was going on in the media and wanted to know what to expect," Galantucci said.

The shooting has sparked peaceful demonstrations and charges that the State Police habitually discriminate against motorists in making traffic stops. Last weekend Rev. Al Sharpton led black off-duty law enforcement officers in using video cameras to monitor State Police traffic stops on the toll road.

Galantucci said, "This is not planet Hollywood, and Sharpton, Cochran and Scheck are not going to try this case in the media. This is New Jersey. People do things a little bit differently here."

Together, my new best friend and I learned that the investigative meetings continued throughout the summer of 1998 and were now held exclusively at the New York City office of Johnny Cochran. Along with his team of Scheck, Nuefield and Greenfeeder, the Dream Team 2 were given photographs, statements, reports of the crime scene, and anything else they wanted. In exchange for these materials, the state received full access and cooperation from their clients, who, by now, were referred to as poor, defenseless victims in the media. Like celebrities, the "victims" were reportedly chauffeured by state investigators to the various appointments, reenactments, and interviews that were being conducted as the state strategically built its case against Kenna and me.

As the summer of '98 concluded, we learned that the van's occupants were interviewed on several occasions. It was reported that their statements regarding their actions continually changed, but ironically, none of these inconsistencies were documented. In the meantime, their attorneys were continually forwarded pertinent evidence such as ballistic and lab reports, as well as photographs and other privileged information affiliated with the investigation.

Furthermore, on June 3, 1998, lab results confirming that Keshon Moore was driving under the influence of marijuana the night he struck me, and caused this entire travesty, had came back positive. Amazingly, instead of forwarding this report to the media as they did with any information detrimental to Kenna and me, this report was mysteriously buried.

Meanwhile, a frustrated Mr. Galantucci continually advised me that he was stymied in each attempt he made to gather information concerning the progress of the investigation. He openly admitted to being stonewalled by the state and that in all of his years in practicing law, he had never seen such a one-sided investigation. The writing was on the wall!

Publicly, pressure from the minority community continued to mount, and more questions regarding the practice of alleged racial profiling by New Jersey State Troopers surfaced. A group calling itself the Black Minister's Council of New Jersey appeared from nowhere. Almost daily, they took center stage on New Jersey 101.5 FM radio; channel 5's New Jersey network news; and major network-news affiliates from channels 3, 6, and 10. This group instantly began making demands as if they controlled puppet-string attached to Governor Whitman, Attorney General Peter Verniero, and state-police hierarchy. Incredulously, it seemed that every time they insisted on an action, it was granted. This group, led by Reverend Reginald Jackson, began holding daily press conferences in which they denounced the state police and its, "years of harassment of minority motorists". Suddenly, with podium, microphone, and camera placed at his every movement, because of the media attention given to him, Reverend Reginald Jackson became not only an expert, but a self-imposed prophet on the issue of racial profiling.

Reverend Reginald Jackson makes demands at one of his countless press conferences; this time he is obviously calling for U.S. attorney general Janet Reno (*inset*) to respond.

In November 1998, the council questioned why state-police cruisers were not outfitted with dash-mounted cameras and demanded they be installed immediately to combat "further acts of racial profiling." Paradoxically, for years prior to the April 23, 1998 incident, the NJSP had lobbied for the money to have these cameras installed, but reportedly, Governor Whitman always stated they were too costly and never included them in her budgets. Miraculously, just one month after this demand was made, the money was "found," and in yet another attempt to appease the Black Minister's Council, cameras started to initially appear in the dashboards of turnpike cruisers. Within months, *all* state-police cruisers utilized for routine patrol would be equipped with these cameras.

As '98 ended, the investigation into the shooting headed into a new year, but 1999 brought more of the same from the media. Each day more negative press splattered the front pages of New Jersey's largest publications. Demands were being made for Attorney General Peter Verniero to speed up the course of the investigation, and minority activists accused the attorney general of stalling the investigation to protect the state police as well as Kenna and me.

Throughout January and early February, protests and demonstrations denouncing the furor over racial-profiling were widely held in front of the statehouse in Trenton, as well as other high-profile venues across the state. Minority activists even threatened that there would be riots if Kenna and me were not soon indicted. Contrary to what the members of the STFA told me, which was, "Don't worry, Troop; it'll die down," the ruckus over racial profiling only grew more intense by the day. Ironically, as the controversy gained momentum, purposely or not, the more isolated and distanced I became to any members of the state police. Is this where the phrase, "hung out to dry" would appear fitting?

Part II

A Shift in the Political Tide

Unexpectedly, on February 17, 1999, United States Senator Frank Lautenberg announced to the public that he would be retiring his position on Capital Hill. Governor Whitman, who had previously been accused of using her governorship solely as a stepping stone to DC, immediately formed an exploratory committee and began a fund raising platform to support her ambition to replace Senator Lautenberg. Without hesitation, Reginald Jackson denounced the governor's campaign and claimed, "She should not be able to leave New Jersey until her administration admits that the New Jersey State Police engages in racial profiling." This admission, however, would completely and utterly contradict what she and her attorney general(s) had been saying for years when defending the NJSP against this allegation. Furthermore, Whitman and Verniero insisted on appealing the *DeSoto v. State of New Jersey*, where a judge ruled that minority motorists **were** unfairly targeted for stop, search and seizure on the southern end of the New Jersey Turnpike (Moorestown Barracks). Up until now, as individuals, Whitman and Veniero—like true politicians—played both sides of the fence. As the demands made by the Black Minister's Council, continually increased, the governor and attorney general soon found themselves at the center of this debate—right next to Kenna and me—but, in no way were we all on the same team!

On February 26, 1999, though embroiled in the turmoil over racial profiling, Governor Whitman nominated her longtime friend and current attorney general Peter Verniero to a recently vacated supreme-court-justice seat. Though he was barely qualified to serve as attorney general, she attempted to make the inexperienced Verniero the youngest justice to ever serve on the supreme court. Also, on this same day, Colonel Carl Williams was quoted in the *Star-Ledger* discussing the drug market and who controls each facet of it. In the article, Colonel Williams made references to certain ethnic groups, both black and white, who were thought to be associated with the manufacturing and distribution of certain narcotics.

The following morning, the Black Minister's Council once again took center stage. Surrounded by microphones and cameras, Reginald Jackson took it upon himself to blast the governor for her proposed nomination of Attorney General Verniero. In speaking for the entire minority community, he also chastised the colonel of the state police for his insensitive comments regarding ethnicity and drug trafficking, even though these facts were made public by the Federal Government. What a mess!

The Black Minister's Council immediately demanded that Whitman fire Colonel Carl Williams and also vowed to block the nomination of Attorney General Verniero unless they admit that the state police engaged in racial profiling. Almost comically, less than forty-eight hours after these demands were made, Governor Whitman publicly called for and was immediately granted the official resignation from Colonel Carl Williams. Though he merely quoted statistics from federal crime reports, she claimed, "His comments today are inconsistent with our efforts to enhance public confidence in the state police." With resignation in hand, the Black Minister's Council now cited the governor to not only appoint a new colonel from outside the ranks of the NJSP, but insist she appoint the first minority colonel in state-police history.

As Whitman and Verniero's push toward higher office continued, minority politicians began to enter the volcanic fray. Appearing at press conferences with activists and ministers from their respective voting districts, black and Latino politicians publicly declared they would block both Whitman's and Verniero's appointments, solely because they had yet to admit that racial-profiling is, "an epidemic" within the state police.

Caught in a catch-22 because of the *DeSoto* appeal, Whitman and Verniero remained quiet and at times even subtly defended the state police as a whole from racial-profiling allegations. (Because of DeSoto, it was blatantly obvious they had no choice.) As the threat and likelihood of their political advancements became evident, so was their complete shift in support for the New Jersey State Police. Despite her previous claims that "the state police does not train, teach, condone, or practice racial profiling," the governor, with the realization that her political future hang in the balance, had a mysterious change of heart and went public with it.

On February 28, 1999, Whitman publicly announced she had directed Attorney General Peter Verniero to investigate allegations of racial profiling against the state police. *Why all of a sudden? What about the years of complaints prior to this? What about the* DeSoto *appeal that she insisted upon?*

Unknown to everyone, this "directive" meant that an unprecedented investigation of state police patrol practices and policies was about to be launched. A thirty-man investigative unit was immediately formed and headed up by the NJSP's Internal Affairs Bureau who, in turn, reported directly to the Attorney General's Office. Broken down into teams, the investigators were dispatched like wildfire across the entire eastern seaboard armed with legal pads, video cameras and microphones. It was rumored that an audit of all turnpike troopers' motor-vehicle stops had been initiated. In reality however, we quickly learned that the "task force" had been split into two teams and focused solely on two young junior troopers. Any guess as to who they were? That's right—Troopers James Kenna and John Hogan each received a fifteen-man unit who investigated us individually, unlike any other trooper in the history of the state police.

Part III

Double-Barreled Investigation

While Gerrow, Cochran, his buddy Henry Lee (who was comically hired to be "a neutral figure" in the shooting investigation), and the remainder of investigators and lawyers decided *how* the shooting occurred in Cochran's Manhattan office, this second investigation was launched full-throttle. Reportedly, these investigators were directed to find any discrepancy possible on our patrol charts, investigation, or arrest reports and immediately prepare any *administrative mistakes* found for presentation to a grand jury. This audit would cover from January 1, 1998, to the night of the shooting on April 23, 1998. Every person stopped by either Trooper Kenna or me was contacted; questioned; and, if at all possible, videotaped. Any deviation in race, time, license plate, demeanor, search, or incident that occurred during these stops was documented and immediately reported back to the attorney general, who was now hell-bent to prove that he addressed the issue of racial profiling. With his nomination to the Supreme Court guaranteed to meet resistance by minority politicians and the Black Minister's Council, rumors immediately surfaced that Verniero planned on combating the allegation that he did not address racial profiling simply by indicting Trooper Kenna and me. By doing this, it would prove to the minority community that he not only dealt with, but handled the issue of racial profiling, thus, clearing the path for his seat on the state's highest court.

To coincide with Verniero's actions—which now started to take shape as a conspiracy much as the shooting case did—the governor too bolstered her obvious negative shift in sentiments toward the state police. Almost as if she were setting up the public at large for what was to come next, on March 1, 1999, Whitman made the following statement: "Unfortunately, the specter of racial profiling has had the effect of questioning the motivations of the state police. I will not have their ability to fight crime compromised by the perception of racial profiling or insensitivity. It is not fair to the men and women of the state police or fair to the residents of our state who rely on them for safety and protection. In addition to the search for a new superintendent, we are in the process of the most thorough review the state has ever undertaken of state-police practices and policies." At the conclusion of this speech, she announced the formation of a committee to help select a new colonel to lead the NJSP, and Secretary of State Reverend DeForest "Buster" Soaries (a black minister) was introduced as the leader of this committee. The governor added, "I am counting on this committee to recommend individuals who share my belief that neither race nor ethnicity should ever be used to define the essential character of a person."

In response to her revelations, uniformed road troopers, in an initial and brief sign of unity, went on an unofficial "slow down" in making arrests and writing tickets. It was reported that an estimated two million dollars in revenue from the issuance of motor-vehicle tickets was lost by the state, and rumor had it that the governor was infuriated with the state police and troopers in general.

As her crusade to gain favor with the minority community continued, the governor appeared to toss aside the common folks as well as the NJSP. Having pitted the minority and law-enforcement communities against each other, in an attempt to straddle fences, she audaciously issued this statement on March 11, 1999: "I am concerned about reports that morale among state troopers is down. Unfortunately, our troopers are getting caught in the crossfire of what has become a partisan political attack directed at me. The men and women of the state police put their lives on the line every day and every night to protect the people of New Jersey. It is wrong for those who are trying to score partisan points to smear the reputations of the vast majority of troopers who do their jobs and do them well." *Is that a political crock or what? How these politicians so eloquently talk out of both sides of their mouths is astounding to me!*

With the abrupt formation of the thirty-man "task force" and the reasons for it dominating the headlines, the shooting investigation lingered on and took a backseat. >From Mr. Galantucci, I learned that Peter Verniero egregiously planned to indict Trooper Kenna and me to *prove* that he addressed the issue of racial profiling. The initial idea for our indictments surfaced when the operator of the car we stopped prior to the shooting was reported on our patrol chart as white, but in reality, he was black. Though this "error" was known immediately to state investigators, it was a non-issue for nearly a year. It wasn't until Mr. Verniero's critics accused him of not doing anything about racial profiling, thus, leading them to block his appointment to the Supreme Court, did he realize he could use this mistake to his advantage.

In a formal statement, Christopher Woodly, the last individual Kenna and I had contact with before the shooting, stated, "They were both gentlemen and professionals. They treated me with the utmost respect when they could have towed my car and given me a ticket. You know, if they wanted to stick it to somebody that night, I would have been their man!" (This is referring to the fact that his car was reported stolen, and he did not possess his driver's license.) Scandalously, the state never introduced Christopher Woodly or his statement to the grand-jury-hearing testimony in the shooting case. *Surprised?*

By the end of March, Mr. Galantucci mentally began to prepare me for the state's intention to indict Kenna and me for administrative mistakes. Despite being fully aware of the political motivations behind the indictments, I was hysterical. The mere thought of being indicted, let alone facing two separate sets of indictments, was surreal. *How can this be happening to me?* Though testimony in the "shooting case" grand jury had begun, it was abruptly halted, and without explanation, the investigation into the shooting was deemed "incomplete." The grand jurors previously selected were given a hiatus as Gerrow advised them that "further investigation" was required. *Talk about doing whatever the hell you want!*

In reality, however, the shooting case mysteriously ceased so that the attorney general could proceed with a new grand jury that was selected to hear testimony on the hastily created "falsifying documents" case. Regardless of case, Whitman and Verniero personally and blatantly manipulated the timing and presentation to perfection to ensure they could both move forward with their political aspirations. I had never felt so much like a human shield before in my life!

Though the grand-jury members were given a hiatus from hearing testimony, the investigation into the shooting continued. On April 10, 1999, for the first time in its history, the busiest highway east of the Mississippi was shut down between exits 8A and 7A on the southbound side for a Hollywood-style reenactment of the shooting. This high-profile debacle was open to the media and reporters alike. This would also mark the first time media were allowed to observe any grand-jury proceedings in the state of New Jersey. This entire "production" was videotaped, recorded, and staged as if it were a movie script. Despite contradicting the most basic evidential facts, it was this glorified and inaccurate depiction of the shooting that was shown to the members of the grand jury when they reconvened several weeks later.

For me personally, the reenactment marked the first time I realized how eager the state was to shove it up my ass. That cold and blustery night began at 9:30 PM where I met Mike Strug, an investigator from Mr. G's office. Present with Mike was renowned ballistics expert Lucian Haag, whom we hired and wanted present in hopes of keeping the state and Dr. Henry Lee honest during the reenactment. *Damn that Mr. G was smart!* Over the course of the next several hours, I observed a horrid depiction of the alleged shooting incident. It was in no way, shape, or form even remotely close to what happened that tragic night. Worst of all, I had to stand next to that runt little Barry Scheck the whole night. Scheck was present on behalf of "Dream team 2" and the van's occupants.

For starters, the state made the incident into one continuous motion even though all evidence indicated that the van had struck the troop car on at least two and possibly three occasions. Despite being "stonewalled" from obtaining information and evidence, even we knew that there were a minimum of two, and quite possibly a third set of permanent indentations found on the bumper of the troop car. These marks lined up perfectly with the license plate of the van proving that this incident could not have been one continuous motion. This fact alone disproved the state's theory and as we later learned, the state chose not to present the multiple indentations on the bumper to the grand jury.

The state's reenactment also showed me firing from the ground even though I distinctly stated I was not certain in which position I had fired from. I made this claim during the reenactment that was held at the Cranbury Barracks on May 5, but investigators chose to ignore me and apply their own logic. I also learned that the only purpose for having Jimmy Kenna and I participate in the reenactment was to detail any inconsistencies between this day and our official statements given roughly twelve hours after the shooting. In essence, the state turned the grand-jury proceedings into a "credibility" contest between the van's occupants and Jimmy Kenna and me. Astoundingly, only Trooper Kenna's and my deviations were pointed out and presented to the grand jury, though. Comically, Mr. Gerrow's opening statement to members of the grand jury hearing the shooting case commenced with Gerrow claiming he would take them, "On a journey to the truth!"

The most sickening portion of the state's reenactment came when I watched Detective Kevin Dunn stand at the top of the berm, holding an H&K 9-mm pistol in his left hand. I had no idea what they were trying to depict, but I knew full well that Jimmy Kenna was right-handed. Detective Dunn aimed his weapon at the van, which was painstakingly lowered down the embankment by a tow truck. Eventually, the van ended up in the drainage culvert. Inch by inch, the van was lowered. With every movement, investigators armed with trajectory rods approached the van and attempted to implicate the likelihood of when I could have fired into the van as it slowly rolled away from me. Frozen, shocked, and in a panic, I cried out to Mike and Lucian, "I swear I didn't shoot into that van after it passed me! I swear! I swear! I swear!" Completely bewildered and sick to my stomach, I was convinced that I was being framed for attempted murder. It was nearly 5:00 AM when everything concluded, and I was weary and dumbfounded. *How in the hell did they conclude that this was what really happened? I am going to prison for something I didn't even do! Why did Deputy Attorney General Chuck Grinnell constantly bring Barry Scheck and his girlfriend hot coffee but never offer any to us or even acknowledge our presence? So much for being fair and impartial!*

Just hours after witnessing the state's incredulous and completely bogus reenactment, the front page of the *Star-Ledger* detailed how an anonymous source called and stated that the trooper standing at the top of the berm recklessly and unjustifiably fired at the van's occupants as they rolled harmlessly down the embankment. Obviously, Scheck or someone in his entourage from the scene called earlier in the night because these tests didn't even occur until just before 5:00 AM. *Where will people draw the line for money? This was jury-poisoning to the fullest extent, and it was my life and liberty they were sacrificing all for a larger settlement; that is despicable!* Along with Mike and Lucian, we met Mr. Galantucci at the Newark Airport for breakfast. To put it mildly, I was sickened by the reenactment and the negative, misleading media coverage that followed. *How in the hell am I ever going to get a fair trial?*

By the middle of April, I knew it would be just days before I was indicted, but it wasn't for the shooting. The charges were going to be official misconduct for misidentifying the race of motorists whom I stopped and, even less frequently, searched. By going public with these indictments, critics of the attorney general would forever be forced to remain silent. As she had done every step of the way, Governor Whitman continued to spoon-feed the media in preparation for the indictments. On April 15, 1999, she stated, "Obviously, there is something wrong within the state police, and we plan to root out any racial profiling."

On April 17, 1999, a news report was released, claiming that a preliminary vote taken by the New Jersey State Bar Association concluded that Peter Verniero was not qualified to serve on the New Jersey Supreme Court. This report infuriated Whitman, who claimed the leak compromised the appointment process. The governor indicated she would continue to push Verniero to the state Supreme Court, even if the bar association opposed him. This arrogant claim marked the first time a governor ever threatened to override the state's historical process. Meanwhile, on this same day, the Black Minister's Council publicly reaffirmed they would continue their crusade to keep Verniero from his nomination until he proved that he had addressed the issue of racial profiling within the state police.

Part IV

Indicted

Sensing his nomination was at risk, just two days later, Trooper Kenna and I were indicted on official-misconduct charges. In announcing the indictments at a widely publicized and live press conference, the attorney general portrayed Kenna and me as, "bad apples." I was formerly charged with official misconduct and fifteen counts of falsifying documents for either, "purposefully deceiving race on police documents or conducting illegal searches without receiving written permission." In essence, I was charged with racial profiling. The indictment was based on the **hundreds** of motor vehicle stops we had made in the four months leading up to the night of the shooting, which basically covered a sixteen-week period. Though no reporter had the common sense or intelligence to ask this question, the indictment was based on me averaging *one mistake per week*. (Fifteen mistakes over the course of sixteen weeks means I made one error per week on my patrol chart. Kenna, on the other hand, averaged one mistake every *two* weeks!)

Even more amusing about these indictments was the fact that some of the counts in our indictments were based on traffic stops Kenna and I made when riding with other troopers, yet, and rightfully so, only Jimmy and me were indicted for these administrative mistakes. In concluding their 4:00 PM press conference, which preempted all other programs on the major news networks, both trooper Kenna and I were officially suspended from the New Jersey State Police without pay and benefits. As expected, the STFA made no public comment in support of us against these criminal charges which, at best, were New Jersey State Police SOP violations.

During the discovery phase, to prove my fifteen mistakes, the state handed over to Mr. Galantucci more than **four thousand pages** of discovery. In hopes of draining us financially, the state also billed us for each and every page of discovery they turned over to Mr. Galantucci. *If I can't make one mistake per forty-hour workweek, then send me to jail!*

On the very next day following the announcement of our indictments, April 20, 1999, Attorney General Peter Verniero had the balls to announce that his office had completed its investigation into allegations of racial profiling within the state police. Amazingly, though his office oversees the state police, he assumed no personal blame or responsibility for failing to properly guide the NJSP. To *prove* that he had indeed addressed the issue of racial profiling, a ninety-six-page report was released and became known as the "Interim Report on Racial Profiling." Throughout this report, no member of the attorney general's office or the New Jersey State Police was identified or held accountable for, "The years of disparate treatment of minority motorists" except for James Kenna and John Hogan.

Governor Whitman followed this announcement by proclaiming, "Racial profiling is a national epidemic that is real and not imagined, and *some* New Jersey state troopers engage in the practice." Within the same breath, Whitman also revealed that she and Attorney General Verniero were ordering the immediate dismissal of the *DeSoto* appeal. To hide the obvious fact that our indictments were a blatant case of selective prosecution, she stated, "as many as ten other troopers may be criminally charged because they had identical mistakes on their patrol charts." Six-plus years later, as I finalize this incredulous chain of events, no other trooper has ever been indicted, or even suspended, for these types of administrative mistakes.

To continue the public barrage, three days later, on April 23, 1999, Reverend Al Sharpton led a peaceful demonstration to mark the one-year anniversary of the shooting. The New Jersey Turnpike Authority paid for each attendee's lunch as well as the buses for the rally. They also agreed to temporarily halt traffic so the demonstrators, lead by van driver Keshon Moore, could congregate for a prayer vigil at the exact milepost of the shooting. During a press conference that followed the rally, Reverend Al Sharpton threatened that if Trooper Kenna and I are not indicted soon for the shooting, he would begin to hold "sit-ins" on the front steps of the statehouse and other high-profile venues until we were prosecuted. *How's that for a busy week!*

Despite our indictment, and the release of the interim report, as a result of his refusal to accept personal responsibility for problems within the state police, minority politicians and activists continued to lobby against Verniero's appointment to the Supreme Court. To further complicate the matter, on April 30, 1999, (Democratic) United States Attorney General, Janet Reno, announced that a three-year probe into the NJSP by the Federal Department of Justice had been completed. The results of this probe, which was launched following the DeSoto case, concluded that New Jersey State Troopers had illegally targeted minority drivers for traffic stops on the New Jersey Turnpike as far back as 1995. Though no superior or individual trooper was identified or *ever* disciplined over this investigation, Mrs. Reno announced that the federal government would sue the state of New Jersey to end the practice of racial profiling.

Realizing this lawsuit could be long and drawn out, ultimately harming their political advancements, Whitman and Verniero immediately attempted to work out a plea bargain with the federal government, and when promising reform, Whitman professed, "We already know racial profiling exists; now New Jersey will be a model for other states to follow." To avoid being sued and having their own actions questioned, the governor and attorney general hurriedly agreed to enter the New Jersey State Police into a federal monitoring program that presently garners all existing reforms in today's "new" NJSP.

The following week, however, the nomination of Attorney General Peter Verniero to the NJ Supreme Court suffered another major setback when an official vote by the New Jersey State Bar Association ruled Verniero "not qualified" to serve on the high court. This action marked the first time that the association had ever voted down a governor's nominee to the high court. Despite this ruling, newspaper accounts on May 9 suggested Governor Christie Whitman, who has stood by her nominee despite a barrage of criticism over his qualifications and his handling of the racial-profiling issue, had been secretly lobbying senators the past few days. It was further divulged that John Farmer, the governor's chief counsel and man who would succeed Verniero as attorney general, had also been indiscreetly phoning key senators in hopes of currying a favorable vote for Verniero.

Despite the growing revolt against him, the very next day, Peter Verniero was confirmed to the New Jersey Supreme Court after a bitter bipartisan fight. The vote tally was 21-18. Following his appointment, the governor stated, "I am pleased with today's action and look forward to Mr. Verniero's service on the court." With him secured on the state's highest court, Mrs. Whitman was now on her own to deal with the continually mounting pressure to choose the first minority colonel to head the state police while maintaining focus for her own Senate campaign. *But was Verniero really safe?*

As for me, once indicted, the damage to my reputation and credibility was instant. The Middlesex County Prosecutors Office joined the onslaught of publicly burying me and announced on May 25 that they were immediately dismissing all pending criminal cases that I, in retrospect, foolishly risked my life for. More than twenty cases, including a suspect arrested for $160,000 worth of heroin who additionally turned out to be a fugitive wanted for murder in Pennsylvania, were among those cases dismissed! Subjects previously prosecuted and convicted were also immediately released, and their sentences were overturned. *Shit! Why not give them back their drugs and guns too!*

Because of the state's blasphemous press conferences and intentional (mis)handling of this travesty, I had been vilified to the point that I was already guilty in the eyes of the media and the public. *So much for the premise of innocent until proven guilty!*

On May 27, 1999, Trooper Kenna and I were arraigned in a media-frenzied Mercer County Courthouse. Prior to entering the courtroom, I was fingerprinted and photographed like a typical criminal, but I still had not been advised of my Miranda rights. This processing was staged at the Hughes Justice Complex, which sits adjacent to the Mercer County Courthouse. As I walked outside, toward the courtroom with Mr. G at my side, reporters and cameramen shoved microphones and lenses in my face. It was a pathetic, humiliating and despicable scene.

Once inside, Mr. Galantucci spoke on my behalf, and we waived the reading of the indictments. Though we each faced up to twenty years in prison and several thousand dollars in fines, (suspended) Trooper Kenna and I were released without even having to post bail. Knowing full well that hundreds, if not thousands, of other troopers had identical mistakes on their patrol charts, Mr. G and Jimmy's attorney, Jack Arsenault, emphatically denounced the indictments during a press conference that followed the hearing. Our defense was simple: not only was this case blatant and selective prosecution but, entirely motivated by the political ambitions of Whitman and Verniero. Simply and obviously put, we were *scapegoats* for the state's racial-profiling controversy! Days later, John Farmer was sworn in as the new attorney general, replacing Peter Verniero.

A typical court appearance

Reporters and photographers surround James Kenna's attorney, Jack Arsenault, after one of our many court appearances.

Part V

Governor Whitman, the Profiler

Though things slowed down slightly in the days following our arraignment, it was reported that Governor Whitman chose an African American male from the Illinois State Police to become the next superintendent of the New Jersey State Police. Andre Parker apparently interviewed and verbally accepted the position. Before his official introduction as the new Colonel, however, Mr. Parker declined the appointment after realizing the intense scrutiny, media hype, and controversy that surrounded his selection. Once this announcement was official, another name immediately surfaced. From out of nowhere, Federal Agent Carson Dunbar—who, ironically, is also black—was rumored to become the next colonel. Publicly, Governor Whitman was ridiculed and accused of ***profiling*** for minority males who possessed the qualifications to become the next colonel since they were the only individuals she considered when looking to fill the void atop the ranks of the state police.

In the meantime, as my face remained plastered on both newspapers and television news reports on a daily basis, I again contacted the STFA. In light of the governor's lack of popularity, several attempts were also made by my family, fellow troopers, and even Mr. G himself in hopes that my "union" would finally take a stance and publicly denounce our indictments. Pathetically, each attempt was met with the same negative results, and their only response was, "It's too political for us to get involved in!"

Oddly, another development during this same time was the revelation that Governor Whitman had recently given Reverend Reginald Jackson, her part-time friend and part-time critic, a $125,000 "grant." This grant was alleged to be a payoff to have Mr. Jackson's support in her upcoming Senate campaign! *Dirty, dirty, dirty politicians!*

Finally, on June 17, 1999 (fourteen months *after* the shooting), Kenneth McClelland, vice president of the STFA, called my sister Dot. This would mark the first time that the union had taken the initiative to reach out to us. In speaking on behalf of the STFA, he apologetically stated that, as a whole, they didn't realize just how big this case was. Kenneth McClelland vowed that from this day on, the STFA would become more active and verbal in supporting Kenna and me.

Little did he know we were well informed that numerous troopers were disgusted with the union's lack of care, attention, concern, and initiative over our case, as well as the governor's selection process for a new colonel. As a result of their lack of action in these critical issues, numerous troopers left the STFA and joined local FOP and PBA unions within the state. Unlike the STFA, these unions already had a legal-defense system in place and were far more verbal and supportive of their members if someone got jammed up.

A few days later, we returned to court and made our first appearance before the assigned judge, Andrew J. Smithson. This initial hearing addressed upcoming motions, the discovery process, and future court appearances. In a frugal attempt to show support, a few officers representing the STFA were on hand, but not one of them took the opportunity to address the swarming media that flooded the steps of the courtroom to show support for the ludicrous charges. Mr. Galantucci, on the other hand, went on the offensive and announced to the world that Verniero and Whitman would be his first two witnesses at the trial, which, as luck would have it, was slated to begin in November, the same month as Whitman's Senate election!

Due to the saturated media coverage and "bad-apple" label the attorney general pinned to my chest, receiving a fair and impartial hearing before the shooting grand jury now appeared impossible. Every court appearance for the "falsifying documents case" was widely publicized, and our faces were plastered onto newspapers and television stations across the country. Even worse, I had already been accused of *lying* by the attorney general, the governor, and lead prosecutor James Gerrow who now, with the first wave of indictments fresh in everyone's mind, immediately *reconvened* the "shooting case" grand jury. Like a well orchestrated movie plot, Mr. Gerrow appallingly continued to take the grand jurors on his, "journey to the truth!"

In late June, 1999, Reverend Al Sharpton seized the opportunity to keep the pressure on and announced he would shut down the Atlantic City Expressway on the Fourth of July weekend. Sharpton, incensed that Kenna and I had yet to be indicted for the shooting, threatened to close down the Expressway on its busiest travel weekend in disapproval of the slow action of the "shooting case" grand jury.

Through friends close to the investigation, I learned that Gerrow continued to present evidence, including the bullet fragment he supposedly found, to the grand jurors. It became very evident that the state was adamant on indicting me for attempted murder. *The mere thought of being indicted or "framed" for something I didn't do frightened the hell out of me.*

Out of pure disbelief over these events, I sought the advice of a higher power and on June 28, 1999, I had a private meeting with Monsignor DuBell at a local Roman Catholic parish. I divulged to him the events of that tragic night and informed him of my fear of being indicted, or even framed, by the prosecutor. The monsignor said a special prayer over me, and I was assured that the truth would eventually come out. The following day, my father was admitted to the hospital after suffering a series of mild, undetected heart attacks.

As promised, Reverend Sharpton led a protest on the Fourth of July weekend. He and seventy-five others were arrested for blocking the main road into Atlantic City on its busiest day of the year. In another development, two separate bumper stickers surfaced. These stickers mocked Christie Whitman's handling of the state police and racial profiling controversy and further inflamed the national debate over this issue. In the colors of the NJSP, they stated, "Hey, Christie, prosecute drug dealers, not TROOPERS!" And the second was "Hey, Christie, I support the New Jersey State Police, and I vote!" Though my family and support-staff were accused of having them printed, we later learned troopers from the Cranbury Barracks initiated the sticker campaign in support of Jimmy and me.

Fighting back

As the summer progressed, so did the governor's obsession to appoint a minority as the next superintendent to head the state police. Her choice, Carson Dunbar, initially refused to leave the federal government to accept this position for fear of forfeiting his federal pension. To circumvent this, Governor Whitman and newly appointed attorney general John Farmer entered negotiations with Janet Reno. Like true political geniuses, they successfully secured Dunbar's pension, thus, clearing the way for him to become the first minority colonel, just as the Black Minister's Council had demanded. Though not officially announced yet, it appeared that Whitman had cowered to the vast demands of Reginald Jackson yet again.

Meanwhile, the grand-jury investigation into the shooting case continued to meet weekly. As it neared closure, the state had the incredulous audacity to invite Kenna and me to testify as the final witnesses. *Let's see. We have already been indicted for lying, our faces have been plastered all over the country as racial-profilers, and his investigation was based on a "credibility contest" between us and the van's occupants. No thanks, Jim I'll pass!*

As Mr. Galantucci pointed out, my sworn statement had already been read and picked apart by Gerrow, the grand jury believed we were liars because of the first indictment, and now the State hoped to set a trap by inviting us to testify and use any further contradictions he may find in our testimony against us during the trial. *Did he think we were idiots?*

As the first week of August ended without our indictments, Reverend Jackson made more demands and again accused the state of stonewalling. The great reverend, who by now had become a public icon and clairvoyant on the issue of racial profiling, continued holding daily press conferences and always had the hypocritical media at his beacon call.

A week later, a news report revealed that drug arrests on the turnpike were down 71 percent, and the pressure and backlash against Governor Whitman's failure to formally announce that a minority colonel had been selected became more evident.

In response to Reverend Jackson's demands and the mounting pressure on her, the state "leaked" that they were very close to wrapping up the "shooting" grand jury, and a decision would soon be announced. It was reported that a preliminary vote was taken and in complete dismay, I began to receive calls from friends who heard the grand jury's initial vote "no billed" us or, voted *not* to indict Kenna and me. Allegedly, the thought of on-duty police officers being charged with *attempted murder* was a little excessive, even with Gerrow presenting false, slanted and misleading evidence. For some unknown reason, even after the State announced a decision was close, the grand-jury members were given an abrupt two-week hiatus in mid-August.

During these two weeks, my sister Mary Jane (who had become the unofficial spokeswoman for my family) and Mr. Galantucci began receiving calls, confirming the same rumor. We were not going to be indicted! Even a few retired troopers who were now working at the Attorney General's Office indiscreetly and anonymously relayed this wonderful information to us through mutual friends. It was suggested that the governor (as sick as this is) wanted, "a black face," i.e, new colonel, Carson Dunbar, to announce the verdict in hopes of quelling the backlash within the minority community.

Apparently, this same rumor began to surface to others as well. On August 31, 1999, Reverend Reginald Jackson was quoted as saying, "There will be extreme tension in the black communities if Hogan and Kenna are not indicted!" The reverend also publicly lobbied for Carson Dunbar to now turn down the superintendent position. Jackson hinted that Whitman was *using* him as a minority to save face. Caught in the middle, Dunbar continued to waver on whether he would take the position, and as the verbal assault between Whitman and Jackson lingered, she was forced to announce that Dunbar's confirmation was still weeks away.

On September 7, 1999, exactly one week after Reverennd Jackson's threats, the grand jury mysteriously reconvened for the final time. Apparently, an alternative spin was added to the conclusion of Mr. Gerrow's, "journey to the truth." A new vote was taken, and at approximately 4:40 PM, I received a call from Mr. Galantucci's office.

My heart sank, as it always did upon seeing his number appear in my cell phone. At that instant, I pointed my computer's Web browser to: *www.nj.com*—where my fate and life had been played out for the past seventeen months. As usual—Breaking News on NJ.com—knew my fate before I did.

As I saw my face plastered yet again on the world-wide-web, the words from Mr. G's lips were worse than a dagger through my heart. I was in complete shock and disbelief as I read, and vaguely listened as Mr. Galantucci advised me that I had been formally charged with one count of attempted murder (for firing a shot that never occurred) and two counts of aggravated assault. *Call it political, skewed, or flat-out wrong; but I was now an accused* MURDERER? *I went from a cop with an unblemished record to this? How did this happen?*

Crying hysterically, I abruptly left my miserable office job and contemplated driving my car off the Burlington Bristol Bridge to end both my families' misery as well as my own. Suicide seemed the only and logical thing to do! There was no doubt in my mind that I was going to prison for something I did not do . . . but who would ever believe me?

To deflect attention from herself, merely three hours before announcing our indictments to the world, Governor Whitman officially removed her name from the U.S. Senate race. Her mishandling of the racial-profiling controversy was irreversible; and by announcing her withdrawal just hours before our indictments, she insulated herself from questions, knowing full well that two white New Jersey State Troopers being indicted for attempted murder against minorities would dominate the headlines. Once again, the Queen had used us as her whipping boys!

Part VI

Post-Indictment Politics

As time went by, Jimmy Kenna and I spoke less and less. Though we probably should have been best friends at a time like this, the reality was that there was nothing we could do about what was happening to us. Left abandoned by our employer, we turned to our families and attorneys for support and guidance. Plus, how much could we really talk about the same thing? Repeatedly discussing the incident, the charges and all the other wrong-doings was not healthy—mentally or physically—so in essence, we had all but stopped speaking.

Fortunately for me, as part of workers' compensation, the state had not revoked my weekly visits to my psychologist, Dr. Carl Chiapetta. At least once a week I would vent, cry, scream, cuss and even openly discuss my desire to end my life while visiting with Dr. Chiapetta. These therapy sessions helped me stay strong and not mentally break down in front of my family or friends.

In the days leading up to our arraignment on the attempted-murder charges, the boisterous race-mongers were quiet. Now that we were indicted for the most heinous crimes possible, I guess everyone was happy and satisfied. *Gee, Reverend Jackson and crew get their desired indictment, and all of the sudden, the demands stop!*

With the exception of ousted colonel Carl Williams filing a lawsuit against the governor for unlawful termination, the newspapers and television were equally dormant. Mr. Galantucci had made arrangements for me to secretly go to the Justice Hughes Complex on October 7, 1999 to get processed (arrested) for these new charges. In addition to the initial charges, I was now facing a total of forty years in prison and several hundred thousand dollars in fines; but yet, I had never been advised of my Miranda rights, placed in handcuffs, or been forced to pay one penny in bail money! Something wasn't right!

The next wave of media-bashing came without warning. On October 6, 1999, it was broadcasted that Trooper Kenna filed a civil suit against the state of New Jersey and the NJSP for not properly counseling him after his first shooting, which was three weeks prior to the April 23 incident. This suit came as a huge and bitter surprise to both Mr. Galantucci and my family.

For the past year, we were publicly identified as *political scapegoats* by our ever-increasing supporters and now this! To say the least, we instantly lost a lot of momentum and support. The tide turned drastically, and everyone now assumed Kenna was looking to blame others for his actions. As imagined, the newspaper headlines were TROOPER SUES BOSSES. Even worse, they had a picture of me—not Kenna—on the front page when identifying the trooper who filed the suit. One of our largest support systems, radio station 101.5 FM, had callers blasting Kenna for filing the suit. *How can a scapegoat now blame others for his actions?*

On October 12, 1999, we were formally arraigned before presiding judge Andrew Smithson, who was now responsible for overseeing both cases. As would become the norm for all future proceedings, Mr. Galantucci did all the speaking for me both in court and outside the courthouse, where the largest press corps I had ever seen amassed itself. After pleading not guilty to the new charges, Judge Smithson postponed our November trial on the falsifications indictments. The purpose of this delay was to allow the state and our attorney's time to decide which case should be heard first.

Once outside the courtroom, I realized how monumental and historical it was for white police officers to be charged with the attempted murder of a minority. Satellite trucks from CNN, MSN, Fox, and every major news station were present. *Vultures!* They were everywhere, rushing at me, literally inches from my face, thrusting microphones and cameras down my throat! One jerk-off reporter even fell and got trampled on by his "colleagues." I was quickly escorted from the scene by my squad mates who were dressed in civilian clothing. Circled by my peers, we literally had to push through the droves of cameramen and reporters to get away from the scene. *What about the monsignor's promise that the truth would come out? I was charged with attempted murder for a shot that was never fired!*

With Kenna and I safely buried by the same legal system we once risked our lives for, defense attorneys from across the state began insisting that all twenty-one counties review every state-police-trooper arrest. These pathetic windbags insisted that all charges against their clients should be dismissed since the governor herself proclaimed that the NJSP practices racial profiling. *The can of worms she opened just continued to get bigger! Way to go, Governor!*

Now in the national spotlight, the debate over racial profiling raged on. Television and radio networks across the country featured programming almost daily, highlighting this most sensitive and controversial issue. Every program I watched or heard about all stemmed back to the igniting point: The April 23, 1998 Turnpike Shooting!

To add further insult, even Johnny Cochran had now become an expert on racial profiling. He audaciously appeared on a documentary called DWB (Driving While Black), which aired nationally on *MTV*. During this interview, he spoke directly about our case and professed, "One of the troopers was at the top of the hill, just shooting at the kids in the van for no reason!" By the end of the 1999, not only were "Hogan and Kenna" nationally identified as "racist troopers and attempted murderers," but the bitter debate over the issue of racial profiling had exploded across the country. Even presidential candidates George W. Bush and Al Gore were put on the hot seat concerning our case and, even more specifically, how they intended to combat the despicable law-enforcement tactic known as racial profiling.

On November 19, 1999, I attended a benefit for Trooper Francis Belleran who tragically died in the line of duty a few days previously while chasing a fleeing motorcyclist. While there, I ran into a classmate of mine who was close to the shooting investigation and also witnessed the state's bogus reenactment back in May. He stated that his unit, the Fatal Accident Investigation Unit, had been summoned by Gerrow's investigative team to independently reconstruct the events of April 23. With great detail, precision, and utilization of the identical evidence that Gerrow's team had, extensive and comprehensive reports were prepared by the state police's fatal-accident unit. Once completed, these reports, prepared solely by troopers classified as "experts" in accident reconstruction, were forwarded to Mr. Gerrow for review. On the night of the reenactment, the Fatal Accident Unit was asked to assist with the scene. As Gerrow led the reenactment, along with yet another high-dollar expert the state hired named Steve Batterman, a bitter argument apparently broke out. Though it wasn't visible to me from behind the roped off area where I was forced to stand, Gerrow told members of the NJSP's Fatal Accident Unit to, "shut the fuck up!" when they attempted to point out obvious and blatant inconsistencies with the reenactment based on the physical evidence. The most egregious inconsistency, even to them, was that Gerrow's version had the van striking the troop car only once. The physical evidence was indisputable that it had struck the troop car, at the absolute minimum, twice and, quite possibly, a third time. Yet the videotaped version of the "state's" reenactment that was shown to the grand jury proved just how badly the true facts of the incident were manipulated.

By showing the accident as one continuous motion, my statement about having time to fire after being struck by the van was blown out of the water, thus, leaving no doubt that I had to fire at the van after it passed me and crashed down the embankment. *I was being framed!*

Just as I thought things could not get any worse, I woke up on the morning of November 30 to learn that a new witness had surfaced for the prosecution. As was the norm, I learned this from the sensationalized media that printed new and unsubstantiated stories just about every day. This new witness came forward more than nineteen months after the shooting and claimed to have observed the shooting from a turnpike overpass, roughly three tenths of a mile from the spot where the tragedy took place. The new witness, an oral surgeon named William Kenny, stated, "The troopers panicked!" Though he admitted to not witnessing the gunfire, Mr. Kenny stated he heard a final shot seconds *after* the van came to rest down the embankment. *I am going to prison for something I didn't even do!* In sheer disbelief, I began to wonder if I was so screwed up that maybe I did fire into the van after it stopped and had no recollection of it! I really began to question myself and my mental state!

To refute this new claim, a few nights later, two of my closest friends who were still assigned to patrol the turnpike conducted their own investigation.

After lighting a flare at milepost 62.8, exactly where the incident occurred, they then left the turnpike and drove up to the overpass where Mr. Kenny claimed to have witnessed the shooting. According to them, unless this guy was Superman, it was impossible for him to have seen anything. Furthermore, from Mr. Galantucci, I learned that Dr. Kenny attempted to meet with minority politicians as well as Reverend Al Sharpton before going to the state with his version of the incident. Though his motives were never ultimately revealed, we soon learned that this individual had, "issues," and the state had no intention of ever having him testify at a trial. Once again however, the damage was done! The general public of course didn't know any of this, and if it were even possible, the potential jury pool was further poisoned by the widespread front-page articles this sensationalized portrayal of the incident obtained. I was certain I would never be able to receive a fair and impartial jury!

As if the overwhelming criminal indictments weren't enough, the "Dream Team 2" further complicated my flailing mental well-being by filing a kazillion-dollar lawsuit on behalf of the van's occupants. Almost daily, I was bombarded by certified letters, packages containing legal documents and demands for discovery. Hundreds of trees had to have died to account for the masses of paperwork I received, and I am certain my mailman—who had to deliver these heavy files, sometimes boxes—hated me! Though we tried diligently to postpone the civil case, the presiding judge Paulette Sapp-Peterson shot down each attempt. Even O. J. was treated better than we were in this respect. If you'll recall, his wrongful death civil-suit was put on hold until the adjudication of his criminal trial. From every angle, I felt bombarded, and the mental and psychological toll these events had on me were overwhelming to say the least. Not only was I deeply depressed and withdrawn, but thoughts of suicide and outlandish acts ran prevalent. Waking up and trying to face the endless barrage grew even more difficult with each passing day!

As the new century began, the early months of 2000 were spent with Mr. Galantucci sifting through the mountains of discovery the state turned over and simultaneously billed us for. While my attorney's fees were estimated in the hundreds of thousands of dollars, it was an issue that Mr. G refused to speak to me about. *Only my family will ever know how wonderfully incredible Robert L. Galantucci is!*

Behind the scenes, a grassroots campaign to raise money for my rapidly mounting legal fees was established and directed by my sister Mary. Letters; signs; articles; and, eventually, *www.trooperhogan.com* was launched all in an attempt to gain verbal and financial assistance to keep up with the state's overzealous pursuit to incarcerate me.

Nearly two years had now passed since the shooting. Legally speaking, the only thing we knew for certain was that the shooting case would be tried first. With the exception of a few status conference hearings, no formal dates were imposed. Though I was in no position to feel this way, it almost appeared that the state, knowing full well how despicable their investigations and presentations before the grand jury were, now began to back off. With the indictments secured, the likes of Reginald Jackson and Al Sharpton all but faded into the sunset. It soon became obvious the state was in no rush to prove beyond a reasonable doubt that Kenna and I were guilty of anything other than being sacrificial lambs!

Even the media coverage dulled, and aside from having to answer subpoenas concerning the civil trial, all was quiet in the media. With the exception of receiving a lot of stares and finger-pointing from strangers when I was in public venues, my life almost seemed to go back to normal.

In mid-February, I was forced to attend a video-conference call with the attorneys representing the state, the turnpike, the van's occupants, and the state police. *Talk about feeling out of place!* Each participant had to identify themselves on the record, and lastly, there was *me*! Because I was pro se, meaning I was representing myself, (Mr. Galantucci served more as an advisor than an attorney in the civil suits—thus saving me from hiring another lawyer that I could not afford), I had to appear alone during these proceedings. Our hope was that once the criminal trial was over, the state would settle out of court with the injured men so there was no need for me to hire a costly civil attorney—plus, I was now working in an office making less than half of my trooper-salary so I was barely staying afloat financially as it was.

As I sat alone in a large conference room inside the Bergen County Courtroom, I wondered how I found myself in the midst of a video—conference with the likes of Cochran, Scheck, and Nuefield. Once the video camera shied away from my face, I actually chuckled in disbelief as to what was going on. Here I was, actually introducing myself on a live video feed as John I. Hogan, pro se, to some of the most recognized and powerful attorneys in the country. This marked the first time I actually smiled (to myself, of course) in nearly two years! *From tiny Florence to video conferences with Johnny Cochran and Barry Scheck—this has to be fiction!*

While racial profiling remained a political football nationally, Mr. Galantucci and his partner, Phillip DeVencentes, were hard at work preparing our official "motion to dismiss" application for the shooting indictments. In April, the Newark *Star-Ledger*, who relentlessly pursued the allegations of institutionalized racism in the state police, reported that the "ten other troopers" who Whitman claimed would be indicted for having the same mistakes on their patrol charts as Kenna and me, were referred back to the NJSP's Internal Affairs Unit for "administrative sanctioning" as opposed to facing criminal charges. Had it not been for the *Star-Ledger's* relentless pursuit, I am certain this fact would have never been publicized.

Though they were identical in nature to me and Kenna's mistakes, when forced to address what the Star-Ledger had reported, Attorney General John Farmer claimed, "The troopers' mistakes reared no criminal intent" and remanded the cases back to the state police's Internal Affairs Unit for disciplinary action.

This broad announcement left two young troopers as the sole law-enforcement officers in the country ever indicted for administrative mistakes that were somehow twisted into criminal allegations paralleling racial profiling! Personally, I was delighted that no one else was to be charged mainly because the charges were bogus to begin with, and furthermore, it gave further proof of Whitman's and Verniero's vindictiveness. Additionally, it bolstered our claim that this was a deliberate case of selective prosecution.

On April 17, 2000, Mr. Galantucci filed our motion to dismiss and eloquently cited the abundant reasons why Judge Smithson should throw out the shooting indictments. Citing "prosecutorial misconduct," the lengthy brief detailed the state's ill-advised and distorted presentation before the grand jury. He also singled out numerous critical factors like, Gerrow loquaciously failing to inform members of the grand jury that Keshon Moore had tested positive for marijuana.

Ironically, two days after submitting our brief, we received a written subpoena from the Attorney General's Office, Division of Consumer Affairs. This subpoena advised the Trooper Hogan Legal Defense Fund Committee, which initiated from the *www.trooperhogan.com* website, that a formal investigation into our fundraising activities had been launched. *Can you believe this shit! By now, just about every branch of state government was attempting to screw me!*

If fathomable, the next morning marked yet another unbelievable twist in this phenomenal travesty. Mr. Galantucci called me to inquire if I had heard any rumors from fellow troopers regarding a UPS or Fed-Ex truck driver who supposedly got stopped on the Garden State Parkway and professed to the trooper that stopped him he witnessed the April 23 shooting. After answering him in the negative, as was his style, Mr. G was vague in regard to what this truck driver stated to police. Aside from telling me it was favorable to our defense, he insisted that I keep this very quiet because the longer the state hid favorable witnesses, the more explaining they would have to do. The important thing for us was to locate and identify this driver. Based on this new information, Mr. G led me to believe that our claim of prosecutorial misconduct against Prosecutor Gerrow was about to be bolstered tremendously. *Would the state really bury favorable witnesses? Just how bad were they gunning for me and why?*

Every time something positive occurred, it was quickly erased by new information or demands that only brought further anxiety and depression to my family and me. The day after learning the state was purposely withholding information critical to my defense; I received an official letter concerning the civil case. This letter insisted that I immediately turn over all personal financial documents from 1996 to present. These documents were to be forwarded to the plaintiff's attorneys. Talk about an eerie feeling! All the hard work, savings, deferred compensation, and investing I had done was about to go down the drain! My house, gym equipment, automobile, stocks—you name it—I had to provide info about it. The realization that my life, dreams, and goals were over immediately set in, and I dove deeper into depression. How I didn't end it all is still a deep, dark internal mystery to me; but I can only thank God, my parents, family and Mr. G for giving me the strength and courage to endure all this misery on a daily basis.

Three days later, Squad Six had a reunion of sorts and attended a police benefit dinner in New York City. Surprisingly, everyone from the old squad went, and it marked the first time in nearly two years that we were all together. In a gesture of support and sympathy, the guys rented a limo as a surprise for Kenna and me. After meeting at the Cheesequake Rest Area on the Garden State Parkway, we hopped in the limo and partook in some "Buszard specials." Our senior man Scott Busz fed us Stoli O (orange flavored vodka) on the rocks with a slice of orange the entire ride up and back. During the formal dinner, the crowd acknowledged my and Kenna's presence and even gave us a standing ovation when we were introduced.

It was rare—but nice—to see Jimmy out with the guys. Even rarer was the fact that Jimmy partook, like we all did, in multiple Stoli O's. At the end of the night, Squad Six hugged one another, gave Jimmy and me words of encouragement, and walked independently to our vehicles. Kenna and I however stopped to talk as the rest of our old squad departed. This would mark the first time in several months we had spoken to one other aside from our court appearances where only pleasantries were exchanged.

As we stood in the parking lot of the Garden State Parkway's Cheesequake Rest Area, both intoxicated, Jimmy Kenna informed me of things that transpired between him and his attorney, which nearly caused me to run in front of the Parkway traffic.

To this day, I am not certain if it was out of guilt or if the alcohol truly affected him. Possibly, he may have assumed that I knew from Mr. Galantucci, but the truth is, I had no idea and stood there, silenced and stunned.

Jimmy proceeded to confess to me that before the reenactment had taken place back in May, the state (Gerrow and Assistant Deputy Attorney General

Chuck Grinnell) asked him and Jack Arsenault to come to Trenton for discussions. He admitted to me that they offered him immunity from prosecution if he would testify against me. All they wanted Jimmy to say was that I fired into the van after it had come to a complete stop down in the culvert. In exchange for his testimony, Jimmy would have his criminal charges dismissed!

In his own words, Jimmy said he felt that the state didn't care if it was perjury, just as long as they got their conviction of attempted murder against me! Kenna added that following the reenactment, and after we were indicted, he and Jack again went back to Trenton at Gerrow's request. This time however, Gerrow and Grinnell stated that they no longer believed I fired that last shot but still wanted Jimmy to testify against me. As he was offered immunity a second time, the state wanted Kenna to profess that since I was the senior trooper, *I* stopped the van without justification and based it solely on the racial composition of the occupants. *What bastards! They lied to get the indictments, and now that their conspiracy is falling apart, they attack a different angle. Mr. G told me that Gerrow didn't like me from day one because of my arrest stats and aggressive patrol tactics, but when and where does it end?* I was in utter disbelief. All of my gut—feelings and premonitions that I was being set up and conspired against instantly came to fruition. Unfuckingbelievable!

Obviously and thankfully, Trooper James Kenna remained truthful and, in his own way, stood by my side when he could have lied and threw me under the bus to save his own ass. Though we are very different, I owe him forever because he could have very easily taken the state's offer, lied, and sent me to prison for up to forty years! Thank You—Trooper James Kenna—Badge no. 5170!

On May 18, I was back at the Bergen County Courthouse for another video-conference regarding the civil suit. It was an absolute joke—all these big-shot attorneys and *me*! Cochran was in Los Angeles, Nuefield in New York City, and Greenfeeder was somewhere up in north Jersey, as were the attorneys representing the turnpike and the state police. *I believe Scheck was there too but, because he is so short, I don't think the camera could find him!*

Hysterically, once again, I sat alone for several hours in this conference room as they spewed all this legal bullshit. Just as was the case in our initial conference, the TV split into four screens, and I could control whom I wanted to see. Whoever was speaking instantly popped up on one of the four screens. As I sat there, pondering my life experiences, I asked myself, *How in the hell did a little tiny Florence boy end up in this shit?* After introducing myself at the onset of the call, I again remained silent for the duration of this fiasco.

On June 1, the state submitted their rebuttal to our motion-to-dismiss brief. Though it was my ass on the line, I thought their refutation was very weak.

Knowing full well they screwed us, the state even admitted they scrutinized my and Jimmy's statements and, in essence, turned the grand jury into a credibility contest. To me, it was very evident the state put no effort into their brief. After reading it and comparing it to ours, even though it is supposedly the hardest thing to do in criminal-defense work, I believed wholeheartedly that Mr. G and Phil had done the impossible. As we prepared for the ruling before Judge Smithson, I felt his only choice was to dismiss the indictments. In reality, the state had no defense for their deliberate and misleading presentation of facts when securing our indictments for the shooting case.

On June 27, oral arguments on the dismissal motion were held before Judge Smithson. As usual, Mr. Galantucci was flawless in his approach, wording, and charismatic style. The judge hammered the state on their conduct during the "shooting" grand jury, and to add insult to the injury, a female deputy attorney general named Christine D'Elia humiliated herself and the entire state when concluding that our lives were never threatened. Judge Smithson interrupted and poignantly asked her, "Wouldn't a van hitting Trooper Hogan be considered a threat?" Completely embarrassed, she was stymied and didn't answer his question, which proved that I justified in firing my weapon. As a whole, it was a great moral victory and proved just how weak the state's case was. In a repulsive attempt to garner sympathy, state investigators drove up to New York and brought three of the van's occupants to the court. Judge Smithson decided to reserve announcing his decision on whether or not to dismiss the indictments until July 26.

Part VI

The Queen Gets Her Payback

On July 8, I awoke to an image—other than my own for a change—on the front page of every major newspaper in the tri-state area. *Today was going to be a great day!* Every publication in the state had on its front page a huge, blown-up photograph of Governor Christie Whitman **smiling** while patting down a young black male. Apparently, she pissed off the wrong person, and this photo, taken during the Camden City initiative back in 1996, surfaced as a result of her total abandonment of the state police.

This photo quickly became national news, and every news channel in the country was talking about it. Paybacks are a bitch! Just four days later, a collage of photos titled, "Payback" was on the front page of the *Trentonian* newspaper. It showed individual pictures of Kenna, Verniero, Whitman, and me surrounding the now infamous pat-down photo. In true Whitman fashion though, she refused to apologize for her actions in the photo. This refusal only further infuriated the Sharpton's and Jackson's of the world, who demanded she explain the photo (and smile) she donned when the camera captured her despicable act.

Governor Christie Whitman smiles as she mimics patting down an innocent man in the city of Camden.

Though he didn't tell me everything, Mr. G advised me that he had recently been sending the state a weekly letter requesting "any additional evidence." We knew they were grossly violating their oath of office as well as the rules of discovery by withholding the truck driver's name and statement. The longer Mr. G's letters went unanswered, the deeper the state dug itself into a hole.

The web of lies was finally starting to catch up to the same individuals who created this catastrophe! In response to our continued requests, in a bid to stall the inevitable, the prosecution requested a delay before Judge Smithson was to rule on the motion to dismiss. The judge granted the state more time, and the ruling was now rescheduled for August 2. The fact that the state was now withholding evidence crucial to my freedom only further shocked my family and I, proving there was no limit to their malice.

As wonderful as Mr. Galantucci was about always taking or returning my calls, I got a grapefruit-sized lump in my throat when *my* phone rang very early on the morning of *Saturday*, July 29, and he was on the other end. *What in the heck did I do that would warrant him to call me on a Saturday morning? Shit! This has got to be BAD!*

To the contrary, the monsignor's prayers had come to fulfillment! Mr. G called to notify me that the state finally admitted to Judge Smithson that they had (or intentionally withheld) *new evidence* that could result in, at the very least, the dismissal of my attempted-murder charge. Completely backtracking because of this revelation, the state once again petitioned Judge Smithson for more time to investigate the *new* witnesses' claim of having witnessed the shooting. The new date for our ruling on the motion to dismiss was now set for September 7, 2000.

By Tuesday, August 1, due to favorable media leaks for a change, the fact that the state was sandbagging witnesses beneficial to my defense became public. Gerrow, in a frugal and deceitful attempt to do damage control, stated the new witness just "recently" came forward, but he refused to expound on dates. Amazingly, now caught red-handed in their trail of lies, Mr. G called me three days later to advise that the Director of Criminal Justice, Kathryn Flicker called and asked if he would consider meeting with state officials. Almost laughably, the state now wanted to discuss a possible resolution to all pending criminal and civil matters with us!

After he agreed, it was decided that the meeting would be held in Trenton on August 22. Prior to that meeting, as was the case from the start, I reiterated to Mr. G that under no circumstance would I consider pleading guilty to any charges! *Imagine that, their bogus, multimillion-dollar investigation falls apart, leaving them with a bullshit case of selective prosecution, and now they want to attempt to work things out!*

On the morning after meeting with state officials, I drove up to Hackensack and met with Mr. G. It was learned that the state made no formal offers, and he in turn, informed them that I was firm in my decision to not plead guilty to anything. Their hope was that I would plead out, thus, allowing them off the hook, but that was not *ever* going to happen. To say the least, not a whole lot was accomplished in this meeting, and as a result of this possible resolution failing miserably, the state again asked for and received yet another postponement. The motion-to-dismiss ruling was now slated for Halloween Day, October 31, 2000. In announcing this new date, Judge Smithson sternly ruled there would be no further delays!

Behind the scenes, plea negotiations between the state and Mr. G. continued through September and October, but both Kenna and I stood fast, unwilling to give in. The state wanted us to plead guilty to two separate fourth-degree (very minor) charges. One charge would account for the shooting and the other for the falsifying indictments. Basically, the state needed to justify their investigations and wanted us to take the fall. I was advised that I could even pick the crimes in which to plead guilty to. How messed up is that?

As talks intensified, I received a formal letter from Mr. Galantucci's office, stating that the proposed plea-offer was in my best interest. I was risking my freedom, maybe ten to twenty years of freedom, but I just couldn't do it. The thought of letting my supporters down and permitting the state to get away with all the lies and bullshit that took place throughout this entire investigation was not even a consideration. My family, mainly my father and sister Mary Jane, supported my decision wholeheartedly. I had to stand up for what I believed in, even if it meant going to prison as an innocent man. Mr. G thought I was making a huge mistake, but he vowed to stand by me and continue fighting.

On the surface, compared to what I was charged with, it was almost a no-brainer that I should accept the plea-deal. I was too caught up in the principle of the matter, however. The rage and anger I felt at being "railroaded" left me feeling that I would rather go to prison as a scapegoat than give in to the ruthless, lying bastards that put me in this predicament. The state, realizing my unwillingness to cooperate, finally and unwillingly relinquished the discovery materials regarding the "new witness" they had kept concealed for so many months!

By the time Mr. G. reviewed this new discovery, he knew the state had both a legal and moral obligation to dismiss my attempted-murder charge. Not only did the physical evidence at the scene not support this charge, but the witness the state withheld detailed exactly where Jimmy and I were during the shooting, even when and where we dropped our magazines. Most importantly, this witness bolstered our claim that neither Kenna or me fired at the van as it rolled away from us, or it had come to a complete stop down in the drainage ditch. **Much to the chagrin of the state, this witness proved that the statements we willingly gave to investigators the night of this tragedy were, to the best of recollection given the circumstances, truthful, accurate and honest!**

We soon learned that the reason the state continually asked for more time was so they could hopefully find a way to discredit this individual. For months, the state pathetically tried to find weaknesses in this man's story and even gave him a polygraph test in hopes of discrediting him. *Why didn't they give favorable witnesses, like the oral surgeon, a polygraph?*

Had he not been directed and forced by Whitman and Verniero to indict us, Gerrow's sixteen month, "journey to the truth" could have been concluded in weeks. An unbiased and non-politicized investigation would have exposed what April 23 truly was: a tragic and horrifying accident that will forever haunt six decent human beings! Maybe the day will come when Gerrow will find it in his heart to openly and truthfully address what really took place behind closed doors at the AG's office. Personally, I won't hold my breath though!

On October 26, completely out of time and options, the state officially dismissed the attempted-murder charge against me solely as a result of failing to discredit the "new" witness. Area newspapers and reports besieged this new development and the state had no choice but to take it on the chin from everyone, especially the Black Minister's Council. The Council, like most, including Cochran and Sharpton who blasted the state upon the dismissal, couldn't understand how after sixteen months and several million dollars, a new witness came forward to clear me of this very grave and heinous criminal charge. In a press conference following the dismissal hearing, Gerrow put the best possible spin on his lies concerning the "new witness and information." While standing before the mass of reporters, cameras and microphones Gerrow had the audacity to laud his investigations' "thoroughness and fairness." The truth, however, was that he lied, conspired, and manipulated evidence to wrongfully charge me with attempted murder—a charge that carried a penalty of twenty fucking years in prison!

Even scarier for me, had Kenna taken their offer and testified on behalf of the state, I would be sitting in prison right now as a result of the state's politically motivated conspiracy to find me guilty of something that never even happened! *What if we never learned about the "new" witness? There's a good chance I could be sitting in prison right now for something I didn't even do. That is frightening!*

Finally, October 31, 2000, had come. No more delays, postponements, adjournments, or bullshit plea offers from the state. And hopefully no more surprise witnesses or unfavorable evidence was to be pulled from the states bag of fallacies! Today was the day. Though I was no longer an "attempted murderer," this day could prove once and for all that we truly were scapegoats.

Did Judge Smithson have the courage to truthfully rule on the motion, or was this just going to be another political whitewash? Mr. Galantucci felt as difficult and unlikely as it is to have an indictment dismissed; it was even more unlikely in this case due to all the pressure and media hype that surrounded it. Even though there was substantial evidence to quash them, no one around me, including my family, thought Judge Smithson would put his own career on the line and rule in our favor. Unfortunately, Mr. G couldn't make it due to an ongoing trial; so his partner Phil DeVenecetes ushered me, my family, and a large group of supporters into the jam-packed courtroom to hear Judge Smithson's verdict.

When Judge Smithson entered the courtroom, everyone rose to their feet. Once seated at his bench, we too sat. My heart was fluttering, and my stomach was in knots. Cameras clicked, and reporters observed my every movement. I sat between Phil and Jimmy's attorney, Jack Arsenault. Kenna sat on the far left-hand side of the old wooden defendant's table that we all shared.

Judge Smithson began the hearing by reading a summation of the case history up to this day. He read a "factual finding" statement and then gave the courtroom a detailed recapitulation of the shooting incident based on facts that were known to the court at this time. He referenced our official statements and talked about the sharp contrasts in everyone's recollection, further stating this occurrence is normal and even expected in a traumatic event. Halfway through the hearing, I still had no idea where Judge Smithson was going with his ruling. Truthfully, I wondered why he was reading all of this—as opposed to concentrating on the actual motion-to-dismiss brief we filed. My heart and optimism began to sink as each moment passed. In all honesty, I figured he was providing himself an out and was going to rule that since the events of our tragic incident were still so much in question, it was necessary for the case to proceed to trial, thus, allowing him off the hook by having a jury to decide our fate.

After the description of events was completed, the judge then went on to explain the legal issues involved with dismissing an indictment. He stated, **"Courts in New Jersey and elsewhere have said that dismissal is the most severe sanction a court can impose; it is to be used with the greatest caution and deliberation."** When he said this, I knew we were done. There was no way he was going to dismiss these indictments now!

I sagged down in my seat and mentally started preparing myself for a trial. The judge then addressed the prosecutor's rights and responsibilities in presenting a fair grand jury. Judge Smithson clearly stated that as long as there was "some evidence" of the offenses, then the indictment should stand. SHIT! *We're screwed!* The judge concluded this part by saying, "The prosecutor enjoys broad discretion in presenting a matter to the grand jury so that a presumption of validity attaches to these proceedings." Judge Smithson's final broad statement detailed the extreme mal-intentions a prosecutor must be guilty of for an indictment to be dismissed based on the finding of prosecutorial misconduct.

As I sat there listening halfheartedly, I figured our trial would be in six to nine months. I assumed by my next birthday, I would be incarcerated in some prison, hopefully, in solitary confinement so real criminals won't harass me upon finding out I was a police officer. In a panic, wild thoughts of fleeing the country set in. Where will I go? Can I get away with it? Who do I know that'll help me? I cannot go to prison especially for something that didn't even happen! The anxiety medication that I had been taking for the past year was in no way strong enough to handle the overwhelming sense of fear and panic that controlled me both mentally and physically at this point.

Barely listening and overcome with the apprehension of going to trial—then prison—Judge Smithson started rambling on about the function of a grand jury and the rights a defendant has. *Blah, blah, blah as far as I was concerned! Just get this over with and let me enjoy the last few months of freedom I'll ever have!* As I peered over at the prosecution table, I could see the pride and joy swelling in both Gerrow and Grinell's faces.

The judge then spoke of case law governing the presentation of evidence by the prosecutor, saying that it is up to the grand jury, not the prosecutor, to decide if the defendants were guilty of the allegations being heard. *Wow! What was that he just said? Where in the hell is the judge going with this?* I perked back to life and instantly sat upright in my hard wooden chair, now listening intently. A warm sensation overcame my body as my heart began racing again. The judge was now doing a complete 360-degree turn! I was confused, but I really liked what I was now hearing. The momentum was changing, but mentally, I continued to get lost in all the legal jargon being spewed by the judge. I really wasn't certain what or where Judge Smithson was going, but the playing field appeared to be leveling off.

Suddenly, the judge went on the offensive and verbally attacked the prosecution. >From out of nowhere, he began to berate Gerrow for turning the grand jury into a mini-trial, pitting our credibility (knowing full well we had already been accused of lying in the other indictments) against the van occupants' credibility. The state was then further chastised by Smithson for being "selective" in their description of case law governing the justification of deadly force by police officers.

During the grand jury proceedings Mr. Gerrow instructed the jurors that I had a "duty to retreat" when the van came at me in reverse. Absurdly, Gerrow misled the grand jurors into believing that cops are supposed to run the other way when a crime was being committed. The state was then reprimanded for purposely failing to introduce Kenna and me as uniformed police officers—authorized in using deadly force. Judge Smithson's tirade continued when he went-on to criticize the state for allowing the return of the first set of indictments to be made public. *Holy Shit! I was in shock!*

By this point, I looked over at Mr. Arsenault and whispered, "He is going to dismiss it!" Tears began to fill my eyes, and I couldn't sit still. My legs and hands were shaking; my palms started sweating profusely. I couldn't help but to break down and cry despite Arsenault's insistence that I remain poised. What I really wanted to do was tackle and kick the shit out of Grinnell and Gerrow for their actions, but of course, I couldn't. Choking back tears, I just couldn't wait to hug my family who were seated directly behind me in the first row of the courthouse.

Judge Smithson's outburst against the state continued, now blaming the Attorney General's Office for, "caving into powerful and intimidating forces." He added, "It means the motivation to allow the return of the falsification indictments at that time was considerably more a matter of political expediency than of concern for the substantive rights of defendants Hogan and Kenna." Astoundingly, Judge Smithson then complemented our attorneys for properly instructing us to not testify before the grand jury. In the same breath, he reprimanded the state for posturing, by even inviting us to testify—two months after our first indictment was announced. The hearing ended with Judge Smithson saying, **"Members of society engaged in law enforcement deserve no less protection from the criminal-justice system then that which is afforded to other citizens. In this case, that protection deserves the most severe sanction, a sanction based on the clearest and plainest of grounds—a dismissal of the indictment in its entirety."**

As Judge Smithson's gavel sounded, the courtroom exploded with disbelief. Hugs, kisses, tears, and emotions of incredible joy overran my body. As much as I didn't want to because of the cameras, I couldn't help but cry—blatantly and openly—as I hugged my mother, father and entire family. Once outside, the media coverage was so intense that I got dizzy from the microphones, cameras, reporters and photographers that swarmed me. My only regret was to not have Mr. Galantucci present.

Some truth finally!

Deputy Attorney General Charles Grinnell and James Gerrow plot their next course of action as Judge Smithson dismisses the indictments, citing prosecutorial misconduct.

Immediately following the dismissal, my family and friends all went to C. Reeds Place for drinks. As we departed Trenton for C. Reeds, I spoke to Mr. G on the telephone and he advised me to come up to his office for a press conference at 6:00 PM. After a few quick drinks, my family was escorted up the turnpike by a trooper, and the press conference took place in the foyer of Mr. G's Hackensack office. It was an overwhelming, exhausting, and unbelievable day to say the least.

Sadly, by the time we returned home, news had shifted from our victory to Governor Whitman, who was already on TV, demanding an expedited and immediate appeal to Judge Smithson's ruling. When asked about her involvement in our case during the press conference, the ever-crafty Mr. G whimsically stated, "Why is the governor, who continually says that politics aren't being played in the case, even commenting on this matter?"

One of several "jokes" that surfaced regarding the state's prosecution of James Kenna and me.

Part VII

A Little Help from the Feds . . .

The following day, instead of reading all the good new concerning our dismissal, the governor and Reginald Jackson dominated the headlines. In demanding the charges be reinstated, the governor went a step further. Backed by Attorney General John Farmer, they announced they would now seek federal assistance in this case and asked the federal government to take over the investigation. *Son of a bitch! When does it end?*

At Whitman's request, the Feds immediately began pursuing a civil-rights case against Kenna and me. Even worse, we soon learned that Attorney General Farmer's close friend, Robert Cleary, was tabbed to oversee the investigation against us! Furthermore, the Black Minister's Council demanded and was granted a meeting on November 15 with the Federal Civil Rights Division in Washington DC. *Talk about three strikes!*

Through news reports, I learned the Council was assured that a fair and impartial investigation would take place, and if evidence was found, Trooper Kenna and I would be indicted yet again. This time, however, it would be for federal civil-rights violations. *Whatever happened to my rights?* In retrospect, Judge Smithson's favorable ruling only further buried us in the legal system. I immediately realized I would never get out of this incredulous predicament. I was going to have to be the fall guy for these crooked, spineless, and ruthless bastards no matter what!

Just two weeks after Judge Smithson's ruling, a friend forwarded an e-mail to me that was sent throughout the Attorney General's Office by Director Flicker. The e-mail stated that her department just received word that the appellate division granted the governor's request for an immediate appeal. The note assured everyone of an early Christmas present when our indictments are reinstated! Unfreakingbelievable! Under normal circumstances, an appeal takes up to two years, but ours somehow was miraculously placed at the front of the pile! Despite saying politics were not involved, only the governor had this kind of power!

We did receive some good news on this day, though. Referring to a report known as the Troop D audit, we learned that of the 162 troopers assigned to the Turnpike, 159 of them had similar mistakes as Kenna and me on their patrol charts. Of course, during this entire debacle we remained the only ones ever indicted or even sanctioned for these administrative mistakes but now, we finally had hard evidence proving the "falsifying records" indictments were a blatant case of selective prosecution—and it was all released to the general public. This report substantiated a fact that had already become blatantly obvious: We were SCAPEGOATS!

In the weeks that followed, the momentum of the entire profiling controversy turned back toward newly appointed New Jersey Supreme Court Justice Peter Verniero. With the pending release of thousands of *dated* documents chronicling years of racial-profiling complaints, Verniero was now on the hot seat. Accusations that he failed to thwart racial profiling when he was the attorney general surfaced. Better yet, with Kenna and me already completely buried and indicted for everything under the sun, he had no one to deflect the criticism to like he had methodically done up to this point.

Having denied any knowledge of racial profiling until it *"crystallized"* in his mind *after the turnpike shooting*, Verniero was now caught in a swatch of deep, dark lies. Knowing full well these dated documents bore his name and signature, it became very evident that Verniero lied during his confirmation hearing when questioned by senators on his knowledge of the entire profiling controversy.

By Thanksgiving, the burden on Attorney General Farmer to release the massive array of documents concerning racial profiling grew unbearable. Democratic legislatures, minority clergymen, and citizens across the state demanded he turn over any document regarding racial profiling. On November 27, without further hesitation, Attorney General John Farmer ultimately did open the floodgates. At a public press conference that permitted the media to read through the volumes of materials, Farmer released over one hundred thousand documents relating specifically to racial profiling in the State of New Jersey and more specifically, the New Jersey State Police.

To everyone's dismay, each dated memo came directly from the Attorney General's office and plummeted Justice Verniero, who laughably claimed he never even heard of racial profiling until **after** the April 23, 1998 shooting right into the firestorm.

Dating back as far as the 1980s, these memos had been compiled and passed on by the numerous attorney generals who held that office prior to Verniero. Despite the obvious, Verniero had the audacity to emphatically deny any knowledge of these documents despite a majority of them being signed, initialed or orchestrated directly by him.

In a transparent attempt to do damage control, Governor Whitman played spin doctor; commending Verniero for being the first attorney general to address the issue of racial profiling. In defense of her long-time crony, Whitman claimed that Verniero's critics were using him as a scapegoat and political pawn! *The impudence of this woman is sickening!*

Despite her support, actions regarding possibly impeaching Justice Verniero instantly surfaced as it was now clear to everyone that he deliberately lied to senators while under oath during his confirmation hearing. In the midst of this, oral arguments regarding the states desire to re-indict Kenna and me on the shooting charges took place at the Bergen County Courthouse. The three-judge panel, allegedly handpicked by Governor Whitman herself, heard verbal arguments from both sides but declined to issue a verdict.

Ironically, with the appellate decision being held over our head, the state surprisingly initiated plea negotiations with our attorneys again. In essence, they had us by the balls and probably assumed we would finally cave in to their demands. After all, the deck was never so stacked against us. In addition to the pending appeal by handpicked judges, a second trial on the falsification indictments awaited us; and once these trials were adjudicated, if we were to somehow win them—the state all but had a guarantee from their friends within the Federal government to indict us on civil-rights violations. *Where do I sign?*

The distinction of being the most highly prosecuted member of the NJSP got old very quickly!

The states latest resolution attempt supposedly came to fruition because newly elected Republican president, George W. Bush was going to offer his political crony—Governor Christy Whitman—a cabinet position. As these reports surfaced, the likes of Reverend Sharpton, Reverend Jackson, and their constituents immediately threatened to block her appointment until the firestorm over racial profiling subsided. Presumably, if we plead guilty, the controversy would fizzle, allowing the Queen to then move forward, leaving New Jersey as quickly as possible to work for President Bush.

Once again, however, both Kenna and I declined to accept any plea offers. I must admit though, I was getting worn down. I was wavering like never before. Additionally, I was scared to death regarding what I heard about the federal criminal system and how it worked. More importantly, just what were civil-rights violations and what if race enters the trial? Did I really want to face the possibility of enduring three separate trials? I was beginning to break down like never before!

As the year 2000 ended, this debacle now entered its fourth calendar year. The state's latest proposal assured us no jail time or excessive fines in exchange for our guilty pleas. My internal fortitude remained the same. I was still more willing to go to prison than give into Whitman, Verniero and Gerrow's multiple lies and bullshit criminal charges.

Despite not having spoken in months, I learned from Mr. G that Jimmy Kenna felt the same way as I did. Though I am certain he too had to be weakening, neither of us was quite ready to throw in the towel.

On January 2, 2001, through our attorneys, Kenna and I again formally turned down the state's offer in these latest plea negotiations. Amazingly, without warning, just two days later, we learned that the Whitman-selected appeals court overturned Judge Smithson and reinstated our indictments in the shooting case. *What a vindictive BITCH!* As usual, we asked the STFA to make a statement on our behalf, but contrary to their promise to be more vocal, they failed to publicly denounce this occurrence and instead just stated, "It's just too political!"

Three weeks after overturning Judge Smithson's decision to dismiss our indictments, we were back in court once again and the charges were officially reinstated. Before setting a trial date, in yet another bizarre twist, an annoyed and bitter Judge Smithson completely recused himself from our case. Before doing so, however, he lashed out at the judges who reversed his ruling. This marked the first time since being appointed to the superior court that Judge

Smithson had been overruled by the appellate division, and he made it perfectly clear that he was seething mad. During our hearing, Judge Smithson openly accused the appellate division of questioning his integrity and admitted that his ability to fairly and impartially hear the remainder of our case was damaged as a result of their actions in rebuking his ruling. Before storming off the bench, he remanded the case to Judge Delahey, and now, after almost three years, we were forced to start over with a new judge.

As you can only imagine, for the first time, I really started to seriously consider pleading guilty—just to end this true-life soap-opera. It was becoming laughable! I was mentally exhausted, as was my family—as we also dealt with the declining health of my father. Where and when was it going to end, and what am I going to gain by fighting? Maybe it was time to just give up!

In light of these latest developments, I turned to my best friend—Mr. Galantucci.—and asked him to see if the state's offer still stood. I needed out! I was ready to take the deal! I could no longer stand the idiotic and endless charade that my life had turned into. I was waving my white flag in defeat. I just wanted a way out without going to prison for something that never even happened or for making stupid administrative mistakes that nearly every other trooper had also innocently made.

At my request, Mr. Galantucci met with Gerrow and his henchmen on the twenty-fourth of January. I learned that the offer still stood, but now the state insisted I read a prepared statement. Even more pressing, however, was obtaining assurance from the federal government to not prosecute me if I agreed to plead guilty to the state's charges. The very next day, Whitman drove another nail into our guilty label, agreeing to a civil settlement of 12.9 million dollars with the van's occupants. Once again, for the first time ever, a civil case was resolved before a criminal case. Cochran and his entourage took what was rumored to be the largest police settlement ever in the State of New Jersey and were never to be heard from again in regards to this case.

Comically, this settlement served as her last act as the governor of New Jersey. Whitman abruptly left New Jersey, accepting President Bush's appointment to be the director of the Environmental Protection Agency. Many speculated that she couldn't get out of New Jersey fast enough. Instead of fighting her appointment as promised, Reverend Jackson mysteriously had a change of heart and applauded it. He stated that since she would now have President Bush's ear, she could encourage him to make racial profiling a top priority within his administration. Obviously, the settlement money was spread across the desks of many individuals!

Splitting Headlines

State settles 'pike-shoot case for $13 million

Trooper lawyers: Fair trial impossible

As Cochran, Reverend Al Sharpton, and the van's occupants announce their multimillion-dollar settlement, it became even more evident that obtaining a fair trial would be impossible.

Though I assumed it would just fade away, state senators continued to push for Verniero to come clean regarding his knowledge and awareness of the racial-profiling issue. At the request of his political enemies, a special investigation into Verniero's actions while the attorney general was launched by a specially appointed Senate Judiciary Panel. Also, in early February, as a result of the volumes of documents released, Attorney General John Farmer dismissed seventy-seven more criminal cases across the state where "profiling" against the arresting trooper was alleged by the respective defense attorney. Through it all though, Kenna and I remained the only troopers indicted or even disciplined for allegations of racial profiling. With Verniero in his own world of hell and Whitman removed from the state, all future court dates for Jimmy and me were now mysteriously suspended. At the state's request, our attorneys were hard at work trying to secure the best possible plea deal for us—a fact that I was very happy about and strongly supported. I was drained and on the brink of a mental breakdown!

Nevertheless, by March 1, all talks regarding a possible plea deal ceased. The state's demands were incorrigible and I refused to accept their despicable offers. I would have jumped at anything decent—but, we were not even on the same page when discussing a mutual resolution.

Left with no other options, Judge Delahey was notified that no plea agreements were to take place and he set a trial date for September 4, 2001. In doing so, and without consulting anyone, Delahey paralyzed us when deciding the "falsifications" case should be heard first—simply because it was older. This was a complete setback for us because for the past two years, Mr. G. and his staff were hard at work preparing for the shooting case! Furthermore, in light of the state being forced to dismiss the attempted-murder charge once all their lies caught up with them, we felt the state had no case against me whatsoever. Aside from the several thousand dollars in legal and expert-witness fees that accompanied it, I welcomed the shooting trial. Privately though, I knew finding an impartial and unprejudiced jury was all but impossible given the years and volumes of negative press this case garnered.

On March 6, a ninety-one-page report was released to the public. It detailed the investigation that surrounded the Senate judiciary's probe into racial profiling. Focusing in on Verniero, the report concluded he purposely mislead senators during his confirmation hearing and accused him of posturing to politics when indicting Kenna and me on the "falsifying" charges. As a result of this investigation, open-forum hearings were then scheduled. Several high ranking officials from the Attorney Generals Office as well as the NJSP were subpoenaed to testify regarding the history of complaints regarding racial profiling. Despite exhaustively fighting to be excused from testifying, Verniero was subpoenaed and slated to be the final witness.

As this was transpiring, behind the scenes, Mr. G filed a petition to the New Jersey Supreme Court in hopes they would hear our case and ultimately overturn the appellate divisions' ruling in the shooting case. After all, this was the biggest and most controversial case in recent state history—how could the y NOT hear our case right?

Pathetically, just one week after filing our petition with New Jersey's highest court, they supposedly voted and rejected our request. Imagine that—what could arguably be the most sensitive case in the history of New Jersey regarding law enforcement and the state's highest court refused to even look into it! Sounds bizarre to me, but considering that two-thirds of this court was comprised of Whitman-appointees, including former attorney generals Verniero and Deborah Poritz, we could only assume that politics once again reared its ugly head and controlled the decision makers thought process in this ruling.

On March 15, Verniero's former first-assistant Paul Zoubek testified before the Senate Judiciary Committee investigating Verniero. When questioned about the timing of my and Kenna's indictments, Zoubek did not stand by his former boss. Instead, Zoubek professed he informed Verniero that it was improper to announce the falsification indictments against Kenna and me back in February 1999 because it would affect the outcome of the shooting grand jury. He further stated that Verniero blatantly disregarded his advice and demanded they move forward with announcing the falsifications indictments to appease the outcry from the minority community. Zoubek even agreed with the committee when asked if this was done to help Verniero advance his appointment to the supreme court. *Wow, this Zoubeck guy is all right! In listening to him, it almost sounded as if he felt bad for Kenna and me.*

One by one, all of Verniero's former deputies testified to these same facts. All indications showed that it was just a matter of time before impeachment hearings to remove Verniero from the bench would initiate. Even his predecessor, Deborah Poritz, testified that she specifically advised Verniero of the numerous accusations regarding NJSP profiling complaints. Upon replacing her as the attorney general, Poritz claimed to have told Verniero he should make accusations regarding racial profiling in the NJSP a top priority. *So, when exactly did racial profiling crystallize in your mind Peter—you heartless coward?*

As these hearings continued, a director from the United States Department of Justice flew to Newark and agreed to secretly meet with Mr. G and Jack Arsenault concerning our plea negotiations. Though the meeting was positive, Mr. G informed me that the Feds declined to back off their pursuit of civil-rights violations against Kenna and me. Without a guarantee from the Feds, it was senseless for us to plead guilty to the state charges. In other news, two East Orange police officers shot and wounded two unarmed black teens sitting in a parked vehicle. Ironically, it was classified as an "accident" and never made it to the front page of the newspapers!

On March 28, judgment day for the former attorney general had finally come and Peter Verniero was the last witness called to testify before the Senate Judiciary Committee. Based on his thirteen hours of testimony, I was surprised that he remembered his name or how he drove to Trenton on this day. "I don't recall" was Verniero's response on more than *three hundred* occasions while facing direct questioning by the committee. What he did admit to, however, was that our indictments were driven by politics and that he instantly terminated the Troop D audit, which proved that hundreds of troopers had identical mistakes as Kenna and me, the day *after* we were indicted. That was good enough for me! In light of Verniero's testimony, I was certain the state would now be forced to dismiss the remaining charges against both Kenna and me. For Christ sake, he just admitted that the charges we faced were completely driven by politics! At the conclusion of his marathon testimony, Committee Chairman, Senator William Gormley, verbally lambasted Verniero and accused him of "purposely misleading and being untruthful" with the committee.

Verniero's actions finally called in to question!

While Peter Verniero appeared cool and calm before testifying, this comic clearly identified his abysmal performance before the Senate Judiciary Committee—lies, lies, lies!

Over the course of the next few weeks, demands for Verniero to resign or be impeached dominated the news. On April 5, acting governor Donald DiFrancesco, in a live news conference, publicly accused Verniero of lying and asked for his immediate resignation from the New Jersey Supreme Court. Verniero, through his attorney, bitterly rejected the call for his resignation and vowed to fight any attempt to remove him from the bench.

By the end of April, it became obvious that the Feds were unwilling to go along with our plea deal. Because of this, we, in turn, advised the state that we would not settle. Four long, tumultuous years had now passed and no one knew what in the hell was going on. To put it mildly, there was no end in sight—we were now further from a resolution then we were two years previous.

As for Verniero, every person in the Senate and Assembly called for his resignation except for one: Republican Jack Collins. As fate would have it, as the head of the Assembly, Mr. Collins was the only person who could draw up impeachment proceedings, and he refused to do this to his longtime political ally. As a result of this, it appeared that Verniero was safe for the time being. Is that incredible or what? Every person in the state, politician or not, demanded that Verniero resign, but yet, despite his lies and blatant misconduct, he not only retained his job but was promoted to a better-paying and more prestigious position! To this day, when reflecting over all the bizarre happenings, that is still the one thing that troubles me most! Maybe I would have been better off being a crooked cop? When considering some of societies latest blunders, including OJ, Gary Condit, President Clinton—maybe I should have just stolen the drugs and money I confiscated. Foolishly, I actually thought I was making a positive difference.

Once Collins rescued Verniero, the issue of his impeachment all but died, as did every attempt to resolve our criminal cases. Judicially speaking, nothing but further delays and postponements took place as my life and future hanged in the balance. *Did anyone really care about Kenna and me? For everyone else, it was their job. At the end of the day—they went home. But for us—it was 24 / 7—their actions, or lack of, controlled our lives, our families, our personalities and our futures and I bet none of them cared in the least bit.*

From my perspective, it was obvious that the state did not want to try these cases, and in return, I wanted no part of possibly losing a trial that was going to be based on race as opposed to the facts of the case. For the next few months, my attorney and the state went round and round, attempting to hammer out a deal that would appease everyone, but no progress was made. Years, yes—three entire years—had now passed since the incident occurred, and pathetically, we were no closer to a resolution than when the tragedy first happened. Bitterness, stress, and animosity were the only things that grew between the state and us and I was certain this travesty would never be resolved.

With the exception of being invited to be the "Grand Marshal" of a controversial white-supremacy parade that was being held in Morristown, New Jersey, on July 4, 2001, the summer months were uneventful. Mr. G even had to forward a press release to the media denouncing any alleged involvement with this KKK-like group once it was reported in the newspapers. *Just how out of control has this thing gotten?* The parade was "pro-profiling" and portrayed Kenna and me as heroes for our actions on April 23. *People are NUTS!*

By the end of July, even the perennial optimistic and upbeat personality of Mr. Galantucci had become frustrated and utterly annoyed at the lack of progress that was being made. Behind close doors, the state willingly admitted that this entire charade was a political fuckup in plain English (especially now that Whitman and Verniero had abandoned them). Ultimately, though, the state needed someone to blame for the years of profiling allegations and the hysteria our incident created. Mr. G informed me that even though they didn't agree in principle with the premise of it, somehow, and some way, Kenna and I had to be the fall guys. They knew our charges were selective and held no weight, but the state vehemently refused to drop the charges. Facing two long drawn-out and costly trials with the state, only to have the Feds waiting in the background to indict us, Mr. G and I were convinced that we were even further from a resolution than anyone in the general population could have deemed possible. What a freaking disaster—and comically, the assholes who created this entire mess are no where to be found—both now making more money and holding more prestigious jobs! *Life truly is a bitch!*

On the last day of July, in what was thought to be a last-ditch attempt to hopefully resolve our multiple criminal charges, I agreed to a private "debriefing" with Gerrow and state investigators. Ironically, at the same time, the state was also secretly asking the Feds to back off from prosecuting Kenna and me in hopes that our plea agreement would appease every branch of government investigating allegations of racial profiling. Having just returned from a family vacation in Cancun, I learned that Kenna was debriefed a few days prior to me. At this point in time, I really didn't care what they asked Kenna or how he responded to their questions in this latest, surreal development. Personally, I had nothing to hide and actually looked forward to facing my accusers who by now had all but destroyed my life, reputation and credibility. My goal was to be truthful; answer any questions these hypocrites asked; and hopefully, finally be able to put this nightmare behind my family and me. Even to a very experienced attorney like Mr. G, with criminal charges pending, this "debriefing"—like everything else in this debacle—was a first and completely unheard of. Yet out of sheer desperation, we agreed to this interview and only imagined how the state would somehow end up using it against us.

For nearly four straight hours on July 31, 2001, I was interviewed and questioned about the events of April 23 as well as my entire career as a New Jersey state trooper. Seated in a conference room at the Hughes Justice Complex, I was interrogated by Gerrow, Grinnell, and other investigators from the state.

Addressing everything from my training in the academy to what transpired (off duty) at Trooper Emer's wedding, these knuckleheads scribbled endlessly on their legal pads as I explicitly depicted my vast experiences as a general road-duty trooper. Focusing mainly on patrol practices and the April 23 shooting, I calmly and confidently divulged my work ethic, how and why I made so many arrests, and what specifically I looked for when on patrol. What I did refuse to answer, however, was any question relating to a trooper's activity **other than myself**! Admirably, as did Trooper Kenna, we refused to discuss names, patterns, or activities relating to other troopers or supervisors with whom we worked in the past. We were willing to take the fall—and through our attorneys—we both first agreed not to bring any other member from the NJSP down with us. If only our Union had been as strong, we probably would have never been in this position!

Admittedly, at times during this grilling—and throughout the tumultuous years since being sacrificed as a political pawn—I felt like bringing down the entire state police like these interrogators desperately tried to get me to do. There were moments when I wanted so badly to spew certain names of hard-core troopers and superiors alike whom I felt were ultimately responsible for all the negative criticism bestowed on the NJSP and trust me, it extends way beyond all the lawsuits, claims of racial profiling, bigotry, defamation, nepotism, claims of racism within the ranks etc. Names such as—(Don't worry guys—you know who you are—and be assured your names are safely tucked away in memory! Enjoy your pensions and those large new homes you all built—I just hope each room is mirror-less because spineless pricks like yourselves should never be permitted to look in the mirror!)

As we quickly learned, the underlying goal of this "debriefing" was for the state to acquire enough information regarding the mindset of a trooper and learn the inner workings of the state police. They then hoped to present their findings to the Feds, thus, proving that the numerous abrupt and dramatic policy changes implemented over the past few years were adequate. If accepted by the Feds, the underlying hope was they would then have a change of heart and not be so dead-set on seeking further criminal charges against me, Kenna, or any other trooper for that matter. All of this was bizarre, unethical, risky, and absurd; but it had become the norm in this case!

In mid-August, I learned that Gerrow and Attorney General John Farmer went down to DC in an attempt to again try and convince the Feds to back off and promise not to indict Kenna and me if we plead guilty to the state's charges. Obviously, our "debriefings" failed, and in fact, it was rumored that because of our refusal to acknowledge other troopers, the Feds were going to launch their own full-scale investigation into racial-profiling as a results of the "thousands" of trooper mistakes uncovered during Verniero's Troop D audit. Way to go, Peter—now you fucked over every trooper assigned to the Turnpike!

As fate would have it, Gerrow and Farmer returned from DC without securing a deal or garnering assurance from the Feds that they would not prosecute Kenna and me. Instead, it was rumored that the Federal Government—who in previous years instructed troopers on profiling techniques—were now reportedly preparing to initiate a massive investigation that could have far-reaching implications within the state police. Before I knew it, the fall of 2001 was upon us. Aside from status conferences, trials, bizarre inquisitions and a pending federal indictment, a new Philadelphia Eagles football season was all I had to look forward to. In my heart and mind, I was certain this would be the last year I would watch football as a free man! *Would football games be televised in my prison?*

Part VIII

Divine Intervention (?)

As the autumn leaves changed colors and fell from the trees, the issue of racial profiling remained a highly explosive issue nationally. Though they were infamous for training, practicing, and establishing criminal profiles, I learned from friends assigned to Troop D that the Feds were hard at work compiling paperwork in preparation to indict Kenna; me; and, possibly, other troopers as the first law-enforcement officers in the country for crimes consistent with racial profiling. Using the Verniero ordered "Troop D Audit" as their basis and backbone for their investigation, no one knew just how far-reaching the scope would go. Rumor had it there were tons of scared troopers, but the mere thought of the Feds conducting this type of inquiry appeared to be the epitome of hypocrisy.

Just days after this latest witch-hunt was initiated, the world as we knew it forever changed, as did society's view on this volatile topic. As I exited my Mount Laurel residence for a work-related appointment in Philadelphia, my phone rang. It was Ashley barely audible and crying. Hysterically, she advised me that a plane had just crashed into the World Trade Center. Like most, I assumed it was just a tragic accident. By the time I got into my car and headed for Philadelphia, a news radio report announced that a second plane had just crashed into the adjacent tower. Then the third plane—targeting the Pentagon—struck. Like everyone around the world, I got an eerie and uneasy feeling in the pit of my stomach. Terrorism hit home—right here in the United States!

As I crossed the Walt Whitman Bridge, I wondered if Philadelphia was the next target. Ironically, as this calamity unfolded, a two-day symposium was taking place between lawmakers and law-enforcement officials in Atlantic City, New Jersey. The symposium's topic was how to end the practice of racial profiling. As news of the national tragedy broke, the summit ended abruptly and never reconvened. The world's view on the practice of profiling would never be the same!

In the days following the greatest national tragedy in history, the word "profiling" again took center stage. Most people now had a different opinion of this suddenly "needed and accepted" law-enforcement practice. By mid-September, most of my former colleagues were either positioned on dismounted posts at the tunnels leading into New York City, the Newark Airport, or some other main corridor, "profiling" Arab and Middle Eastern-looking males. In conversations, they hesitantly admitted to me they were searching more cars and trucks without probable cause than any five thousand troopers could ever do on the Turnpike. Suddenly, profiling and conducting undocumented searches was not only accepted but encouraged. From my research, I found only one reporter who addressed this drastic swing in the "political correctness" of racial profiling (excerpts from Newark *Star-Ledger* article).

Racial profiling Returns to Fore

On the morning of Sept. 11, New Jersey law enforcement officials and lawmakers were gathered in a conference room in Atlantic City, praising the great strides made in the fight to end racial profiling. Then the terrible news arrived shortly after 9 a.m.: Terrorists had crashed hijacked planes into the World Trade Center's Twin Towers and the Pentagon. A visibly shaken Attorney General John Farmer Jr. and State Police Superintendent Col. Carson Dunbar hurried out of the room. The two-day symposium on racial profiling ended abruptly—and with it the way New Jersey and America have talked about racial profiling for the last 10 years. Some say a certain level of profiling should be tolerated—particularly in airports.

"It would be a dereliction of duty to the American public to forget the fact that the people who committed these terrible crimes all spoke Arabic to each other," Abrams said. "At the same time.... we don't want to be in a position where we're pulling every Arab-American out of line for detailed strip-searches. At the same time, we have to protect ourselves." This is how the new debate is framed.

"It seems to me, being questioned by the police is a relatively minor inconvenience compared to what over 5,000 people experienced on Sept. 11, what their families are experiencing and what our economy will experience," said Heather MacDonald, a fellow at the Manhattan Institute and outspoken critic of those who accused the police of racial profiling. MacDonald said that scrutinizing Arabs more closely is not racial profiling if law enforcement agents are taking other factors into consideration. "The chance a 60-year-old Euro-American mother is a terrorist is virtually zero," she said. "What we do know about these (terrorist) cells is that they are tightly controlled, only deal with people extremely familiar, and I'd be willing to bet the membership is 100 percent Muslim and Arab."

Yet since the attack, Jahshan said, Arab-Americans across the nation have been victimized by vigilante attacks, and others have been hauled in for questioning by federal agents.

"It is more ethnic profiling than racial profiling," said Sohail Mohammed, a Clifton immigration attorney. "This tragedy has too many victims, besides the injured and the dead. Immigrants, particularly Arab-Americans."

Farmer, who has been to the devastated site of the World Trade Center several times in the last week, said there is no doubt that the events of Sept. 11 have changed the debate over racial profiling.

Forgotten in this lengthy article was the fact that two lone New Jersey troopers remained as the only law-enforcement officers ever indicted for alleged acts of racial profiling. As could be imagined, the Feds' concentration and interest in prosecuting Kenna and me vaporized immediately following the unforgettable events of September 11. It can only be assumed that the same FBI agents assigned to the Cranbury Barracks that were rifling through our paperwork in the days prior to 9/11 were instantly reassigned to "profiling" duties like most of the troopers I remained in close contact with. Sadly, unlike the state of New Jersey, at least the Feds realized the hypocrisy in attempting to prosecute Kenna and me.

On October 7, American troops began bombing the Taliban, and closer to home, we were hit with our own bombshell. My family learned that our father was diagnosed with inoperable lung cancer and required immediate chemotherapy and radiation treatments. Due to his previous heart problems though, the doctors refused to radiate his left lung due to its closeness to the heart. By late October, my father's chemo treatments had begun, and now, with the Feds in hot pursuit of true criminals, plea negotiations between the state and our attorneys resumed.

To end the Feds overall involvement in our case, it was now required that I resubmit to yet another secretive, closed-door debriefing. This time, however, it would be with a federal prosecutor and FBI agents. *When does it end?* Before agreeing, the one constant variable was that Kenna and I *again* vowed not to identify other troopers or supervisors in our debriefings or implicate or accuse any other trooper of wrongdoing.

Unknown to everyone, especially the public at large, on October 30, 2001, I drove to the US Federal Courthouse in Newark, New Jersey where I met Mr. Galantucci. Together, we entered and were directed to a plush conference room occupied by two agents and a federal prosecutor from Washington DC. After formally advising us that he was sent to New Jersey personally by President Bush and U.S. Attorney General John Ashcroft, I spent the next three hours being questioned by this prosecutor. With each break in questioning, I pondered; *Did President Bush and John Ashcroft really know me by name? Had this debacle gotten that big? Apparently so! Remember, if you want a politician to act, you had to garner public attention. Who better to do this than Cochran, Sharpton, and Jackson? Wow! How can this happen to a non-assuming Florence kid that despised politics?*

Similar to the state's debriefing, this interview addressed trooper training; barracks life; patrol tactics; and, of course, allegations of racial profiling in the NJSP. Though no guarantees were made (because he stated Bush and Ashcroft were ultimately the ones to decide), we hoped this interview wound conclude the federal investigation and, in turn, ensure that the Civil Rights Division would not pursue unjustified charges against Kenna and me, as the minority community had demanded after Judge Smithson's dismissal.

Deceitfully, as this interview was taking place, these same guys knew as well as I did that their colleagues worldwide were now profiling Arabs. In a bizarre twist of fate, the FBI now had their own problems with the ACLU and Muslim community for allegations of illegally targeting Arabic citizens at airports and other high-profile venues across the country. *A twisted mess and I was somehow stuck dead-center!*

Nearly three weeks following the federal debriefing, I received a call from Mr. G. He stated that we received official notification that the Feds agreed not to prosecute. Now, it was just a matter of how the state would proceed and, more importantly, when would this abysmal prosecution be completed. In the interim, I heard nothing but knew Mr. G was attempting to secure the best deal possible. Truthfully, I was emotionless; completely drained of any willpower. I didn't care what it was going to take! I just needed to get it over with. I had no fight left!

As November came to an end, I learned the state was just waiting for the opportune time to announce that our deal was completed. Though I didn't even know the details of the agreement, I was informed that the state wanted to keep a lid on our deal in hopes of avoiding any backlash from the likes of Reverend Jackson. As it leaked however, Reverend Jackson broadly announced the minority community would be highly critical of a plea agreement and demanded that Kenna and I go to trial.

For the next several days, lawyers on both sides went back and forth—arguing over what should be said in court and by whom. Foolishly, Gerrow insisted Kenna and I read prepared statements that he personally devised based on the information obtained through the investigation and our "debriefings".

Designed specifically to publicly justify his lengthy, costly, and slanted investigations, I refused to accept several proposed drafts. Not that I would ever feel sorry for him, but with Whitman in DC and Verniero on the supreme court, Gerrow was left to be the jerk-off holding a bag of shit for those assholes. Ultimately though, with our careers and reputations forever ruined, it was Kenna and me who were sacrificed by those dishonest, manipulative, greedy, backstabbing scumbags!

By Christmas, the deal was all but finalized. All that remained pending were signed papers from the federal government confirming they would not seek indictments once our guilty pleas were entered. Just as everyone had hoped, news of the deal remained quiet, and a new year was upon us.

Unbelievably, this catastrophe entered its fifth calendar year as 2002 dawned. Now thirty-two years old and totally unhappy at my current job, I had no idea what the future had in store for me. Just for being in the wrong place at the wrong time and, as most would suggest, because of the pigmentation of my skin, I was soon to be forever labeled a criminal. This was a far cry from the good old days with Franco and how this front-page news article depicted my life to be—talk about digressing in life!

Trooper Hogan Had It All Going for Him

In State Police terms Trooper John Hogan was a superstar. Newly released papers from Attorney General John Farmer's office include memos to State Police superiors urging that the Florence resident be considered for the agency's highest award because of his aggressive work and drug seizures on the New Jersey Turnpike.

Galantucci said the news media and critics of the State Police subsequently whipped up outrage over racial profiling and hypocritical politicians like former Gov. Christie Whitman "just turned tail and ran."

"There can be no question but that they are scapegoating John," Galantucci said. As soon as the media turned this to be a very bad thing, they turned away from John Hogan and James Kenna and left them out there."

I can't help but wonder how this would have played out if those men in the van were white. Better yet, what if the likes of Whitman and Verniero chose to let the legal system work as opposed to interjecting and manipulating the process?

On January 14, 2002, Mr. Galantucci and I, along with my family and few remaining supporters, entered the Mercer County Courthouse for the final time. As we approached the courthouse's entrance, the same jackass reporters and cameramen who by now had hundreds, if not thousands of these same photographs from the previous appearances swarmed us like never before.

Once inside the courtroom, Reginald Jackson and a few of his entourage were already awaiting our arrival, and as luck would have it, I was forced to sit near these swindlers as our attorneys met and hammered out the final details. As was the case from day one, beginning on the morning of April 24, 1998, **nothing** during this entire charade ran the way it was supposed to. Every step of the way—meetings, conferences, and backdoor politics—superceded the legal process and determined how and when this fiasco would be played out. It was like a well-orchestrated game of chess, with Kenna and me being used as the pawns to deflect blame from Whitman, Verniero, and the decades of racial-profiling complaints against the New Jersey State Police.

Here we were almost five years later, and no one except Kenna and me had been sanctioned, suspended or punished. Giving up a job I never planned on returning to was the easy part; being labeled as a criminal, knowing full well that

159 of 162 troopers had the same mistakes on their patrol charts, was the unnerving part of this farce.

Tragically, I had no options, choices or other way out of this cluster-fuck. Had I chosen to keep fighting the state's charges, our deal with the Feds would have been revoked. Facing two lengthy and costly state trials, I was certain that at least three to five more years of my life would have been consumed. Assuming we won both of these State trials, I would then have to play wait and see until the Feds decided whether or not they would seek civil-rights violations against me. Talk about being backed into an inescapable corner!

Financially speaking, my savings had all but evaporated, and my family and supporters already donated every cent they could to my defense. Additionally, my father's health was quickly deteriorating, and I could not allow him to go to his grave wondering how this disaster ended.

Though I am certain the STFA officers and few troopers who openly chastised me for accepting this deal didn't consider any of this—or have the balls to put themselves in my shoes—pleading guilty was the *only* choice I had left.

With this in mind, I held my head high as I stood before Judge Delahey on this brisk January morning. I was not ashamed, embarrassed, or nervous. I knew the truth! We had fought as long and hard as we could have. Purposely dressed in a navy blue suit, yellow dress shirt, blue and gold tie, and black accessories (identical colors of the infamous NJSP uniform), I hoped my attire would send a subliminal message to my fellow troopers. John Ignatius Hogan was a trooper's—trooper until the end. I did not cave in or dime anyone out. Trooper Kenna and I took the fall for an entire organization, refusing to implicate any individual member of the NJSP despite the relentless hounding from the state and federal attorney generals' offices. Unlike the numerous individual troopers who sued, claimed discrimination, lied, or pointed the finger at someone else to get out of the jam(s) they were in, Kenna and I remained truthful throughout this entire persecution. At times, I felt the state attorney generals office wanted us to lie or make stuff up just so they could blow the doors off the NJSP but, aside from having a shitty Union—I really didn't know what they wanted or hoped to hear when questioning us.

As the proceedings began, Judge Delahey labeled Kenna and me, "not only victims of our own conduct but victims of the system that employed us." After Jimmy and I individually read the lengthy statements that Gerrow prepared and insisted upon, Gerrow then addressed Judge Delahey.

Prosecutor Gerrow gave a lengthy summation regarding racial profiling and detailed what the state learned throughout the course of their investigations. He assured the court that the investigation proved that our actions, and subsequent shooting, were in no related to—or a result of—an act of racism. Furthermore, he reaffirmed to the court that the mistakes identified on our patrol logs, prompting the Troop D audit, "were commonplace throughout the ranks of the New Jersey State Police." Gerrow concluded his summation by admitting that our indictments regarding the falsifying charges were precipitated by "a rush to judge error" by the state's Attorney General's Office. *Then why did he insist we plead guilty?*

In closing, Gerrow admirably ended his lengthy abridgment of the tumultuous five-year saga by admitting that Kenna and I were not criminally culpable for the shooting. Instead, he blamed the hard-core training and attorney general's policy regarding the use of deadly force for sending mixed signals. (Both have since been completely revamped during the myriad of reforms imposed by the federal government.)

Though we both faced forty years in prison and hundreds of thousands of dollars in fines (despite never being Mirandized), when discussing punishment, Gerrow suggested merely probation for us.

In rebuttal to his suggested punishment, Judge Delahey stated that, "the conduct we exemplified and the adverse extenuating circumstances we faced for the past five years were punishment enough". After imposing a court fee of $280 to both Kenna and me, Judge Delahey verbally stated he did not even feel probation was required. Weirdly, we were immediately released on our own recognizance. After all the lies, backstabbing, rumors, fallacies, jury poisoning, evidence tampering, protests, demonstrations, rallies, threats, and utter bullshit for five incredulous years, I wrote a simple check for $280 and instantly became a free man. To say the least, it felt surreal and anticlimactic.

Of all the unbelievable events that occurred during this marathon prosecution, the fact that we concluded this deal on the final day of the Republican (Whitman) administration was obviously more than a coincidence. The very next afternoon, Democrat James McGreevey was sworn in as the new governor of the "great" state of New Jersey. I am quite certain the files regarding the Troop D audit, the shooting investigation, and every other malicious and crooked dirty-doing conjured by the Whitman administration during the racial-profiling controversy are buried in the same untraceable vicinity as the body of Jimmy Hoffa.

As expected, the fallout from the minority community concerning our lenient sentence was immediate. Reverend Jackson openly and boisterously cried foul, stating, "Justice was not served!" He demanded that the newly appointed Democratic attorney general (Peter Harvey) open yet another investigation based on the statements we were *forced* to read, as well as the entire plea agreement.

Basically, when all was said and done, I realized no matter what, some people were not going to be satisfied until we were in prison! Giving up what once was a flawless and promising career in addition to serving as the "poster boy" for an entire political administration just wasn't enough for some, not even an alleged man of peace and love like Reverend Reginald Jackson. Despite his constant torment and insistence that I be severely punished, I never became resentful, bitter, or angry. Not a day goes by when I don't pray for all six young men whose lives were forever altered as a result of this tragedy. Regardless if the scars are emotional, physical, or psychological, the fact that we all suffered greatly in our own way appears lost as the debate rages on.

With the most sincere intentions, I would like to thank every individual who stood by my family and me during this travesty. I can only hope you find the actions perpetrated by our elected officials as appalling and atrocious as I did when forced to continually remain silent as they occurred.

With the World Trade Center Towers in the backdrop, this comic synopsized how most of society felt regarding only Kenna and me being forced to give up our careers.

CHAPTER 10

Racial Profiling: Real Or Imagined?

Part 1

The Academy

In September of 1999, the self-serving governor of New Jersey, Christine Todd Whitman, along with her Attorney General, Peter Verniero proclaimed to the world that, "racial profiling is real, not imagined!" the question that should be asked is, as citizens, should we just accept this myth as truth from two individuals who never once patrolled the highways, cities, or municipalities of our state?

After years of personally listening to jackasses who never donned a bulletproof vest or police uniform describe and depict this alleged act, it's appalling to me that society as a whole never challenged this assertion. Since no one from the STFA, the NJSP, or the law enforcement worldwide tackled this debate, is it safe to assume the next time a similar incident involving racial overtones happens, the controversy will undoubtedly reignite? Will more careers, reputations, lives, and police departments sadly be ruined all for political gain? Since Whitman's and Verniero's accusations went unopposed, does it mean racial profiling must exist?

Or was this travesty really just a case of bad timing as most pro-law-enforcement persons suggested? Was the fact that this tragedy occurred during an election year the sole reason Whitman decided to turn her back on Kenna, me, and the entire NJSP? Better yet, if we are blaming the political process, let's go a step further. Maybe we go way back and say this is all Howard Stern's fault!

Most New Jerseans will recall the only reason Christie Whitman became governor in the first place was because she befriended the shock jock. After appearing on his morning radio show, her popularity catapulted. This appearance, and the support she subsequently received from Stern, became the sole reason Whitman won her initial gubernatorial bid. In turn for his loyalty, Whitman named a rest stop (urinal) in Howard's honor on Interstate 295 (northbound), ironically, just minutes from my hometown.

Like a true politician, however, she later removed the plaque dedicated to Howard when pressured by Stern detractors who claimed it offensive that she did this.

Presently, the same Republican administration Whitman worked for under President George Bush is seizing every opportunity to attack the *Howard Stern Show*. The government-backed FCC has all but censored his right to free speech and is unwaveringly attempting to remove him from public broadcasting. In theory, isn't this a form of profiling? *To think Howard, she once thanked and patted me on the back too, only to screw us both over!*

Having been publicly indicted for what Attorney General Verniero categorized as "crimes consistent with racial profiling," was he suggesting that I was a racist? As I grapple with the totality of what transpired over the years, I am forced to wonder if he or Whitman ever once considered how their newfound position on racial profiling would affect my family, my personality, or my reputation for the remainder of my life. In retrospect, did my life matter at all to these two?

I'd like to think if I had character flaws or was a racist, all the tests, background checks, oral interviews, and personality screenings I endured throughout the NJSP's selection process would have weeded out me, or any other person, exhibiting negative qualities.

Ironically, some members of society have even suggested that the entire NJSP, at its core, is a racist organization. I often wonder what the current state of the NJSP would be had the tragic events of April 23, 1998, never occurred. Depending on whom you ask, some may try and convince you into believing that by now all troopers would be donning white hoods, riding horse-back, and positioned at the entrance to every toll plaza, strictly searching minority-driven vehicles.

Despite what transpired and the years of finger-pointing that followed the infamous "turnpike shooting," it pains me to grasp the public's sole perception concerning racial profiling. Somehow, the stereotypical definition only depicts white police officers stopping minority drivers. Ask yourself, the last time you boarded an airplane, what were you looking for and why? If you are honest with yourself, you must admit that the tragic events of 9/11 subliminally made everyone a profiler regardless of your beliefs.

Despite what side of this debate you are on, the sad truth is, I never had a chance in hell. Once the Whitman administration decided "racial profiling is a national epidemic," I was toast. These same politicians then methodically spoon-fed the media craze that relentlessly exploited the hell out of this sensitive and explosive issue. Within days of announcing the indictments, my human right of "innocent until proven guilty" was revoked. Because of the intentional mishandling of our indictments by the attorney general himself, it automatically became *assumed* that Jimmy Kenna and I were racial profilers, and in the court of public opinion, we were immediately deemed *guilty*. From that day forward, with every public appearance I made relating to these charges, I was relentlessly quizzed regarding the state police's "policy" on racial profiling.

Every pinheaded reporter, newscaster, and author covering this topic called Mr. G in hopes of gaining permission to speak with me. Much like Gerrow, they hoped to get in my mind and hear when, how, and where the state police taught troopers how to profile. Was it taught to me at the academy? Was I given a book called *BLACKFACE—Stop That Car No Matter What*? Did my Caucasian coach teach me? Was I pulled into a dark alley after work by senior troopers wearing white hoods and forced to participate in racial profiling?

The popular misconception often portrayed publicly by the masses, who pretend to be experts on this issue, was that cops observe minorities' driving fancy—new BMWs, Lexuses, or Mercede Benzes—and think they are *drug dealers* and immediately pull these individuals over.

On the contrary, from a law-enforcement perspective, that theology is preposterous, stupid, and idiotic. In fact, to the best of my recollection, I can honestly say I never once made or witnessed an arrest involving a brand-new luxury car. From my perspective, knowing the truth about this controversial issue, permitting ministers, senators, assemblymen, and lawyers to publicly crusade against this societal demon with their wild, uneducated, and absurd accusations did more harm than good to any true victims of this alleged practice.

Most people driving these types of vehicles are professionals, who rarely get stopped and are even less frequently subjected to search. In my opinion, the continuous ranting and uneducated portrayal of this practice by accusatory civilians only diluted the core of this so-called epidemic. In turn, their ignorance only opened the floodgates to anyone hoping to fallaciously sue the state of New Jersey for a quick buck. To put it mildly, it was sensationalism at its evil best, and the media craved for more!

As we now know, the New Jersey State Police had been accused of racial profiling for decades. Yet prior to Attorney General Farmer's release of hundreds of thousands of documents relating to this subject, only circumstantial evidence such as a bullshit training video about the Jamaican Posse—which, to my knowledge, was made by the federal government—had previously surfaced. Given what's known today, how can the numerous political figureheads who denied this practice existed and intentionally withheld the volumes of documents, complaints, and allegations not be punished or held accountable for their malfeasance? How can it be that after all is said and done, two young Caucasian troopers became the first and only law-enforcement officers in the nation accused of the horrid act of racial profiling? If the repeated claims of institutionalized racism and systemic problems relating to profiling were true, wouldn't more troopers have lost their careers?

With that said, could it be that Kenna and I were simply made examples of? The answer to these questions simply lay within one's belief concerning the legitimacy of this most sensitive and debatable topic. After all, if there were a clear-cut answer, it would not be considered a controversy!

Individually, I first became aware of the term "racial profiling" in the wake of the aforementioned Gloucester County case of *DeSoto v. the New Jersey State Police*. Admittedly, I never read the entire decision. Hell, I wasn't even a trooper yet. In a nutshell, without having spent hours researching this topic, I know a superior-court judge was summoned to hear a case concerning numerous subjects claiming they were illegally targeted, and ultimately arrested, on the southern end of the New Jersey Turnpike. The state police was ordered to turn over thousands of documents including summonses, warnings, arrests, and investigation reports even though race was not identified on most of these documents.

After weeks of testimony by various troopers and superiors alike, the New Jersey State Police, as a whole, was dealt a crushing blow. Judge Robert E. Francis ruled that members of the Troop D Moorestown Barracks had unfairly singled out minority motorists for stops, searches, and seizure. The defense, which consisted of seventeen individuals, had their convictions immediately overturned. Any pending indictments were also dismissed.

The state police and individual troopers named in the suit were, per policy (until *our* shooting of course), represented free of charge by lawyers from the Attorney General's Office. Deborah Poritz was the acting attorney general and, like the formidable backbone that her office ***was*** to the state police, immediately denounced Judge Francis's ruling and ordered this decision be appealed by her legal staff.

As I entered and dredged through the academy in 1992, this case remained under appeal. The *DeSoto* case, however, was rarely, if ever, mentioned in a block of instruction to the members of the 113th Recruit Class.

But was racial profiling discussed, and what ever happened to the troopers who were singled out in the *DeSoto* case? What were the far-reaching results for the members of the state police found guilty of racial profiling at that time? Who were they? Were they all white? Do they all have shotgun racks in the back of their pickup trucks and attend Klan rallies on the weekends? How much time do they have on the job? Were they all big "lock up" guys? Do they all chew tobacco and speak with a Southern draw? Do they really hate African Americans? Did they get fired? Did these individuals lose their jobs, pensions, homes, families, identities, careers, and children as a result of this ruling? Or were they transferred and buried at another barracks as far from the turnpike as possible?

The truth is, I don't know for certain, but I am positive no one was ever disciplined and, certainly, not terminated. These troopers had the backing of the colonel, the governor, and the attorney general's office, thus, rendering them untouchable. My point is, had we not been abandoned by our elected officials hoping to advance their careers and been backed by our union and peers, this entire debacle most likely would have unfolded and been properly addressed for what it was, a horrific tragedy—no indictments, no poster boys, no perfectly timed press conferences, no "bad apple" labels, and certainly no scapegoats!

I believe most troopers caught up in the *DeSoto* case simply asked for and were granted immediate transfer off the turnpike. Who needed the aggravation? Why risk getting jammed up to make criminal arrests if you have a judge who is just going to let the bad guy(s) walk away? Who cares about the kilograms of cocaine and heroin, bundles of marijuana, dirty money, assault-style weapons, and paraphernalia the dregs of society possess as they travel through New Jersey?

Wouldn't it have been preposterous and immoral for a judge, jury, attorney general, governor, or anyone for that matter to hold five, ten, or even twenty troopers accountable for what the defense repeatedly claimed was decades of disparate treatment of minority motorists? Fortunately and rightfully so, to the best of my knowledge, the ruling by Judge Francis did not affect any individual trooper's life or career because they were shielded by their employer. Is it fair to suggest that Kenna and I ultimately accepted punishment for any alleged wrongdoings of those affiliated with the *DeSoto* case too? Had Whitman and her attorney general confronted this issue in light of Judge Francis's ruling, its very likely that our tragic saga would have never occurred. Shit, many believe Whitman would have been the vice president to George Bush had it not been for her complete over indulgence in the racial profiling controversy.

Instead, as I graduated from the academy, my colleagues and I wholeheartedly began pounding the roadways as foot soldiers in New Jersey's war on drugs. I was certain that I had the support of my employer. Regarding racial profiling, the only thing I knew about this issue was the tidbits I read in the newspapers regarding the *DeSoto* case. Much to the chagrin of certain reverends, lawyers, and activists, I assure the world that racial profiling was never discussed, taught, or trained to the recruits of the 113th Recruit Class.

As my career in the NJSP began, attorney general Debra Poritz was soon replaced by Peter Verniero. Though she later testified to briefing Verniero on the *DeSoto* appeal and "the constant accusations of alleged acts of racial profiling by troopers on the New Jersey Turnpike," none of these was known to junior troopers such as me. All I knew was that during his tenure, Mr. Verneiro, by order of Governor Whitman, continued to appeal this case. Even more important to us road troopers, like each of his predecessors had, along with the governor, they denied that racial profiling flourished, existed, or was taught, trained, and practiced by New Jersey troopers.

Upon graduating from the academy, though I had a constant deceit for politics and politicians alike, it was reassuring to know these two individuals supported, backed, and encouraged us to continue to do the daunting task of patrolling the roadways of New Jersey to the best of our natural abilities. Beginning my career as a general road-duty trooper in the early 1990s, I cannot sit here in good conscience and tell you when, where, or how the term "racial profiling" entered society. Obviously, it existed long before I ever became a trooper. For you rap enthusiasts, even LL Cool J documented New Jersey's reputation for searching minority motorists in his song entitled "Illegal Search", released in the late 1980's: (excerpts)

> *On the turnpike, and everything's right*
> *In the background is flashin lights*
> *Get out the car in the middle of the night*
> *It's freezin cold, and you're doin it for spite*
> *Slam me on the hood, yo, that ain't right*
> *You pull out your gun if I'm puttin up a fight*
> *You're a real man, your uniform is tight*
> *Fingerprint me, take me name and height*
> *Hopin it will, but I know it won't work*
> *Illegal search*
> *And them cops out there*
> *That did the wrong thing to one of my brothers*
> *In Jersey*
> *Keep on searching*

In retrospect, who am I to admit, deny, or expound upon this most controversial topic? Shouldn't a retired colonel or high-ranking officer be the one to tackle this societal demon? Better yet, why hasn't anyone from the state police openly talked about it?

Deep down, I often wonder if anyone really wants to know the truth. Maybe it's just such a bitter, controversial, and agitating topic that it should remain as such. This way, television and radio talk-show hosts, journalists, pro or antipolice spokespersons, reporters, lawyers, ministers, and race-mongers can continue to get headlines while the debate rages on. Is society ready for the truth about racial profiling and just who knows the truth?

Do cops or, more specifically, New Jersey State Troopers stop cars based *solely* on the race of occupants as widely alleged? This is the apparent definition and claim made by minorities, ministers, lawyers, and even troopers that have or are currently suing the state police over this issue.

What gives me a thirty something-year-old Caucasian and former trooper, now with a criminal record, the right to address this issue? For Christ's sake, I was only assigned to the turnpike for a little more than four years. Who is going to, and why should anyone believe me? What god-awful experiences did I endure that makes me feel I can openly, honestly, and eloquently—with great detail—

depict what goes on in a cop's mind the second he decides to make a motor-vehicle stop? The answer is simple and cliché in nature! I have been there; done that; and, most importantly, have nothing to gain or lose from being the first trooper who isn't suing someone to openly address the issue of profiling in the NJSP.

I cannot, will not, or even attempt to speak for any trooper other than myself. I spent my short but adventurous career doing what I thought exemplified a squared-away New Jersey state trooper. In the academy, I took the advice of my instructors who said, "A good trooper will take one thing [good or bad] from every other trooper they come in contact with throughout their career." As I left the academy, that piece of advice was tucked away in my bulletproof vest.

After twenty-three weeks of sheer misery, only two other sentences stuck with me from my training. While studying Title 39, New Jersey's Motor Vehicle Laws, the instructor stated (purposely or not), "A good trooper can find a reason to stop any motor vehicle in which he chooses to. Do not stop a car if you cannot articulate what you are stopping it for."

I can only wonder if these statements had the same, or any, impact at all on my fellow classmates. What I did know for certain was that I had no interest in being a good trooper. John Ignatius Hogan, badge no. 5068, was going to be the best trooper!

Though everyone aspires to become a member of law enforcement for his or here own reasons, I believe the underlying truth is we feel, or assume, that we can have a positive impact on people's lives. I will be the first to admit that I brought certain feelings, emotions, and stereotypes to the academy. It is impossible for any person—black, white, blue, green, or purple—not to have certain prejudices. Does the proverbial, "If you don't like a certain flavor of ice cream, it's considered an act of prejudice" apply here?

Are there racist cops? Absolutely! But are they all white? Absolutely not! Racism is a two-way street. For some reason, white America, with the exception of the extremists who are racist in their own beliefs, are afraid to deal with the subject of racism. Just imagine posing a question with racial overtones to a politician or CEO of a major corporation and see what kind of response you get! White America is afraid to speak about racial issues for fear of sounding like, or being accused of, racism. Frankly speaking, certain members of ethnic cultures know this, and they take full advantage of it. *Isn't that right Mr. Sharpton?*

Why am I not afraid to speak about racism? Again, what experiences have I had? What does a decent-looking, blue-eyed white male with black hair know about racism? Have I ever been discriminated against because of my gender, skin color, looks, religious beliefs, or age? The truth is, probably not! But I can say with great confidence that if I wasn't a Caucasian, this tragedy would have never made headlines! Was I made an example of simply because I was a white police officer on the wrong side of a political hot potato? I'll let you decide that for yourself but numerous people (of all races) have repeatedly approached me about this incident and claimed it was the most blatant case of reverse discrimination they've seen in their life time.

With this in mind, for more than four years I had been publicly embarrassed, humiliated, vilified, and openly called a racist. I have been on the front page of every major news paper in the tri-state area, was pictured in *Newsweek*, *Sports Illustrated*, *Time*, and ACLU newsletters; and for the past four years, had served as the "poster boy for racial profiling in the country."

On the contrary, I have been praised on various skinhead and white-supremacist Web sites and was even invited to be the grand marshal at a white-power rally back in July of 2001 in Morristown, New Jersey. At times, I felt like the Eminem of law enforcement! Somehow, I had become the epicenter of a racially charged controversy despite having never made one public statement or committing an act of racism. *The power of the media is frightening!*

Imagine waking up every morning for four years straight wondering if your face is going to be on the front page of the newspaper. Just visualize if you can, for one second, being a white police officer indicted for what (former) Federal Deputy Attorney General Michael Chertoff called, "a crime worse than child molestation because of the racial implications suggested by the attorney general" (Peter Verniero) when our indictments were handed down.

How did I go on living? How did I look at my father, mother, sisters, and brother in the eye? Even worse, what do I say to my black friends? What about my aunts, uncles, and cousins? Did everyone think I was a racist scumbag?

So just what were those law-enforcement stereotypes and perceptions I showed up to Sea Girt with on August 23, 1992? For beginners, like a lot of young and naive "cops to be," I really thought I could change the world! I was certain my addition to the NJSP would make the world a better, safer place.

As for stereotypes, after doing a report on the Jamaican Posse, I was scared to death of any young black person who spoke with a Jamaican accent. Foolishly, I believed, like most of society, that young black males controlled the drug market but that narcotics themselves, in smaller quantities, were purchased and used by just as many whites as other ethnic cultures. Personally, I looked down on "white trash" that drove beat-up cars, didn't shave, or have nice teeth. For the most part, I unintentionally led a pretty sheltered life. Despite having friends of various races, I was far from multi-cultured or street-smart. Sadly, what little bit I did know came from textbooks or television.

YooKun Kim was one of my best friends growing up. Other than him, I had no perception or even gave much thought to the Asian culture. All I knew and cared about was that he was funny, cool, and had a good-looking sister.

Todd Hayes, Andre Moore, Donovan Tucker, Adam Bond, Steve West, and Darrell Fisher were my African American friends. We played sports, hung out, ate, rode bikes, partied, and tried to hook up with girls together. These guys were no different than me. Some lived in apartments, others in homes nicer than mine. They came to my house and I went to theirs. Florence was no different than any other lower middle-class community of mixed races. Shit, my idol when I was growing up was a minority stud that graduated high school with my sister Mary named Lionel Barther, "the Iceman"!

So did I become a racist after getting accepted to the academy? Did they train me to stop and search minorities in the beginning, middle, or end of my training? Still today, as I write this, there are pathetic, money-hungry lawyers all across this godforsaken state awaiting a response from Mr. Galantucci's office. They are hoping to schedule an interview with me and ask that very same question: *Not was it taught* but *when* was I trained on the practice of racial profiling? My response could land them and their self-serving clients millions of dollars! Well, here goes!

Debate me if you wish, but I feel the need to reiterate. The 113th Recruit Class did not, at any point, get specific, detailed, or even subliminal hints that we should target minorities. Hell, the only hands-on tactical experience I received was *one* mock motor-vehicle traffic stop of a car containing five instructors—all of which were white. A sixth white instructor popped out of the trunk and shot me dead as I walked up to their car! In appearance, they were the furthest thing from the Jamaican Posse as could be imagined. Much to the disappointment of state-police detractors, I can honestly say there is no formal, informal, or training of any type at the New Jersey State Police Academy on racial profiling. You don't go there to learn how to be a trooper; you go there to see if you have what it takes to become a trooper!

Part II

Who, If Anyone, Taught Me?

Since the academy did not address or teach me how to racial profile, did I become accustomed to this practice in Troop C? Did it begin on day one with my coach? Damn that Leslie "Rob" Bice! At five feet eight inches and 160 pounds, Rob was probably one of the nicest human beings I met in my lifetime. Upon graduating, I expected my coach to be mammoth in size, have a nasty disposition, and treat me like dirt. In reality, Trooper Bice was kind, courteous, and nothing short of a total gentleman. He never had an internal complaint in his twelve-year career as a trooper and would be the first to admit that he was not very aggressive and never thrived on criminal arrests. So how did I become this god-awful trooper if my coach was so professional?

Was it the guys other than my coach at the Hightstown Barracks? The truth is I left there after just four months. I knew nothing more upon departure than I did after arriving from the academy. I made one criminal arrest and swore to never make another due to the incredible volume of paperwork that was required. I did, however, like the good soldier I was, take one thing from each trooper I came in contact with. From my coach, Trooper I Rob Bice, I learned to treat everyone the same and always be respectful, professional, and courteous no matter how good, bad, or dirty the person I was dealing with. From others, who will remain unnamed, I learned *not* to hawk bars; to "thumb up" the box when testing DWI suspects; and most importantly, to not be a hypocrite. For instance, I never ticketed motorists for the same infractions I committed when driving to work.

As mentioned, my second assignment was the Fort Dix Station, a.k.a., the Wild, Wild West. Sounds like a barracks full of negro-hating rednecks, doesn't it? They must've trained me to stop and search every vehicle being driven by a minority, right? Not quite. Fort Dix was a mixed bag of both troopers and residents. Across the street from the barracks was a section 8 apartment complex. Main Street, Wrightstown, and the surrounding area were filled with lower-income families of all ethnic backgrounds. Sadly, and sometimes comically, this unique composition of various personalities were always fighting, partying, or committing enough mischievous acts to keep all the troopers at Dix very busy. For the most part, traffic enforcement was secondary; and PRAs (patrol-related arrests) were usually a result of some local knucklehead getting caught stealing, breaking into someone's home, or fighting with their spouse or family member. Racial profiling was never introduced, discussed, or even mentioned during my yearlong tenure at Fort Dix.

In fact, if anything, just the contrary was portrayed—but not specifically practiced or condoned. Certain areas—mainly on the other side of the Maguire and Fort Dix military bases, in and around Pemberton Boro—were densely populated by minorities. Speculation was that if you saw a vehicle occupied by a white male or female leaving an all-minority neighborhood, it was likely they may have just purchased drugs. Again, maybe fallacies, false pretenses, or improper stereotyping; but who is to blame? Most television shows, or movies depicting this type of activity concentrate on impoverished neighborhoods so who is truly at fault for societies misconceptions regarding illicit activity?

Allegedly, this same notion, known now as "reverse profiling" was practiced at stations such as Bellmawr, which patrolled the outskirts of Camden City. Did—or better yet, should a police officer's suspicions be heightened upon observing non-minorities departing certain areas of Camden City that are populated by a vast number of minority residents? Better yet, should drug interdiction be emphasized and practiced or completely removed from law enforcement? What are the rewards for the officer? I know what I would tell any aggressive officer!

As I experienced, police officers are baptized with an immeasurable amount of discretion upon graduating the academy. Who should judge where society draws the line on whether law-enforcement should be reactive or proactive? Does society want their police officers to be aggressive or timid? A law-enforcement officer's right to utilize discretion and parameters by which he or she is forced to work under, cannot be fleeting and swayed based on the political climate. Sadly, that's the way it is. The "gray area" every cop works under is constantly wavering. Every critical incident is judged and assessed differently. Prior to our shooting, troopers were aggressive: making arrests, seizing drugs and weapons, and doing what we were paid for. Now, because of the political influence over law enforcement in New Jersey, every trooper is working with handcuffs on, afraid that they may say or do the wrong thing and be penalized, or, worse, fired.

Unfortunately, it will probably take a tragic incident such as an officer being shot or a politician's daughter overdosing on drugs to swing the pendulum back into the officer's favor. I am certain no one will debate me that presently, the millions of dollars in contraband that *used* to be seized annually by turnpike troopers flows freely up and down New Jersey's roadways. Once the most feared roadway, the turnpike is now a smuggler's paradise. It's unfathomable to think that in the current climate, drug dealers somehow have garnered more rights than trained law-enforcement officers in New Jersey, but I stand firmly by this assertion.

Back when I was assigned to the Fort Dix Station, our area of patrol was so small that when you had time to do traffic enforcement, it was on county roads like Route 537, Route 68, or Route 530. These weren't exactly booming with vehicular activity. Troopers at Dix often made arrest for small amounts of marijuana and sometimes cocaine. As instructed, I listened and learned from these troopers. I was always curious and wanted to know why they stopped the car. What questions did they ask? What observations did they make, and what events led them to make the arrest? I learned as much as possible from good, aggressive troopers. There were always several factors that led them to make the stop, arrest, and seizure. Never once did I hear or was I told, "He was black, so I stopped him, knowing he would have drugs!" Yet, that is the ludicrous venom that has been spewed by the multitude of anti-profiling spokespersons positioned throughout our great nation.

Prior to departing the Fort Dix Barracks, I established a few lifelong friendships and the basic knowledge and tactics it took to become an aggressive, smart, and well-rounded trooper. I was not however, introduced to, or ever heard the term, "racial profiling" being discussed or encouraged by anyone while at Fort Dix. Nor did I witness discrimination of any kind, either among the ranks or with the myriad of cultures that entered the station as plaintiff or arrestee. On the surface, it appeared to me that everyone worked well together, got along even better and as a whole station, we were a close-knit group. It was at Dix that I introduced my liver to the hard-partying, queen-filled, and wild-man lifestyle associated with being one of New Jersey's finest; and it was everything I thought it would be and more. *I still wonder where Trooper Getcliffe's glasses are.*

The third round of transfers for the 113th class landed me at Wilburtha Barracks. As I declared, we were not even allowed to enter Trenton City, so it's safe to say I was not taught the concept of racial profiling here either. Other than tickets and an occasional "4-50" (drunk-driving arrest) that was hawked out of Chambersburg, (an all-white section of Trenton), there was no activity at this station. Having served at (3) Troop C Barracks, I assure everyone that the notion or profiling was never addressed, mentioned, or discussed by anyone. Now with nearly eighteen months' experience as a road trooper though, I did notice a change in myself as I prepared to depart Troop C for assignment to the turnpike.

While on patrol, I became more alert and aware of my surroundings. Much like how a professional athlete visualizes things in slow motion, the traffic around me appeared to slow down. I now took the time to look in a vehicle as I passed by. I would note the state and registration of a car that I was behind or passing. I observed the occupants and their demeanor. With just more than a year and a half experience as a trooper, instead of driving at outrageous speeds to go nowhere, I assessed and analyzed the activity that was going on around me. I found myself more curious about others—where they were going, and what they were doing. I also became more confident about what I was doing and in my approach and conversations with individuals I stopped.

With this newfound confidence, I would often see what appeared to be a suspicious vehicle or suspicious-looking occupants or suspicious demeanor or activity. I would follow these vehicles, and Title 39 laws would be quickly shuffling through my brain. I needed a reason to stop that car! I remembered what I was instructed at the academy: *"Good troopers find a reason to stop any car they wish to stop!"* As I transferred to the 'pike, I was beginning to blossom into a good trooper.

When I arrived at the New Brunswick Barracks in December 1994, I was not handed a manual on racial profiling. My first day was spent sitting through an eight-hour orientation hosted by the New Jersey Turnpike Authority. Contrary to the hopes of many, no slides, handouts, maps, photographs, reference books, or guides on how to racial profile were handed out to us "newbies" as we began our turnpike careers.

So if the New Jersey State Police does not train recruits to racial profile at the academy; and while at Troop C, no trooper, sergeant, detective, sergeant first class, or station commander ever provided me with verbal or practical instructions on how to profile, then when did I learn how to do it? The governor and the attorney general proclaimed me guilty of this act, so when and where did my tutorial on racial profiling take place? After all, as the leaders of our state, they wouldn't lie, right?

Part III

My Take

Who a trained New Jersey state trooper chooses to stop and *why* can only be answered by that individual trooper. I have never seen a superior officer hold a gun to a trooper's head and demand that they go out and make an arrest! Once he is dressed; and takes his portable radio, flashlight, shotgun and briefcase, the trooper gets into a marked unit and then decides for himself *who and why* he is going stop!

If this is true, and the state police does not train troopers to profile, then how come the Attorney General's Office has complainants from minorities alleging they were singled out, stopped for no reason and subjected to an illegal search spanning back at least two decades? Even a better question is, why did this only seem to be problematic on the turnpike? I've often heard, "Why is it that we only see young black males pulled over on the turnpike being searched?"

On August 22, 1989, Trooper Anthony DiSalvatore stopped a 1989 red Pontiac Bonneville traveling southbound on the turnpike. It was broad daylight, and the vehicle was occupied by three black males. Within minutes of this routine traffic stop, one of the occupants open fired with a 9-mm handgun and shot Trooper DiSalvatore four times. Fortunately, the other weapon carried by the occupants of this vehicle—a Mac-11 machine gun, capable of firing twelve hundred rounds per minute (enough to easily cut a person in half)—was not fired at him. Luckily, Trooper DiSalvatore survived, and the bad guys were captured and arrested. The guns and three hundred vials of crack cocaine they possessed were seized during the arrest.

It was stories like this, along with JoAnne Chesimard and the Black Panthers—who shot and killed Trooper Werner Forrester, which gave the New Jersey Turnpike its mystique. The "Black Dragon's" reputation for unbelievable and historic events has survived decades of state-police lore. Any time you heard a state police story of a big arrest, seizure, or wild event, it seemed to always happen on the New Jersey Turnpike.

Even at the academy, I recall instructors saying, "If something major happens in the state police, you can bet your ass that it's most likely going to be on the turnpike." Division-wide, I believe every member of the NJSP was aware of the constant dangers associated with the turnpike. Hell, the Drug Enforcement Agency and federal government identified the New Jersey Turnpike as a major corridor for criminal activity connecting Miami, Florida, to New York City. At the height of the nation's war on drugs, Operation Pipeline was established to concentrate specifically on drug trafficking and interdiction. The Feds didn't set up shop on County Road 537, Route 68, or Route 530. Their efforts were aimed straight at the New Jersey Turnpike and targeted groups such as the Jamaican Posse, Columbian cartel, motorcycle gangs, and Dominicans.

Personally, I was never taught profiling of any sorts by the federal government. Rumor has it that the Feds did offer training and informational materials regarding characteristics of drug couriers, the various methods they used to transport narcotics, and other statistics related to trafficking and interdiction to the NJSP. This information was then disseminated through the ranks and left up to the individual trooper for interpretation. All of these happenings preempted my joining the NJSP. Regardless of training, knowledge, and ambition, it is still up to the individual trooper to choose for him or herself if they wanted to be criminally active. Even at advanced-training classes that the state police selectively sent me to such as "Top Gun" and "Narcotic Trafficking Trends," the theology or mention of racial profiling was nonexistent.

Option B for road troopers was simple: just look the other way and focus on motor-vehicle enforcement. Contrary to what numerous lawsuits may claim, no one is forced to do anything in the New Jersey State Police. Why the NJSP did not defend itself during the barrage on lawsuits from the public at large and its minority-members is still anyone's guess!

Was there pressure to make arrests on the turnpike? For me, there was. As a junior guy, you want to fit in and be accepted by your peers. Personally, I chose to be assigned to the turnpike. I wanted to make the big arrest. I wanted the glory that was associated with turnpike troopers. I wanted to be, "King of the Big

Road!" I felt the pressure before I even got there, but I placed this pressure on myself!

Fortunately, the squad I was assigned to thrived on being criminally active, and I loved every minute of it. From day one, I felt compelled to make arrests because everyone else on the squad was doing it. I wanted to fit in, and I wanted to be a part of it! So basically, the only pressure placed on an individual trooper to make arrests is the pressure they place on themselves. Remember, the individual trooper controls *who* he stops for a motor-vehicle violation and *why*.

Sure, there is ball busting. Aggressive and criminally active troopers would take pop-shots at others. Certainly, there's "Your classmate got an ounce and a gun. What about you, ya slug?" Followed by, "Get out there and do God's work, Junior!" Others would suggest, "Hey, Troop, ain't it about time you started bringing in some weight?" The ribbing was always present, but not malicious. No one was forced to buy into it, though. Perhaps in the past, maybe this behavior led some troopers to go out and sporadically stop and search minorities which ultimately may have led to the years of complaints that fell on deaf ears. I don't know. I wasn't there! During my tenure on the New Jersey Turnpike, this was *not* the case.

Should it be assumed that now I was assigned to the turnpike, I just started randomly stopping minority driven vehicles? Truthfully, I never forgot the golden rule from the academy: "Don't stop someone if you can't articulate why he or she is being stopped."

My first few weeks of assignment on the 'Pike were as much a blur as was the speed at which traffic flowed. I couldn't see who was in the car; what state the license tag displayed; or whether it was a male, female, black, white, or green person. It reminded me of playing Madden on Playstation 2 for the first time in "all-Madden mode." Everything was moving so fast and was so much more intense! Admittedly, I struggled to keep up!

Finding people to stop for motor vehicle violations on the turnpike is like catching lightning bugs from a glass jar—not difficult at all! Traffic moves at roughly seventy-five miles per hour at all times. In the beginning, only the most egregious drivers would be stopped by me. Running radar in the Pit—a personalized—paved stretch of blacktop on the southbound-side inner roadway at approximately milepost 72.3—was like shooting fish in a barrel.

Cars whizzed by my marked troop car at 80, 86, 78, 94, 69, 88, and 103 miles per hour—concealed only because of the way a troop car could be set back in the Pit. Bingo! I'd stop the guy going 103 miles per hour. Yes, it was that frequent and easy.

Normally, these stops turned out to be businessmen, doctors, lawyers, nurses, and sales guys running late for appointments. They always had their license, registration, and insurance waiting for me. They were pleasant; courteous; professional; and, most importantly, honest. They knew they were speeding, admitted it, and were ready to accept their punishment. Anyone who knows me or ever rode with me knows I had a very hard time giving tickets to legitimate, hardworking, honest citizens. After all, I, along with most cops, speed in my own car, so I felt it was hypocritical to give a ticket to someone if I drove to work faster than he or she were going.

These stops never quenched my sense for adventure, however. Stopping Biff in his brand-new Corvette going 110 miles per hour because he is late for a tee time wasn't exactly going to get me the Trooper of the Year Award!

When exactly I made the transformation to what some call selective enforcement or criminal profiling is unknown to me. As I gained confidence and experience in what I was doing out there, I started to sense that I was becoming a "good trooper." The reasons for which I started making motor-vehicle stops were vastly different from when I was in Troop C and initially went out to the turnpike. I wanted to make arrests, so I knew I had to allow my preconceived notions and stereotypes to permeate into my mind. I had to start stopping individuals who society taught me *may* be involved in criminal activity. But who are they, and where did I obtain this reasoning? When I observed traffic, mentally, I would ask myself, *Who is in that car, where are they going, and where are they coming from?* I forced myself into using the sixth sense that police officers are supposed to have.

The theory on the turnpike is easy, simple, and full of common sense. New York City served as the hub of illegal activity. No matter what you wanted—drugs, guns, pirated videos, CDs, tapes, paraphernalia, bogus Tommy Hilfiger or Nautica gear, you name it—as long as you had the money, it could be purchased in the Big Apple.

The mentality and knowledge of all turnpike troopers were pretty much the same. The only difference was whether or not they chose to apply this knowledge while on patrol and be criminally active. Every trooper was given the same tools and had the same basic awareness of the negative elements that needed to use the turnpike to conduct their illicit enterprise. Active and conscientious troopers looking to make felonious narcotic arrests believed and held as gospel the following rule: individuals from the South, from Trenton, New Jersey, DC, Virginia, and all the way down to North and South Carolina were willing to risk getting arrested to drive up to New York because of the much-cheaper prices for cocaine, crack, heroin, or whatever their substance of choice was. Like anything in life, the more abundant something is, the cheaper you can get it for. New York City was perceived by both the good and bad guys as "drug heaven."

In interview after interview following a sizable narcotic seizure, I'd ask the same question, "Why drive all the way up to New York to get your shit"? The response to this question was always the same! At that time, an ounce of cocaine for instance, could be purchased for around seven hundred dollars in New York City, then broken down, cut up, and sold by the gram for triple, even four times as much back in North Carolina or Virginia. Someone with enough cash to purchase a pound of cocaine could, in essence, turn an estimated twelve-thousand-dollar purchase into a 400 percent profit. If you do the math, given the bleak alternative some of these subjects had, I not only felt bad for them but learned to understand their logic. *Hell, what would I do if I ever lost my job? Would things ever get so bad that I had to turn to this?*

From experience and the years of reports filed by troopers who patrolled the 'pike before us, we knew the flow of drugs went southbound, with the exception of the "mother load" that may be coming up in a tractor trailer from Miami. Troopers looking to make currency seizures followed the same principle and stopped cars going northbound into the city to make their purchase. Money went north; drugs go south—pretty simple in theory!

From intelligence provided to us by the federal government, Drug Enforcement Agency (DEA), El Paso Information Center (EPIC), as well as drug-awareness bulletins, and daily briefing (BOLOs—be on the lookout), it became pretty evident that young and middle-aged minority men were the main transporters of narcotics. Is this knowledge law enforcements' fault? Are statistics themselves racially biased? Regardless, the trooper concentrating on drug interdiction still needed to initiate and articulate why he or she made the stop before a search could be conducted.

Mentally, in a cop's mind—especially mine, from experience as well as watching, listening, and mentoring myself after the most aggressive troopers—I gathered this: seized drugs always seem to come from Harlem, Bronx, or Manhattan. The driver would normally have an 18W toll ticket and come right out of the Bronx via the George Washington Bridge. If the drugs were purchased from bodegas located in Manhattan, the mules would enter the turnpike through the Holland or Lincoln Tunnel. More experienced mules would go through the boroughs of New York, into Staten Island, and enter New Jersey using the Outerbridge Crossing. Basically, mules knew the game as well as we did and if they were smart, they would take any route necessary to get on the New Jersey Turnpike as far south as possible. The reputation of the NJSP superseded itself.

"If a trooper stops you, you are getting searched"—I heard this constantly during interviews with suspected drug couriers.

As wrong and simplistic as it may appear to be, troopers, in general, justified the search and seizure of minorities with one basic notion: a white person attempting to score a "big load" of cocaine or heroin could not go into the Bronx, Harlem, or Manhattan to make these purchases. They would either be subjected to reverse profiling by the NYPD; or worse, get robbed, beaten, shot, or murdered trying to score the dope. Therefore, in my opinion, it became a common (mis)perception for criminally active troopers to focus mainly on minorities traveling southbound. What transpired once the stop was articulated almost *always* was controlled by the occupants. In most instances, unbelievably, the occupants make the officer's job easier by not having proper identification, a driver's license, registration, or insurance. It always amazed me that subjects carrying thousands, or hundreds of thousands of dollars' worth of drugs would be so inept as to not conjure up a legitimate story just in case they were stopped. Deep down, no matter how many arrests a trooper made, we all knew we only caught the most lax and unorganized dealers or mules. In retrospect, did any of it make a difference?

This does not mean that whites were not stopped and searched. Personally, I witnessed other troopers, and I also tried in vain on numerous occasions, to disprove this theory but never witnessed or affected a sizable quantity of narcotics from a white male. I am not insinuating that all mules are minority; in fact, I would venture to say that just the opposite applies, but I am just relaying my personal experiences. In conversations with intelligent and levelheaded troopers and detectives, we all agreed that whites probably used narcotics more than minorities. But in getting the drugs from point A (New York City) to point B (their hometown or city), the initial large purchase had to be made by someone who a medium-level dealer is going to trust. Ask yourself (because I often did), Could I—a blue-eyed, white Irish-male with a short military-style haircut, go into the Bronx, Spanish Harlem or Manhattan and purchase a kilo of heroin or cocaine and come out alive?

With this in mind, not only did I buy into this perception, but I believed it wholeheartedly. Shit, everywhere around me, the same thing was being said and practiced. To me, the proof was in the pudding. To walk into the barracks on a daily basis and see minorities handcuffed to the bench proved this theory must be correct. We were troopers on the New Jersey Turnpike, *the* drug corridor of the East. Race aside, we thought we were doing the job society wanted and asked us to do! Who cares what color the bad guy was when you remove five kilos of cocaine or a hundred pounds of marijuana from the streets? Race was something that was seldom discussed because my colleagues and I treated everyone with dignity, respect, and class.

History from reading arrest reports, my own practical experiences and observations, loose innocent stereotyping, and information funneled down from various law-enforcement agencies regarding the drug trade *educated* me, not instructors or senior troopers, that in theory, there was a higher percentage of minorities involved in drug trafficking. Right or wrong, that is what statistics proved, and I believe these same numbers serve as the basis for the controversy known as racial profiling. Proponents of racial profiling want everyone to believe that only minorities are stopped and searched, but I assure you that during my tenure, that was not the case. No one, regardless of color, was searched without proper reason or probable cause. Regardless of what one might think, just stopping minorities is not going to lead to drug arrests.

The sad truth is, I have worked with troopers who wanted to make arrest. They believed in these basic principles and, in my opinion, *may have* searched some vehicles based solely on the occupant's race or nervous demeanor. I assure you these individuals did not make a lot of arrests and probably got a lot of 251s (official complaints from motorists that went to Internal Affairs). Furthermore, I can honestly say that these same troopers were justified in making the initial stop and, due to the always-prevalent "conflicting statements between driver and occupants," did, by NJSP policy, have probable cause in searching the vehicle as well. In my mind, stopping and searching someone because of their skin color was not only bad police work, it was stupid in principle. Cops are believed to have a sixth sense, but truthfully, very few have that *knack* to be successful at drug interdiction. My supervisors and, more importantly, I as an individual, knew I was blessed (or in retrospect—cursed) with this talent; and therefore, other troopers began to look up to me. At that point in my career, I reviled in this status—*But look where I am now!*

Several factors had to be satisfied for me to take a motor-vehicle stop to the next step. Obviously, the stop itself was the most important. Being able to thoroughly justify why you stopped someone is absolutely critical. To me, the groundwork for a successful, complaint-free motor-vehicle stop was laid in the first thirty seconds.

This is where good troopers separated themselves. As time went on, I obtained the skill, through no one's fault but my own, of being able to stop any car I chose to once an infraction was observed and substantiate to the driver why I stopped him or her. On average, I would stop ten to fifteen cars a day. In the early part of my career, I saw tons of cars I wanted to stop and possibly search. Remember, I joined the New Jersey State Police to eventually make huge drug arrests on the turnpike, so I knew what to look for but just not how to affect it as a novice trooper.

Never forgetting the golden rule I learned from our Title 39 instructor at the academy, I would let these cars go because I was not confident I could justify the stop. After a few months on the turnpike, I felt I had blossomed into a good trooper. Though I never searched a lot of cars in the beginning, I quickly achieved a status where I was strong enough in my presence, verbal communication skills, and demeanor to precisely and articulately justify any stop I decided to make. The driver and occupants repeatedly made justifying the search easy because they always lied and had conflicting statements when asked the most basic of questions. *You would think someone transporting a couple kilos of cocaine would prepare a story in the event they got stopped.* It was truly amazing, but that's why we always joked that we only caught the dumb ones!

With this confidence, I started to let the businessman going 105 miles per hour pass by. I didn't ask to get assigned to the Big Road to write tickets! After a year or so, I knew who was running drugs, what to look for, and how to justify stopping them. I was a good trooper, and the numbers started to speak for themselves. If arresting criminals or exercising the vast amount of discretion that was bestowed upon me after graduating from the academy is a crime, then I am guilty. But no one was stopped without first having committed an acute motor-vehicle violation that I could articulate to the operator.

I will admit to utilizing every tool at my disposal to help be selective in deciding which vehicles I would stop. The factors that had the most relevance in determining who to stop were the type of car, the state it was registered in, how many occupants, direction of travel, time of day/night, gender; and *yes*, I'd be lying if I say race was not a factor. Of course it was!

As for the allegations that troopers utilized the spotlight and overhead lights to look in passing cars while sitting perpendicular to the roadway, *yes*, it happened. But again, everyone's reasons for doing this were probably different. I did it! The reason—I felt it was my right to get any edge I could. Trust me, very little can be seen when a car flashes by at speeds ranging from seventy to one hundred miles per hour. It's dark; desolate; and, in most cases, 3:00 or 4:00 AM; and only God knows who is in that car. Why should I, or other officers, not be permitted to have this slight edge, and with all things considered, what difference did this act really make?

Most importantly, as long as there was a lawful reason to make the stop, then what harm did this do? Because I was a white police officer stopping a minority, does that constitute an act of racial profiling? Will this controversy ultimately lead law enforcement into a direction where officers can only stop someone of identical race? Is this what humanity wants and needs to end the furor over this alleged practice?

As noted previously, police officers are given more discretion than any other profession known to man. The confusion and fear of being accused of profiling has led many to question if traffic enforcement should be outlawed altogether. Does society want police officers to become robotic in carrying out their sworn duties? Is the nation's war on drugs over? Obviously, because of the political pendulum, it has ceased on the New Jersey Turnpike, once identified as the largest drug corridor on the East Coast by the federal government. Why one of the countless reporters who covered this issue in light of the tragedy aptly named, "the turnpike shooting" has yet to do a comparison regarding drug arrests and seizures from, say, '93 to '97 then '99 to '03 is baffling. I bet society, especially New Jerseans, would be floored by these findings.

Regardless of how one may feel regarding law enforcements right to stop and search, if the operator is composed, has proper credentials, and could answer the most basic of questions, not even the best trooper could take this stop further. No one got searched solely because of the color of his or her skin!

When an arrest and seizure was made, blindly, I thought it was what the citizens of New Jersey wanted and expected from their troopers. Sure, the statistics were great, but more importantly, mass quantities of narcotics were being removed from the roadways. Those of us risking our lives to do this thought we were making a difference in New Jersey and the world. No one forced me to make arrests. I loved it; excelled at it; and with the exception of learning the basics of "common sense" patterns, I hold no one but myself accountable for naively believing my superiors and elected officials supported our efforts to rid New Jersey of illicit activity. I think my downfall may have been growing up in an era where I believed cops were supposed to arrest the bad guys and not knowing the pathetic value of political correctness.

To some, in hopes of reigniting this debate, they may twist these words regarding "selective enforcement or criminal profiling" and consider this racial profiling. Others may come forward to blame or accuse me of profiling in hopes of upping the ante in their pending lawsuits. These individuals, I assure you, are also the same truth-benders who *swear* they were taught and trained how to profile. In their defense, all I know is this: prior to my class graduation, boots would ride with a trooper from the state police's Drug Interdiction Unit (DITU). The methods they used, taught, or trained are unknown to me. Regrettably, I never got an opportunity to go on patrol with anyone from these units. But for those who now complain about this training should ask themselves, "Am I my own man?" It all goes back to what I previously stated: once in the patrol car by yourself, you stop who you want!

Having been called a racist and indicted for "crimes consistent to racial profiling," I take extreme offense to the certain few who now want to blame others for the accusations that troopers or supervisors made them stop cars based solely on the racial composition of a motorist. Laughably, I worked closely with a few of these individuals during my career. Everyone knows as I do, instead of claiming discrimination and suing—you should have been indicted for what was found on your patrol charts during the Troop D audit. You are cowards and disgraceful for your actions, but best of luck with your lawsuits—why not cash in like everyone else did! Again, weak leadership, a ball-less Union and greed lead to the demise of what once was the proudest policing agency in the United States.

With that said, my career ended on April 23, 1998. Up until then, I *never* received one motorist complaint or internal investigation into an alleged act of racial profiling or any other misconduct whatsoever. By simply being professional and treating everyone with class, dignity and respect paid immense dividends for me throughout my tenure with the New Jersey State Police.

Ironically, with my career now reduced to twisted memories, shaking hands and being thanked by prisoners for treating them with respect and dignity are what I am most proud of. Even though these individuals faced five, ten, and even up to twenty-five years in prison, the fact that they respected and thanked me for not being aggressive, abusive, or degrading to them is what I hold closest to my heart. Contrary to Attorney General Verniero's assessment, I was not a bad apple!

As for the decades of alleged complaints of racial profiling by troopers on the turnpike, I am proud to say none of those were mine. Does racial profiling exist? I guess it is up to you to decide. Let the debate rage on!

Society and politicians alike need to tell law-enforcement personnel if the war on drugs is over or not. Either cater to those individuals who claim law-enforcement tactics are prejudiced or stand behind and fully support those law-enforcement officers who have dedicated their lives to make this country safer. For once, citizens need to demand that their elected officials take a position on the issue of drug interdiction instead of the usual constant grandstanding. You can't play both sides of the fence on this issue. Too many lives and careers are at stake!

Upon leaving for work at around 8:00 PM on April 23, 1998, my life revolved around my career. With the exception of my father, who succumbed to his declining health a few months after our plea agreement was entered, no one was prouder of the fact that I was a New Jersey State Trooper. The entire "outfit," known as the New Jersey State Police, was my family—just as Sergeant Kilmurray said it would be. Rumor had it I was a month or so away from the pinnacle of my career, being named as Trooper of the Year. I had a bright future. My career was blossoming. Nothing could hold me back.

As I turned off the lights and prepared to exit 707 Morris Court, I peered at my living-room coffee table. On it sat a silk floral arrangement, coasters I purchased in Tijuana during a vacation with friends, and a thick plain blue binder that my neighbor George had given me.

Originally containing only newspaper clippings from my first shooting, which George neatly included, this binder became a proud chronology of my life and career as a trooper following my first deadly encounter on the New Jersey Turnpike. The binder served as a constant reminder that as a foot soldier in New Jersey's war on drugs, I had the full support of my employer, the attorney general, and the governor. Nearly bulging at the seams, the binder now housed the volumes of personal letters that the State of New Jersey sent to my home. Each letter thanked me for my efforts in making New Jersey a better, safer place. Endorsed by the colonel and acknowledged by Whitman and Verniero, these letters served as motivation to keep up my diligent patrol activity.

More importantly, the colonel, attorney general, and governor were all aware of the statistics. They knew who was being arrested. They received reports categorizing the race and gender of incarcerated subjects. They had full access to any and all reports done by me or other troopers. Not only was my personnel file complaint free and exemplary, never once was I questioned about my activity or statistics. I must have been doing something right!

As arrests on the turnpike piled up, Whitman and Verniero denied that racial profiling existed. Unknown to all of us at that time, they were also busy burying the hundreds of thousands of documents relating to this issue. And as the *DeSoto* case remained under appeal, I was continuously congratulated by the two most powerful people in the state, and I couldn't have been prouder. Almost on a daily basis leading up to April 23, I continued to receive this same congratulatory letter from the two individuals who would later ruin my life, reputation, career and everything I and my fellow members of the New Jersey State Police risked our lives for:

State of New Jersey

CHRISTINE TODD WHITMAN
Governor

DEPARTMENT OF LAW AND PUBLIC SAFETY
DIVISION OF STATE POLICE
POST OFFICE BOX 7068
WEST TRENTON NJ 08628-0068

PETER VERNIERO
Attorney General

COLONEL CARL A. WILLIAMS
Superintendent
TELEPHONE: (609) 882-2000

ADDRESS REPLY TO:

April 17, 1998

Trooper John Hogan #5068

Dear Trooper Hogan:

I would like to take this opportunity to recognize your efforts on April 8, 1998, in Middlesex County which resulted in the apprehension of two subjects for money laundering and the seizure of U.S. currency in the amount of $39,816.

Your actions bring great credit to the Division of State Police and yourself as a sworn member. I congratulate you on a job well done. A copy of this letter has been forwarded to the Human Resource Management Bureau to be made a permanent part of your personnel file.

Sincerely,

Carl A. Williams
Colonel
Superintendent

ro

c: HRM Bureau
    Troop D Hdqts.

New Jersey Is An Equal Opportunity Employer • Printed on Recycled Paper and Recyclable

I only wish they told me the war on drugs was really a fleeting political facade before going out on patrol with James Kenna on April 23, 1998. I guess it's safe to say Peter Verniero buried those documents in the dark since he failed to recollect that they ever existed! With just cause—just like every motor-vehicle stop, search, or seizure I professionally conducted—my first opinion of politicians never changed: lying, shameless, self-serving, career-ruining bastards! Now, with this life altering experience finally behind me, all that's left for me to do is ponder just who truly are New Jersey's bad apples?

Life's Lesson

There are times in one's life when all the world seems to turn against us. Our motives are misunderstood, our words misconstrued, an unkind word reveals to us the unfriendly feelings of others.

The fact is, that it is rare when injustice, or slights, patiently borne, do not leave the heart at the close of the day filled with a marvelous sense of peace—perhaps not at once—after you've had a chance to reflect a bit. It is the seed God has sown, springing up and bearing fruit.

We learn, as the years roll onward and we leave the past behind, that much we had counted sorrow, but proved God is kind; that many a flower we'd longed for had hidden a thorn of pain, and many a rugged by-path led to fields of ripened grain.

The clouds that cover the sunshine; they cannot banish the sun. And the earth shines out the brighter when the weary rain is done. We must stand in the deepest shadow to see the clearest light; and often through wrong's own darkness comes the welcome strength of right.

—Ella Wheeler Wilcox

Printed in the United States
38143LVS00003B/66